T0388304

NATHANIEL WALLICH

In March 1807, Nathaniel Wallich, a young Danish surgeon left his home in Copenhagen towards India. During the troubles of the Napoleonic Wars, it was not possible to foresee, that he was to emerge as one of the most prominent nineteenth century botanists.

Wallich spent most of his adulthood in India and, as the long-time superintendent of the Calcutta Botanic Garden, gained extensive expertise on Indian flora. A truly global communication network emerged from his desk facing the River Hooghly, reaching out to eminent specialists as well as amateur researchers long forgotten today. He conducted research trips to Nepal, as well as to South East Asia and may be perceived as one of the founding fathers of tea production in Assam.

This book is based on the enormous correspondence of Wallich, preserved in libraries across Calcutta, London, Copenhagen, Hamburg, Munich and many other places. It aims to approach a long career marked by biographical ruptures and contradictions, but at the same time by continuity. It furthermore explains the tight links between supposedly neutral botanical studies and the emergence of British colonial power in India.

Martin Krieger serves as a professor for Northern European History at the University of Kiel, Germany. His major fields of research are intellectual and cultural history and the history of science. He has extensively published on the history of the Baltic Sea region, on global intellectual networks and global consumer goods, such as on tea and coffee. He has published *European Cemeteries in South India: Seventeenth to Nineteenth Centuries* (Manohar 2013).

Nathaniel Wallich

Global Botany in Nineteenth Century India

MARTIN KRIEGER

Routledge
Taylor & Francis Group

LONDON AND NEW YORK

MANOHAR

First published 2023
by Routledge
4 Park Square, Milton Park, Abingdon, Oxon OX14 4RN

and by Routledge
605 Third Avenue, New York, NY 10158

Routledge is an imprint of the Taylor & Francis Group, an informa business

© 2023 Martin Krieger and Manohar Publishers

Print edition not for sale in South Asia (India, Sri Lanka, Nepal, Bangladesh, Pakistan or Bhutan)

British Library Cataloguing-in-Publication Data
A catalogue record for this book is available from the British Library

Library of Congress Cataloging-in-Publication Data
A catalog record for this book has been requested

ISBN: 9781032377117 (hbk)
ISBN: 9781032377124 (pbk)
ISBN: 9781003341529 (ebk)

DOI: 10.4324/9781003341529

Typeset in Janson Text 11/13
by Kohli Print, Delhi 110051

MANOHAR

Contents

List of Plates

Acknowledgements

A global project such as this biographical study, has required the support of colleagues and institutions, but also of one's own family in many ways. Over the years of writing this book, I have received much help and encouragement in India, Denmark, Britain, South Africa and Germany. Some of the support related to the provision of specific information and source material, while other assistance involved close cooperation based on trust over a long period. Among the latter was an enormously profitable cooperation with Mark Watson and Henry J. Noltie (Royal Botanic Garden Edinburgh), to whom I owe unlimited valuable advice, hints and sharing of source material, and who always let me share their thoughts and ideas. Professor Ib Friis (Copenhagen) also accompanied this project with expertise, sympathy and provided me with many relevant insights.

I would also like to thank P.S. Ramanujan (Copenhagen) for valuable information about Rasmus Rask; Martin Schwarz Lausten (Copenhagen) for his expertise on Wallich's family background; Milinda Banerjee (St. Andrews) for important insights into the culture of Bengal; and Martin Nickol (Kiel) for his patient explanation about Linnaeus and other companions of Wallich. I am also grateful to Simon Rastén (Copenhagen), Christopher Fraser-Jenkins (Kathmandu), Pakshirajan Lakshminarasimhan (Pune), Paramjit Singh (Kolkata), Potharaju Venu (Calcutta), Adrian Thomas (London), and Charles Allan (Camden).

Institutional support, without which this book would not have seen the light of day, was generously provided by the Central National Herbarium (Kolkata), the Agricultural and Horticultural Society (Kolkata), the Victoria Memorial Hall (Kolkata), the Tocklai Tea Research Institute (Jorhat), the

British Library (London), the Linnean Society of London, the Royal Society (London), the Natural History Museum Copenhagen, the Royal Danish Library, the Danish National Archives and the State Museum for Art (Copenhagen), as well as the West Cape State Archives (Cape Town), the observatories in Cape Town and Edinburgh, the University Library Kiel, the State and University Library Hamburg, the Museum Fünf Kontinente Munich, the Bavarian State Library Munich and the Leopoldina (Halle).

Many thanks go to my team from the Department of Northern European History at the University of Kiel. Tobias Delfs (now in Berlin), Imke Hamann-Bock, Florian Jungmann, Jessica Kunze, Christin Maichrzack and Kerstin Möckel were significantly involved in the creation of this biography. They researched material, made transcriptions from Danish and English sources, compiled a database of all the letters from and to Wallich and tirelessly read corrections. They also made substantial suggestions as regards content.

I gratefully point out the financial support of the Kiel Wallich Project by the German Research Foundation (DFG).

First and foremost I would like to thank those who helped me with the English translation of the text, including Ramesh Jain from Manohar Publishers in New Delhi; and especially Henry J. Noltie and Mark Watson, two extraordinarily helpful, competent and collegial botanists who went to great lengths to help ensure the accuracy and readability of the English translation. Henry Noltie also made major revisions to this initially computer-generated translation from German into English using the package DeepL Translator (www.deepl.com). My heartfelt thanks to all of you!

As always, the professional advice, inexhaustible patience, and constant encouragement from Nimmy, Benny and Paul were invaluable.

Kiel   MARTIN KRIEGER
February 2022

Abbreviations

As. Res.	*Asiatick Researches*
BL	British Library
BSB	Bavarian State Library
CA	West Cape Archives
CNH	Central National Herbarium, Kolkata
FT	Folketællinger/Censuses, Dansk Demografisk Database
IOR	India Office Records
MS	Museet for Søfart/Maritime Museum, Helsingør
SNM	Natural History Museum, Copenhagen
RAK	Danish National Archives, Copenhagen
RBG Kew	Library and Archives of the Royal Botanic Gardens, Kew

CHAPTER 1

Introduction
Nathaniel Wallich:
A Life's Correspondence

On New Year's Day 1848, an old man in poor health was seated at his desk at 5 Gower Street in Bloomsbury, London. In front of him lay an enormous number of letters which he had received or written in the decades that lay behind him. He read them again, because he wanted to put them in chronological order and to create an index. There may have been about four thousand letters in all. The letters stirred up memories: of people who had written those letters, long-time companions, friends, but also bitter enemies. Many of them were long dead. Of the eleven Assistant Surgeons appointed with him to the East India Company in 1814, eight were no longer alive.

The man at the desk was Nathaniel Wolff Wallich. He had only recently retired from India and moved to London to join his family. Born and raised in Denmark, he had spent most of his adult life in India and, as the long-time superintendent of the Calcutta Royal Botanic Garden, had gained extensive expertise on Indian flora. A truly global communication network had emerged from this garden, reaching out to eminent specialists as well as amateur researchers long forgotten today. He was by no means an ingenious theoretical thinker, nor a creator of significant new concepts or systems in the field of botany. He, nevertheless, gained significance and prominence as one of the great global communicators of the first half of the nineteenth century.[1] By the time Wallich, an intellectual descendant of Linnaeus, returned to Europe to settle in Bloomsbury, the world had changed. Natural science had reached new shores in terms of theory and practice, and the continent itself was on the verge of revolution.

The question is who was Nathaniel Wallich? In recent times, he is known to very few people, mainly botanists, pharmacists, and physicians. They may recollect that a number of plants commemorate his name, including *Apostasia wallichii*, *Allium wallichii*, *Valeriana wallichii* and *Rhododendron wallichii*. Among contemporaries, the verdict on him was varied, sometimes, biased. Many had been dependent on his services, and great was the joy when another wooden box with dried, pressed, labelled and carefully packed herbarium specimens or seeds reached Copenhagen, London, Glasgow, Paris, Munich or Hamburg. His fellow Danish countrymen, stranded in India during the Napoleonic Wars, were also grateful to find refuge and assistance with him. On the other hand, Wallich was able to antagonize with an overly direct word.

The aim of this book is to reconstruct the hitherto unknown biography of an outstanding nineteenth century botanist. It aims to approach a long life marked by biographical ruptures and contradictions, but at the same time by continuity. It simultaneously aims to display the embeddedness of Wallich's botanical achievements in contemporary discourses and his personal career strategy. Furthermore, this study intends to highlight the importance of academic communication networks in an age of global expansion.

To write a biography of Wallich bears a certain risk, because the surviving sources are largely one-sided. Although the administrative files of the British East India Company, as well as surviving letters in archives in Munich, Leipzig, Hamburg, Copenhagen and Cape Town, can be consulted, the primary source remains his personal correspondence. The so-called 'Wallich letters', now kept in the Central National Herbarium of the Acharya Jagdish Chandra Bose Indian Botanic Garden (formerly, the Calcutta Botanical Garden) in Kolkata, comprise thirty-three volumes relating almost exclusively to Wallich's professional correspondence. The largest part is made up of letters addressed to him; however, copies of some of his own replies also survive. Wallich used carbon paper from about 1840 onwards, luckily for us, so that many copies of original letters from later years have been preserved. Most of the letters are written in English, but there are also considerable numbers in Danish, German, and French.

Wallich took the letters from Calcutta with him to England on his retirement, had them bound, and prepared an index up to the 1830's. In his will, shortly before his death, he appointed his long-time friend Robert Brown as the executor and trustee.[2] The letters were later sent to the Royal Botanic Gardens Kew, from where they were returned to Calcutta in 1887 or 1888.[3] Many of them are now in poor condition, though they have recently been safely stored in archival quality boxes in steel cabinets. The bindings of the volumes commissioned by Wallich have largely disintegrated and the paper of many of the letters has been severely damaged using iron gall ink (which applies especially to the paper of letters from Germany), by folding, from the rigours of the Indian climate and by the depredation of insects. Nevertheless, it can be stated that the letters which Wallich chose to keep are completely preserved.

These letters provide information about the practices of scientific communication and the transfer of plants, about patronage and scientific credibility, but also about the ideas of a botanist between Europe and India in the first half of the nineteenth century. They also contain much indirect information and raise broader questions: to what extent were local intellectuals or assistants involved? What was the role of the amateur collector in support of Wallich's network? But also, very practical ones: how long did it take for letters from Copenhagen to reach Calcutta in 1815 (a reply to a letter would not normally be expected to be received within a year), and by how much was this shortened in 1845 following the arrival of steam navigation—and what did this mean to his network? Where was Wallich in Nepal on a particular day in the year 1821? His meticulous notes of the receipt of letters also provide information on this and enable an exact reconstruction of several of his itineraries. He himself was a diligent letter writer who often answered letters immediately. But his handwriting, never good, became even worse as he grew older—a fact of which he was all too aware of himself, as he once wrote from Allahabad to a friend in Calcutta: 'prepare yourself with patience & spectacles'.[4]

To reconstruct a life from letters, it is necessary to examine their impact on their recipients and more widely—for letters not only serve to convey information between sender and recipient, but their impact could stretch well beyond such direct interaction. Information obtained from reading them was passed to third parties, just as information from third parties was received and communicated back to the sender. Especially, in the time before the emergence of specialized botanical journals, letters played a crucial role in the exchange of knowledge and ideas. The networks, thus established were multinational and multidirectional, and reached countries like Germany that then had few formal overseas interests. It should not be overlooked that substantial exchange took place informally, but such direct, personal contacts, fruitful as they might have been, are much more difficult to document.

This study rests upon the broad debate of the past decades on the scientific exploration of the colonial world. To an ever-increasing extent, natural science was understood as an element of imperial statehood with botany playing the central role. Those who were knowledgeable about the forest resources of a country, about its food and its medicinal plants, were able to make major contributions to studies of a country in all its social depth and spatial extension. Pioneering work in these areas has been made by Richard Grove in his *Green Imperialism*,[5] by David Arnold[6] and Michael Mann,[7] all of whom refer to Wallich. A wealth of overviews and case studies exist, as well as an equally large number of methodological and theoretical works.[8] This book cannot and does not aim to contribute to theoretical studies, but rather, to provide context, suggestions, and a framework for further work at the interface between theory and practice.

NOTES

1. M. Harrison, 'The Calcutta Botanic Garden and the Wider World, 1817-46', in: U. Das Gupta (ed.), *Science and Modern India*, Delhi, etc.: Pearson Longman, 2011, p. 236.
2. PROB 11/2192/77, Last Will Nathaniel Wallich, 11 April 1854: 'I give to the care and custody of my illustrious friend and patron Robert Brown . . . for his individual use during his life my correspondence whether original or otherwise relating especially to the History of the East India Company's Botanical Garden.'
3. J. Bastin (ed.), 'The Letters of Sir Stamford Raffles to Nathaniel Wallich 1819-24', *Journal of the Malaysian Branch of the Royal Asiatic Society*, vol. 54, no. 2, 1981, p. 1.
4. Landsarkivet for Sjælland, QA-035, Engelholm Gods, 1811-52, Wolff family private archive, correspondence 29-8, Wallich to Benjamin Wolff, 4 October 1820.
5. R. Grove, *Green Imperialism. Colonial Expansion, Tropical Island Edens and the Origins of Environmentalism*, Cambridge: Cambridge University Press, 1997.
6. D. Arnold, *The Tropics and the Traveling Gaze*, New Delhi: Orient Black Swan, 2005.
7. M. Mann, *Flottenbau und Forstbetrieb in Indien, 1794-1823*, Stuttgart: Steiner, 1996.
8. For a systematic overview see M. Sommer, S. Müller-Wille & C. Reinhardt (eds.), *Handbuch Wissenschaftsgeschichte*, Stuttgart: Metzler, 2017.

CHAPTER 2

Copenhagen

FAMILY

There was still peace in Denmark when in October 1800 a young man set off on a walk through northern Copenhagen. His home was in a street called Adelgade, from where it was only a few steps to the royal palace. Further on, around the Norgesgade, lay the genteel quarter of Frederikstad with its spacious baroque houses. Here, the young man reached his goal—the Surgical Academy, located almost at the end of Norgesgade. He was about to embark on his training as a surgeon. However, when this young man, Nathaniel Wallich, first left his parents' house for Norgesgade, nor he nor his kins could have guessed that seventeen years later, as a renowned botanist, he would be appointed as the director of the Calcutta Botanic Garden. He overall, didn't anticipate, neither was it yet foreseeable that the Napoleonic Wars would prove to be a catalyst for his unique career.

The Wallichs had traced their origins in the Jewish community of Germany. For centuries, they had produced merchants as well as doctors. The motivation for Wallich's father and grandfather to move from Germany to Denmark was trade, which, in the last decades of the eighteenth century, offered many opportunities. The absolute monarchy pursued a policy of reform that, in the spirit of Enlightenment, not only ended bonded labour, but resulted in significant economic growth. Foreign policy was in the hands of the wise foreign minister Count Andreas Peter Bernstorff, whose agenda was one of neutrality. On the North and Baltic seas and on the world's oceans, during the American War of Independence and the French Revolutionary Wars, richly laden ships sailed undisturbed under the neutral Danish flag and brought back lavish profits. At that time the Danish monarchy was the leading power of northern Europe and also a global player. It had its own small colonies in the Caribbean, Africa and Asia; and the German Duchies of Schleswig and Holstein, Norway, Iceland and Greenland also belonged to the monarchy.[1]

The economic, political and cultural centre of this small empire was undisputedly Copenhagen. Rasmus Nyerup, a librarian and professor of literature, published a description of the Danish capital in 1800,[2] in which he praised the multinational spirit of the city:

In Copenhagen everything that in other countries you must look for scattered between several cities is united. Copenhagen is a capital and residential city, the seat of the most considerable trade of the whole country, the main fortress of the empire. Here is the only university of the two kingdoms; here is the fleet and the maritime arsenal; all factories are concentrated here; here is the academy of arts and the theatre;—in a word: everything peculiar and interesting that Denmark has to offer can be found in Copenhagen.[3]

The Danish capital was the showcase of the multinational monarchy, to which came merchants, artists, students, scholars and civil servants from all parts of the empire.[4] Nyerup also pointed out that Copenhagen had changed greatly since the reign of Christian VII. He particularly emphasized the founding of new scientific institutions such as the veterinary school, the natural history museum and the botanical garden.[5] Copenhagen was green and bright; avenues were planted everywhere and there was good street lighting.[6]

Wallich was born in the mid-1780s, at a time of economic growth, but also of reforms and tensions within the Jewish community of the city, which were to be felt in his paternal home. A start had been made, and from 1788, Jews were officially permitted to obtain a doctorate from the University of Copenhagen.[7] A royal resolution, commonly referred to as the 'Letter of Liberty', was passed on 18 August 1814, which brought about at least a partial emancipation of the Jewish community in Denmark.[8] The freedom of the press offered opportunities for expressing modern opinions, but on the other hand, also brought forth unrest. Nathaniel himself was to face anti-Jewish discrimination from the German-born theologian and royal counsellor Conrad Georg Friedrich Elias von Schmidt-Phiseldeck, who almost ruined Wallich's career in India before it had even begun. The fruits of liberal reforms were only to be harvested in Copenhagen later, by which time, Wallich had been living in India for many years.

WALLICH'S FAMILY

Nathaniel grew up in a liberal, middle-class environment. The marriage of his parents, the merchant Wulff Lazarus Wallich and Hannah (*née* Jacobson) had taken place in August 1778; and their first child, Aaron, was born in 1779 when his father and mother were twenty-four and twenty-one years old respectively.[9] Aaron—who later used the name Arnold—was to make a career as a theatrical painter.[10] Three years after Aaron's birth, a daughter Nanine was born and, on 28 January 1786, in the middle of winter, the Wallichs were able to celebrate the birth of a second son, who received the name Nathaniel, derived from the Hebrew, meaning 'the gift of God'. In 1787 the couple had a second daughter, Promethe, who appears to have died at a young age. The household also included a maid.[11]

The Judaic faith which Nathaniel and his siblings were brought up by in their Copenhagen home had a modern slant to it, as his father made his own contributions to the enlightened debate then underway. In 1795, when Nathaniel was nine years old, Wulff Lazarus published a paper with the title 'Forslag til Forbedring i den Jødiske Menigheds Forfatning i Kjøbenhavn' ('Proposal for the improvement of the condition of the Jewish community in Copenhagen').[12] Such improvement was to begin with education, which was still a male concern, from which girls remained excluded. An anonymous pamphlet from the 1790s shows the scope of the traditional educational curriculum—in addition to the study of Hebrew and German, the Talmudic and various spiritual commentaries were also read; but hardly any practical skills that might be useful in later life were taught.[13] In the Wallich household, by contrast, the educational ideals of the Enlightenment were attended to, and these focussed on science and other worldly subjects. The father recognized the artistic-cum-scientific talents of his children at an early age and promoted them according to their abilities. There is no doubt that a large part of the education of children took place not in Yeshivas (Jewish schools) or synagogues (prayer houses), but in the parental home. Part of the education was in German, which was essential to launch a career, because government and administration under the Danish monarchy was still a domain of German noble families. Throughout his life, Wallich developed good command of German and he always showed himself to be a connoisseur of German literature.[14]

A rather secular education may have resulted in a certain indifference towards religious matters. Looking at Wallich's long life, it is striking that there is little evidence of a practical exercise of his faith, and his later contribution to British imperial rule in India and the founding of a family in Calcutta led to his complete integration into a Christian colonial context. Only for one moment, when in 1806 it became clear to him that as a Jew, he officially could not enter the Danish civil service, he was aware about the existing inequalities between Jews and Christians in the Danish monarchy.

THE SURGICAL ACADEMY

When Wallich enrolled at the Surgical Academy in Norgesgade, he was just fourteen years old.[15] Undoubtedly, it was his parents who decided not to let their younger son learn the merchant's trade, but to let him follow in the footsteps of his southwest German ancestors as doctors. However, the choice was not to study medicine at the university, rather to obtain training as a surgeon at the Surgical Academy, which as an institution (like the Wallich family itself), was a by-product of Enlightenment and the reform of Absolutism. With the founding of this institution, contemporary with the Collegium Medico-Chirurgicum Josephinum in Vienna, a completely new path was taken in the professionalization of the medical profession. Traditionally, the training of doctors had been in the hands of the medical faculties of the universities, where it was conducted in Latin, and it was generally theory-based and concentrated mainly on the internal diseases. For centuries, it had been guilds of barbers who had been responsible for external ailments and injuries and, if living in the countryside, a sick person could sometimes only consult a poorly-trained doctor or a quack.[16]

The road to the foundation of the Royal Academy of Surgery in Copenhagen on 22 June 1785 had been a long one and two more years were to pass before it was able to move into its

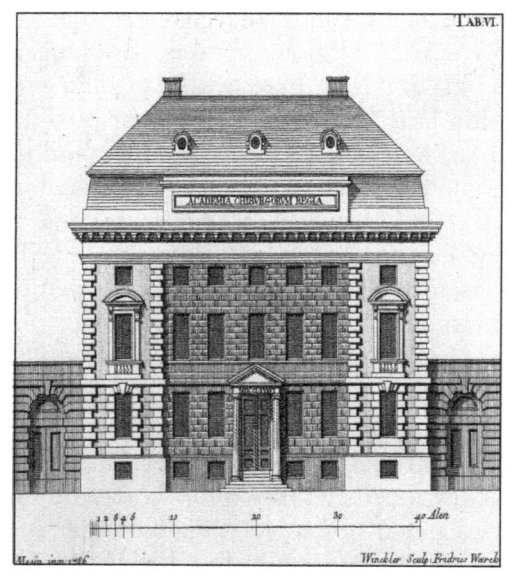

Plate 2.1: The Royal Academy of Surgery at Copenhagen, copperplate engraving, 1786. (Royal Library, Copenhagen)

new, prestigious, neoclassical building in Norgesgade, next to the royal Friedrichs-Hospital. The founding of the Academy meant a considerable boost in terms of professionalization because now it was only by studying there that it was possible to obtain a permanent position as a well-paid public surgeon in the kingdom. Education was practice-based, but nevertheless, students also had to complete academic courses in particular subjects at the university and at the botanical garden.[17]

When Wallich began his studies, Britain and Austria were at war with Napoleonic France, a war that would affect life at the Surgical Academy. In May 1800, sixty-four students were enrolled; six months later not even half of them that were there. While in May twenty candidates were from Germany or the German-speaking Duchy of Holstein, there were now only five.[18] It may be assumed that the decline in the number of students from abroad was due to the increasingly threatening political-military situation in Europe. Napoleon defeated the Austrians at the Battle of Marengo in the summer of 1800, depriving the British of their only serious ally remaining on the continent. However, neutral Denmark also entered dangerous waters after Bernstorff's death, with its increasingly aggressive trading policy under finance minister Ernst Schimmelmann.[19]

By October 1800, twenty-nine candidates were enrolled at the Surgical Academy, including Wallich who was by far the youngest.[20] The students came from all parts of the Danish kingdom. Eleven came from Denmark itself, six from Copenhagen. Students from Schleswig made up the next largest share; from the Duchy of Holstein came two, with the same number from Norway. One student of Danish parents came from the Caribbean Island of St. Thomas and one from India. The student body, thus, formed a colourful kaleidoscope of the Danish state.[21]

At the Surgical Academy, Wallich came into contact with the Danish medical and botanical research elite of the time. First, he attended lectures in chemistry, mineralogy and botany given by Professors Peter Christian Abildgaard and Erik Nissen Viborg. In 1801, he studied proper surgery, which included

courses in forensic medicine, naturopathy, anatomy, physiology, toxicology, *materia medica* and dietetics. Soon, he was
allowed to earn his first spurs in medical practice and in 1803
the register of the Surgical Academy lists him as volunteer at
the neighbouring Friedrichs-Hospital.[22]
Wallich developed an early inclination towards the subject
of botany, which was not taught at the academy itself, but at
the botanical garden of the university. Such an interest was
not unusual among the medical practitioners at the time, since
a precise knowledge of medicinal plants was an absolute
necessity for the exercise of the profession. Soon, Wallich's
passion for plants proved to be far beyond average. The study
of botany had flourished in Europe for many centuries, but
increasingly so during the eighteenth century, attracting the
attention of countless physicians and scholars. From all over
the world, exotic plants arrived in the botanical gardens of
European universities, and in the parks, gardens and conser-
vatories of the aristocracy. Prominent researchers endeavoured
to describe the increasingly well-known European and non-
European plant world and to classify it in a uniform system.
An important landmark was the binomial nomenclature
standardised by Carl Linnaeus. From his *Systema Naturae*
(1735), Linnaeus developed a system of classification, in which
he divided plants into phanerogams (flowering plants) and
cryptogams (non-flowering plants). Other, often more obvious
features, such as the shape of the flowers, leaves or fruit, were
not considered, and reliance on a single character rendered
Linnaeus' classification system to be increasingly contested
during the first half of the nineteenth century. Accordingly,
Linnaeus' artificial system, gradually gave way to a natural
system based on the use of multiple vegetative and floral
characters.[23]
  In terms of botany, Denmark was rather late in catching up
with what was going on elsewhere in Europe, and botanical
studies there concentrated primarily on the local flora.
Professors of medicine at the University of Copenhagen, such
as the ailing Christian Friis Rottbøll, taught broader taxonomy,

but the first impulse for a gradual development came from the research and publication project of a *Flora Danica*, initiated by King Frederick V in 1761.[24] From this gradually arose a younger generation of scholars internationally networked in the Linnaean school. The three eminent plant researchers Martin Vahl, Jens Wilken Hornemann, and Frederik Ludvig Holbøll finally freed Denmark from the botanical torpor and trained a select circle of talented Linnaean 'grand-pupils'. The Norwegian Martin Vahl, who was respected far beyond the borders of Denmark, emerged as the doyen of modern plant research in the Danish kingdom. After studies in Copenhagen, he spent some time with plants in his Norwegian homeland; then, after five further years of private lessons with Linnaeus, returned to Denmark as a convinced Linnaean. Lacking a permanent appointment, he earned his livelihood as a lecturer at the botanical garden of Copenhagen and led unpaid botanical excursions. Later, Vahl took over the editorship of the *Flora Danica* and, after a long wait and several periods abroad, in 1801, he finally received the professorship of botany at the University of Copenhagen, which had been established only a few years earlier.[25]

Vahl worked internationally and under his aegis Danish botanical researchers for the first time received recognition beyond Denmark itself. He himself studied the plants of Europe and North Africa through his own travels but was also in contact with India through the German Lutheran missionary and botanist Christoph Samuel John, a correspondent of William Roxburgh, the Superintendent of the Calcutta Botanic Garden.[26] It may be presumed that, through Martin Vahl, Wallich not only became acquainted with Linnaeus' binomial nomenclature, but also with the advantages of global academic networking.[27]

For several decades, Wallich would be connected with Vahl's successor Jens Wilken Hornemann through a close and frequent correspondence. Hornemann, who came from the island of Aerø in the Duchy of Schleswig, had joined the inner circle of Vahl's students in the late 1780s. After having studied medicine, he then undertook a journey through Germany, and on to France, with the eminent Norwegian philosopher and natural scientist Henrik Steffens. After Vahl's death, his appointment as a lecturer at the Copenhagen Botanical Garden was followed by his succession of the editorship of *Flora Danica* and his appointment as professor of botany at the university. Hornemann described himself as a close follower in the footsteps of Linnaeus.[28]

Wallich's attention to practical work, and an ever-increasing love of botany, was expressed in the fact that he regularly assisted Frederik Ludvig Holbøll, who was the head gardener both of Frederiksborg Castle near Copenhagen and of the Botanical Garden.[29] Like Vahl many years before, Wallich used to volunteer in the Botanical Garden, thereby gaining experience in practical botany. For a while, he participated in Holbøll's seminars on horticulture from which, according to the teacher, Wallich was never absent.[30]

Plate 2.2: Frederik Ludvig Holbøll, lithography.
(Royal Library, Copenhagen)

The Copenhagen botanical school, closely linked to the Linnaean tradition through Vahl, Hornemann, and Holbøll, produced several students who became famous both in Denmark and far beyond. Niels Bang from the town Vejle belonged to the inner circle of Vahl's students in the 1790's. After his studies and a trip to the Pyrenees Bang he undertook a longer research trip to Norway with Hornemann and finally acquired property in Denmark. As the heir to the Hofmannsgave estate, which enabled him to lead an economically independent life, he would become one of Wallich's correspondents.[31]

At the same time as Wallich, the Norwegian Christian Smith maintained contact with Vahl and Hornemann. In 1814, he was appointed the first professor of botany and political economy at the recently established University of Christiania (modern day Oslo). In 1816, Smith took part in an expedition to the Congo organized by Sir Joseph Banks, but it was there that he met his death.[32] Holbøll's practical botanical school, in turn, produced Johann Siebke from Holstein, who, after an apprenticeship as a pharmacist, found employment with Holbøll and, following a trip to London and Paris, was appointed head gardener of the young botanical garden in Christiania.[33]

From the outset professional and family networks were scarcely to be separated from one other. Among Wallich's contemporaries as a student was a J.O. Møller and many decades later, in London, his son Charles was to marry Wallich's daughter Ann.[34] Cornelius Gottlieb Roll from Schleswig was another fellow student.[35] From 1819, Roll worked as a surgeon in the town of Hadersleben, where he died in 1834, but he always took a keen interest in the distinguished career of his one-time comrade Nathaniel Wallich.[36]

Wallich may also have formed a friendship with his fellow student Jørgen Henrik Berner, who was born in the Indian city of Patna. Jørgen's father had established a trading post there for the Danish Asiatic Company in 1773, and served as a Danish representative (chiefly trading in opium) until his death.

Following the death of his father, Jørgen returned to Denmark with his mother.[37] We do not exactly know what Wallich and Berner talked about, but one can imagine that Nathaniel listened attentively when Jørgen recollected his Indian childhood. Of much greater importance for his later network was Nathaniel's cousin Ludvig Levin Jacobson. Wallich's mother Hannah and Ludvig's father Aaron were siblings. During a period when his family lived in the Swedish capital Stockholm, Jacobson attended a school there and began to study medicine. In 1800, he continued his studies at the university and Surgical Academy in Copenhagen. In 1806, he was to find a position at the Academy and gained expertise in the field of surgery. Jacobson was appointed as a professor of medicine in Copenhagen in 1815, and made a name for himself as an anatomist and zoologist.[38] Various contacts with teachers, fellow students and friends offered him inspiration as well as professional contacts. Barely twenty years of age, he had already laid the foundation for his later global communication network that would one day extend from North America to Australia, with its heart in northern India.

While Wallich pursued his studies, enormous changes were taking place outside his small academic world. At the beginning of April 1801, the British fleet attacked Copenhagen as a warning shot to not to lean too closely on the enemy Russia in the matters of foreign policy. Only a little later, in the winter months of 1802-3 and 1803-4, a virtual revolution took place in the intellectual history at Copenhagen. Henrik Steffens gave his famous lectures at the Ehlers College in the city, in which he prepared the ground for the spread of Romanticism and Romantic natural philosophy in Denmark.[39] At that time, Wallich was too young, perhaps the paternal heritage of the enlightened Jewish tradition weighed more heavily; whatever the reason, he seems to have paid no heed to the cultural upheaval. Throughout his life, he remained a practitioner and pragmatist while romantic natural philosophy in the Germanic tradition of Schelling and Humboldt always remained alien to him.

On 21 April 1806 began the three days of his final exams to qualify as a surgeon, in which three grades, or 'characters' were awarded. The first examination took place on the same day at lunchtime about surgical therapy and pathology, in which he earned the first grade. This was immediately followed by anatomy and physiology, in which he also obtained distinctions. There was then a break, but between five and six o'clock, he passed the examination in the field of 'therapia et pathologia chirurgia morborum capitia et thoracis', also with higher grades.[40] The next day, he continued with an examination in midwifery and obstetrics as well as gynaecology and diseases of childhood. This was followed by an examination of medicinal plants; and in the final exam Wallich had to deal with a practical medical problem.[41] Four other candidates took part at the same time, all of whom received the second grade and Wallich alone was awarded the top rank for his overall performance.[42] He had completed his studies at the age of twenty and was now a fully trained surgeon with a passion for botany – it was now essential to find job to earn his livelihood.

NOTES

1. M. Krieger, 'Der dänische Gesamtstaat im Zeitalter der Napoleonischen Kriege', in S. Kinzler (ed.), *Der Kieler Frieden 1814: Ein Schicksalsjahr für den Norden*, Neumünster: Wachholtz, 2013, pp. 32-7.
2. R. Nyerup, *Beschreibung der Stadt Kopenhagen*, Copenhagen: Prost, 1807.
3. Ibid., introduction.
4. E. Gøbel, *De styrede rigerne. Embedsmændene i den Dansk-Norske civile central administration 1660-1814*, Odense: Universitetsforlag, 2000, passim.
5. I. Friis, 'Martin Vahl's videnskabelige løbebane i København og betydning for botaniken', in P. M. Jørgensen (ed.), *Martin Vahl. 250 års minnet*, Bergen: Bergen Museum, 2000, p. 16.
6. Nyerup, *Beschreibung*, pp. 33f.

7. G. Norrie, 'Jødernes kamp for adgangen til universitet og den medicinske doctorgrad i Danmark,' *Bibliotek for Læger*, vol. 87, No. 7, 3, 1892, p. 137.
8. Schwarz Lausten, *Jøder og Kristne i Danmark. Fra middelalderen til nyere tid*, Frederiksberg: Anis, 2012, pp. 154-6.
9. Diary Rasmus Rask, pers. comm. from P.S. Ramanujan, 17 June 2014.
10. S. Müller, 'Wallick, Ahron Wulff' in: C.F. Bricka (ed.), *Dansk Biografisk Leksikon*, vol. 18, Copenhagen: Gyldendal, 1905, p. 227.
11. Promethe was not mentioned in the 1801 census protocol. Cf: FT-1787, C2170.
12. See Schwarz Lausten, *Jøder og Kristne i Danmark*, p. 127.
13. Schwarz Lausten, *Jøder og Kristne i Danmark*, p. 118.
14. For example CNH, Wallich letters, from Martius to Wallich, 6 January 1849.
15. RAK, Kirurgisk Akademi, 3405-1, 'Matricul-Protocoll, Matricul 1785-1839', p. 45.
16. Medicinsk-historisk Museum af Københavns Universitet (ed.), *Academia Chirurgorum Regia. Det kongelige kirurgiske Akademi 1787-1987*, Copenhagen: Københavns Universitet, 1988, pp. 13f.
17. Ibid., passim.
18. RAK, op. cit., pp. 43-6.
19. O. Feldbæk, 'Revolutionskriege und Gesamtstaat. Das Ende der Neutralitätspolitik', *Zeitschrift des Vereins für Schleswig-Holsteinische Geschichte*, vol. 116, 1991, p. 118.
20. RAK, op. cit., pp. 43-6.
21. Ibid.
22. Ibid., p. 52.
23. M. Möbius, *Geschichte der Botanik. Von den ersten Anfängen bis zur Gegenwart*, Jena: Gustav Fischer, 1937, pp. 48-54; K. Mädgdefrau, *Geschichte der Botanik. Leben und Leistung großer Forscher*, Stuttgart, Jena & New York: Gustav Fischer, 1992, pp. 70f., 78-86.
24. Friis, 'Martin Vahl's videnskabelige løbebane', pp. 12f.
25. C. Christensen, *Den Danske botaniks historie med tilhørende bibliographie*, vol. 1, Copenhagen: H. Hagerup, 1924-6, pp. 155-75; Friis, 'Martin Vahl's videnskabelige løbebane', p. 17.
26. B. Hoppe, 'Von der Naturgeschichte zu der Naturwissenschaften. Die Dänisch-Halleschen Missionare als Naturforscher in Indien vom 18. bis zum 19. Jahrhundert', in: H. Liebau, A. Nehring,

B. Klosterberg (eds.), *Mission und Forschung. Translokale Wissensproduktion zwischen Indien und Europa im 18. und 19. Jahrhundert*, Halle: Franckesche Stiftungen, 2010, p. 162.

27. C. Christensen, article 'Vahl, Martin', in Poul Engelstoft (ed.), *Dansk Biografisk Leksikon*, vol. 25, Copenhagen: Gyldendal, 1943, pp. 12-17.

28. Christensen, *Den Danske botaniks historie*, vol. 1, pp. 205-18; id., article ,'Hornemann, Jens Wilken', in Poul Engelstoft (ed.), *Dansk Biografisk Leksikon*, vol. 10, Copenhagen: Gyldendal, 1936, pp. 599-601.

29. C.F. Bricka (ed.), *Fonden ad Usus Publicus. Aktmæssige bidrag til belysning af dens virksomhed*, vol. 2, Copenhagen: C.A. Reitzel, 1902, p. 113.

30. Leipzig University Library, Collection Römer, NL 134 M 62, Holbøll's testimony about Wallich, 28 September 1806.

31. E. Rostrup, article ,'Hofman (Bang) Niels', in Carl Frederik Bricka (ed.), *Dansk Biografisk Leksikon*, vol. 1, Copenhagen: Gyldendal, 1887, pp. 504ff.

32. Christensen, *Den Danske botaniks historie*, vol. 1, p. 220; L. Borgen, *Botanisk hage 1814–2014. Historien om en hage*, Oslo: Press, 2014, p. 53.

33. Borgen, *Botanisk hage*, p. 55.

34. RAK, op. cit., pp. 43-6.

35. A. C. P. Callisen, *Medicinisches Schriftsteller-Lexicon der jetzt lebenden Ärzte, Wundärzte, Geburtshelfer, Apotheker, und Naturforscher aller bildenden Völker*, vol. 16, Copenhagen: Königliches Taubstummen-Institut Schleswig, 1833, p. 274.

36. D.L. Lübker & H. Schröder, *Lexikon der Schleswig-Holstein Lauenburgischen und Eutinischen Schriftsteller von 1796 bis 1828*, vol. 1, Altona: K. Aue, 1829, p. 482.

37. Kay Larsen, *Dansk-Ostindiske Personalier og Data, Dansk Demografisk Database*, http://www.ddd.dda.dk/dop/sogeside.asp, entry 'Berner, Jørgen Henrik'.

38. O. C. Aagaard & R. Spärck, article 'Jacobson, Ludvig Levin', in: Poul Engelstoft (ed.), *Dansk Biografisk Leksikon*, vol. 11, Copenhagen: Gyldendal, 1937, pp. 342-5.

39. B. Henningsen, 'Henrik Steffens Kopenhagener Philosophie-Vorlesungen 1802-3. Zur Einführung', in Henrik Steffens, *Einleitung in die Philosophischen Vorlesungen*, Freiburg & Munich: Karl Alber, 2016, pp. 7ff.

40. Wallich later wrote of Giesemann as 'last—as well as least', cf. CNH, Wallich letters, index, p. 2
41. RA, Kirurgisk Akademi, 3411-02, 'Kirurgisk eksamen, Protokol over de skriftlige specimina, 1792-1842', p. 221.
42. CNH, Wallich letters, index, p. 3.

CHAPTER 3

As a Surgeon to the Danish East Indies

SURGEONS IN THE DANISH EAST INDIES

Europeans developed their colonial power in South Asia from the sixteenth century onwards. While the Portuguese, Dutch, French and Danes established their minor trading settlements, the British East India Company, in the wake of the Battle of Plassey (1757), was effectively transformed into a territorial power. Sickness and death have, since the beginning of the colonial age, been a common complementary to the European merchants, civil servants and missionaries in South Asia. It was not only unknown tropical diseases that caused the largest toll among Europeans, but common ailments already familiar in Europe—from the common cold to diarrhoea or stroke. Some women died in childbirth, while alcoholism and depression not infrequently led to suicidal deaths. Gradually, did the medical knowledge improve during the nineteenth century with a resulting increase of life expectancy among the Europeans in India.[1]

All of this applied to the tiny Danish trading colonies in India: Tranquebar on the Coromandel Coast in south India (Danish from 1620) and Serampore some thirty kilometres north of Calcutta in Bengal (from 1755). Both the settlements were administered by a Danish council headed by a Governor on behalf of the Danish Ministry of Commerce. Trade with Europe was carried out by the Danish Asiatic Company and, to an increasing extent, by private traders. In the second half of the eighteenth century the office of Royal Surgeon was created for both Tranquebar and Serampore to provide basic medical care for Europeans living in the Danish East Indies. In addition, the Asiatic Company had its own doctor in each settlement, but both positions were usually combined in the same individual.

From 1797, Johann Friedrich Lebrecht Quentius, born in the German town of Halberstadt, served as the Royal Surgeon, and later as the company doctor in Serampore, but he died in office on 13 November 1805.[2] A few weeks later, the Danish council there sought a replacement from Copenhagen and requested a well-trained and experienced physician to be sent to Bengal.[3] In addition to high social prestige, a good income was advertised, which was supposed to enable a good standard of living in India.[4]

It took more than six months before a letter from India could reach the Danish capital by sea; however, the request was quickly granted, and the Ministry of Commerce commissioned the Surgical Academy of Copenhagen to find a suitable candidate from among its graduates.[5] For someone to be interested in the position not only a good portion of idealism, but a deep interest in life in a completely unfamiliar environment was required. On the other hand, it meant a secure position in the Danish civil service and must, therefore, have been attractive to a young medical graduate.

What could a young person living in Copenhagen at the outset of the nineteenth century know about India? The architectural evidence of a long and fruitful cooperation between Denmark and the Indian Ocean region was striking. Since the 1640s, the elongated, richly decorated building of the Copenhagen Stock Exchange with its pointed tower made of four oriental-looking dragons had been located adjacent to the venerable Christiansborg Castle. On the other side of the channel dividing Copenhagen, the twin baroque gables of the administration building and warehouse of the Danish Asiatic Company rose into the air. In front of this—clearly visible across the water from the city centre—was the harbour basin where the huge Danish East Indiamen unloaded their precious cargoes:

tea and porcelain from China, spices from Southeast Asia as well as cotton and silk from India. Each year up to five Company vessels, and more private ships, sailed to Asia. In the households of wealthy Copenhageners Chinese porcelain was to be found, tea drunk and textiles from India were becoming more and more fashionable.

Unfortunately, no autobiographical information from Wallich himself exists for this period, so that one can only speculate about the motives for his application to leave for India. Did the young man meet sailors coming home from Serampore, Tranquebar or Chinese Canton? Or did his father or grand-father, as merchants, tell him about the riches to be gained in the East? It is perhaps more likely that his deep interest in botany, inspired by Vahl, Hornemann and Holbøll, played a significant part. A job as surgeon at Serampore would potenti-ally allow studies on the Indian flora since many areas of the vast country still represented blank spots on the map of natural history. Whether botany was the main motive from the begin-ning, or whether his 1830s statement 'My sole motive being Botany!' was a retrospective projection remains uncertain.[6] Perhaps, the fact that he was still without a permanent appoint-ment almost six months after taking the exams proved decisive.

Whatever the reason, on 15 September 1806, Nathaniel applied to the Surgical Academy for the vacant position of Surgeon at Serampore.[7] Within one week the decision must have been made to present him as a suitable candidate to the Ministry of Commerce. The quick selection suggests that he had already been interviewed before applying for the position, perhaps even approached by the professors themselves,[8] and they willingly issued the necessary letters of recommendation.[9] As was soon to become apparent such promotion was not entirely altruistic, for it was hoped not only to share knowledge of natural history, but to be supplied with botanical and zoological specimens from India. In this way Nathaniel Wallich was assigned to a role where he could become an intermediary between Asia and Europe where botanical knowledge was concerned.

However, the next steps on the way to Serampore were anything but a formality, for the candidate in question was of the Jewish faith; and at this time Jews were not allowed to enter the Danish civil service. Thus, before being appointed by the Ministry of Commerce, a royal decree had to be obtained, which proved to be difficult and Conrad Friedrich von Schmidt-Phiseldeck, as a member of the Ministry, sought instead to push through another, and obviously, less suitable candidate.[10] His anti-Jewish resentments were obvious: he argued 'that Jews should generally be excluded from the administrative and judicial offices of the state'.[11] Somewhat a one-sided view, his competitor was a simple barber who had failed the exams of the Surgical Academy as Wallich later wrote. From the outset, Wallich displayed a goodly portion of self-confidence.[12]

The decision of the Ministry of Commerce must have been very close. Even decades later, the world-renowned botanist wrote, 'this Mr von Schmidt-Phiseldeck was nearly frustrating my application for the Serampore Surgeonship' and in the 1840s, against the backdrop of German-Danish national conflict, he wrote, 'such was the disgraceful influence which all that was German had in these days in Denmark'.[13] However, examination marks spoke for themselves; perhaps the father and grandfather had also used their contacts with the political establishment; on 11 October 1806 Nathaniel, held in his hands the royal permission to enter the Danish civil service despite his Jewish roots.[14] Three weeks later, the appointment was made by the Ministry of Commerce, but Schmidt-Phiseldeck, clearly a bad loser, refused to sign it.[15] It was to take another four months before Wallich departed for India.

Immediately after his appointment as Royal Surgeon a veritable marathon of negotiations began, in which the young surgeon first demonstrated his negotiating skills that would later become apparent time and again. Already at a young age, he showed that he was able to promote his own economic as well as intellectual interests. First and foremost, Wallich explored his future field of activity and seems soon to have become familiar with his economic prospects. On 4 November, he applied to the Asiatic Company's Board of Directors to appoint him, like his predecessor Quentius, to the additional post of Company Surgeon of Serampore.[16] This decision took some time to be reached, and it was only shortly before his departure that the Company issued the requisite order to the Serampore administration.[17]

Wallich made preparations to ensure that he would be adequately equipped for future activities. First, he applied for money to purchase the expertise literature for his planned botanical studies. With regard to books, Holbøll advised him to turn to the Fonden ad Usus Publicos, a public foundation that provided financial support to the artists and scientists.[18] Their directors Ernst Schimmelmann and Friedrich Reventlow recognized the opportunity for developing the limited research links between Bengal and Copenhagen. They expressed their opinion that it was of great importance, especially for the Copenhagen Botanical Garden, to be in contact with a man in Bengal who was a zealous botanist and who would in future be obliged to increase the Copenhagen collections of living plants, seeds, and herbarium materials—an opinion undoubtedly dictated to them by Holbøll.[19] Wallich was granted the considerable sum of 200 Rigsdaler (Rd.) for the purchase of books (more than half of his later annual salary as Surgeon of Serampore).[20] In India, he was not to disappoint his supporters by the dispatch of numerous botanical consignments. Some of the books he acquired in Copenhagen have survived in the library of the Botanical Survey of India at Kolkata to this day.

In contrast to the Fonden ad Usus Publicos, the Ministry of Commerce proved to be less generous. Wallich must have known that one of his predecessors had received funds for the purchase of medicines and medical equipment, but when he applied for financing such acquisitions, it fell on deaf ears.[21]

Even if boarding and lodging were free on the voyage to India, an adequate outfit for the journey would be expensive, so he had to seek a personal loan. The Royal Treasury granted a loan for a further 500 Rd, which was guaranteed by his father.[22] Only nine days before Nathaniel's departure his father sought another advance for travel expenses to make some final purchases.[23]

ON THE *PRINCE OF AUGUSTENBURG*

Soon after the start of the year 1807, the young surgeon found out which ship would take him on his long journey. *The Prince of Augustenburg* was still moored in the port of Copenhagen and was just being rerigged. Towards the end of January, Wallich paid the ship a first visit to see the cabin in which he would most likely spend the long crossing. The officer on duty showed him his accommodation and assured that it was one of the best on board and exclusively for his own use. It seemed particularly pleasant that the cabin had a small window through which the daylight fell, which would be good for reading and writing.[24] In the course of the following weeks, he got the cabin furnished according to his social status.[25]

In March, the seventy-strong crew gradually gathered on board. In addition to Captain Christensen and Mr Leisner, the ship's head-merchant, the crew included chief steersman Jørgensen, first and second helsmen Kølle and Petersen, quartermasters Sigbrantzen and Petersen, as well as Boutellier Ferm, responsible for the alcohol supply, chef Holm, chief carpenter Mouritsen, corporal Lund and butcher Wilfardt. The ship's two doctors Simonsen and Knutzen meant that Wallich himself had nothing to do on board as a doctor. Besides a large quantity of silver coins, the cargo consisted mainly of ironware. In terms of food and drink exported for sale in India, the ship carried more than 20,000 bottles of red wine, 1,680 containers of gin, 554 cheeses and a large quantity of salad oil.[26]

The *Prince of Augustenburg* was late. To catch the southwest monsoon to carry the ship to India beyond the Cape of Good Hope, it would have been wise to start in January or

Plate 3.1: Nathaniel Wallich's Danish passport which permitted him to leave Copenhagen, 1807. (Botanical Survey of India, Central National Herbarium, Kolkata)

February. However, it was only on 28 March, that the directors of the Asiatic Company boarded the ship to inspect and swear in the crew. The pilot then climbed aboard to escort the ship through the sound to Elsinore. Finally, the same day, two passengers arrived with their luggage, the merchant John Brown, and the surgeon Nathaniel Wallich.[27]

The Ministry of Commerce had paid a considerable sum for Wallich's journey. In addition to the free passage, he was able to enjoy 1,200 pounds of free freight and was allowed to dine at the captain's table during the voyage.[28] However, the initial joy was not to remain undisturbed for long. The problem was the cabin he had been promised two months earlier, which he had liked and for which he had obtained all the necessities. When the surgeon wanted to make himself comfortable there, he found that his fellow-passenger Brown had already occupied it. The merchant bluntly demanded to vacate the cabin with all his belongings—which in Wallich's eyes represented improper behaviour towards a royal official. While still in Copenhagen, he was told that a high-ranking company functionary had, for an appropriate fee, personally assured Brown of the cabin, and that Wallich would have to move into a smaller cabin that did not even have a small window hatch.[29]

The ship was still in port, so Wallich wrote a strongly worded letter of complaint to the Ministry of Commerce about Brown's misconducts. The language not only indicates, once again, a pronounced self-confidence, but also that he was very upset indeed. The new cabin assigned to him would be nothing more than a prison that he was unable to think of bearing for the passage of many months. The most annoying aspect was probably that he would be unable to read and write in daylight without a window.[30] A day later, two carpenters arrived on board to carry out structural changes to the boatswain's cabin. The boatswain was billeted out and his cabin handed over to John Brown. Wallich had got what he wanted.[31]

A final greeting from land came in the form of a letter from his fellow student and cousin Ludvig Levin Jacobson. With the letter, he sent a medical instrument for the surgical treatment of deafness, the use of which the author described in detail and which he wanted to see used by Wallich in India.[32] The *Prince* lifted anchor and immediately after leaving the Sound and reaching the open sea Wallich began to write letters. From close to the Swedish coast a first letter was sent to Jacobson; two others followed within a week when off the coast of Norway. He reported, inter alia, that he was carrying out zoological studies on fish and was particularly interested in their innards.[33] Fortunately, he did not suffer from the dreaded seasickness that could put many an experienced sailors out of action for weeks. The sea became increasingly rough, a small foretaste of the stormy crossing of the South Atlantic four months later. On 14 April, the first victim of the voyage was recorded—one of the pigs had perished and was thrown overboard. Four days later, the Shetland Islands appeared on the southern horizon.[34]

The journey continued south-westwards across the Atlantic. Frightening was not only the loneliness on the seemingly endless ocean, and the increasingly scarce supplies of drinking water, but also the condition of the food. One day it was discovered that the dried peas stored on board in crates were gradually rotting, though they were still prepared for the sailors until they finally refused to eat them. Following the complaints of the crew it was decided to remove the rotting legumes from the menu and instead serve the sailors with groats and the healthier sauerkraut.

On 7 July the *Prince of Augustenburg* anchored off Rio de Janeiro, where Danish East India vessels on their way to the Indian Ocean were not an uncommon sight. Flags were hoisted and the Portuguese fortress saluted with nine cannon shots; the anchor was dropped, and the ship remained in port for eleven days. The further west a sailing ship travelled over the mid-Atlantic, the more reliable were the winds that would carry it south from there and later, eastwards around the Cape of Good Hope.[35]

For the first time in his life, Wallich practised botany outside his home country. Decades later, he remembered that the stay at Rio had pleased him very much. For some time afterwards, he maintained contact from Serampore with an unnamed 'gentleman' from the capital of Portuguese Brazil.[26] He brought Brazilian plants to India, one of which, a *Malpighia* plant, finally found its way to the Botanical Garden of Calcutta.[37] At Kew, there are drawings made by Wallich after he arrived at Serampore of three species of *Sida* that he collected at Rio. Specimens of five species of ferns collected in Rio are mentioned in the Wallich Catalogue.

The voyage to Rio turned out to have been the easiest part of the journey—the onward one towards the Cape proved dangerous, stormy and uncomfortable. On 20 July, the Tropic of Cancer was crossed. Days with high waves followed and finally the strong wind grew into a heavy storm accompanied by thunderstorms. The air temperature dropped considerably and against the humid cold captain Christensen issued an extra portion of brandy.[38] The *Prince of Augustenburg* passed the invisible dividing line between the Atlantic and Indian Oceans some 250 kilometres south of Cape Town, but the weather hardly improved even here.[39]

Wallich and the other men on board were unaware that at the same time, many thousands of kilometres further north at home in Copenhagen, catastrophe was looming. For too long, Denmark had taken too much advantage of its neutrality, selling large numbers of weapons to the enemies of Britain in Europe and India. The British now wanted to force Denmark to join the anti-Napoleonic coalition; but by using military pressure they achieved the opposite. The Danish capital was attacked by the British fleet in early September. Copenhagen experienced the heaviest bombing raid in its history and Denmark had no choice but to enter the war on the side of Napoleon.[40] Denmark's entering the Napoleonic Wars against Britain was to have a decisive influence on Wallich's latter life in distant India.

As Copenhagen lay in ruins, the *Prince of Augustenburg* again crossed the Tropic of Cancer on 19 September—this time in a northerly direction into the Bay of Bengal. After long weeks of loneliness, ships once again came in sight, and it was probably with no small relief that the crew spotted the coast of Ceylon on the north-west horizon in the early evening of 6 October—the first sight of land since leaving Rio de Janeiro two and a half months earlier. The climate was mild, and the steady south-west monsoon carried the Danes safely towards India.[41]

Three days later, early in the morning, the grey walls of the fort of Dansborg with the Danish flag blowing high above it were visible in the distance and at half past ten in the morning the *Prince of Augustenburg* was lying in the roads off the Danish colony of Tranquebar, alongside three other Danish East Indiamen. There was no harbour there, so all persons and goods had to be transported on small boats, the so-called 'sellings', from the ship to the wide sandy beach—a somewhat risky enterprise in view of the usually heavy surf. Around noon the first selling moored alongside the ship to transport the captain, the ship's assistant and a mail bag ashore; three empty barrels were also sent to be filled with fresh drinking water for the crew. Soon afterwards, Wallich disembarked to step onto the soil of his promised land for the first time. From now on he was to live and work in India for almost four decades.[42]

The few days during which the *Prince of Augustenburg* anchored off Tranquebar were sufficient to give him a good impression of the tiny colony. Right on the beach lay the four-winged Dansborg fortress dating from the 1620s. To the north of it was the tree-lined parade ground, on whose opposite side the neoclassical Governor's building could be glimpsed in the sun. Inland from the parade ground, Kongensgade, today's King's Street, stretched out, on which two churches from Danish times can still be seen; the Lutheran Zion Church of 1701 and the New Jerusalem Church built by the German Missionaries in 1718. Stately private residences of Danish, Dutch and English merchants, and of colonial officials, were lined up along Kongensgade next to the mission house. Hindus and Muslims lived away from the European quarter. The whole of Tranquebar, with its grid-pattern of streets, was surrounded by a town wall and a moat. Of these walls only a few overgrown fragments and the magnificent town gate of 1792 now remain.[43]

Wallich apparently had little contact with the Danish government during his short stay and his attention was directed towards the German missionaries and the local surgeon Anton Wilhelm Friedrich Ruhde, his future counterpart in the Danish East Indies. Two missionaries were of particular interest to him because of their natural history research—Christoph Samuel John and the missionary doctor Johann Gottfried Klein. John had been in India for more than three decades and in 1779 had founded a school for European and Indian children in Tranquebar. His natural history research had made him prominent far beyond India and he had been awarded an honorary doctorate from the German Academia Leopoldina in 1795 for his zoological studies. The missionary Johann Peter Rottler, with whom Wallich was also later to be in contact, was similarly honoured at the same time.[44]

The exchange between John and Wallich was only brief as John had only recently returned from a journey to the south Indian temple town of Chidambaram shortly after the arrival of the *Prince of Augustenburg*. On Wallich's departure, John sent to the ship a short note in German expressing his regret that 'my journey to Sidambaram has robbed me of the pleasure of enjoying your pleasant company more often and for longer!'[45] This brief note was accompanied by a letter to his long-standing friend William Roxburgh, Superintendent of the Calcutta Botanic Garden.[46] Even if this letter itself does not survive, we may presume that it had contained words of recommendation and a request that Roxburgh keep a close eye on the young and promising scholar from Denmark.

The Tranquebar surgeon Ruhde probably explained Wallich the diseases prevailing in India and the options for their treatment. Ruhde was thirteen years older than Wallich and came from a family of gardeners; his father had been royal gardener in Fredensborg Castle north of Copenhagen. Wallich might have first met him in Copenhagen, where Ruhde was Wallich's senior by a few years at the Surgical Academy and already experienced at the dissecting table.[47]

Wallich's visit to Tranquebar marked the beginning of a long-lasting correspondence with Ruhde, which was shaped by many a personal word as well as medical-scientific exchange. The elder surgeon's first letter was addressed to Serampore on 16 December 1807, in which he expressed his delight at Wallich's arrival there, which he had heard about from English newspapers.[48] The respect was mutual and at some point after Ruhde's death Wallich picked up that first letter again and wrote at the top a touching note in his distinct handwriting in English: 'R. was beyond all doubt one of the dearest surgeons who ever visited India. As an anatomist he was *sine pari*'.[49]

That the stay of the *Prince of Augustenburg* at Tranquebar was short was due primarily to the fact that the Danish Asiatic Company no longer had much business there, its main activities now being in Serampore. On 5 November, at half past five in the evening, the Burmese coast of Arakan was sighted at some distance to the north-east. Bengal could not be far away. The first evidence of the approaching country was the strong tidal current, which now made itself felt on the ship. The effect of the ebb is intensified by the enormous mass of water released by the Ganges into the Bay of Bengal. It became more and more problematic to sail against the counter-current, and finally the ship was able to move forward only on the incoming tide, while the rest of the time the ship was anchored.[50] On 11 November, it was finally possible to get a Bengali pilot on board.[51]

Five days later, at noon, the village of Kulpi was passed. The ship's logbook for that day reports that the passengers Brown and Wallich left the ship together.[52] We do not know exactly how Wallich finally reached Serampore, but it can be assumed that he went on a river boat with his travelling companion first to Calcutta and from there on to Serampore. He finally reached the small Danish colony on the Hooghly River on 18 November 1807, some days earlier than the *Prince* itself.[53]

NOTES

1. T. Delfs, 'What shall become of the mission when we have such incompetent missionaries there?: Drunkenness and Mission in 18th century Danish East India', in H. Fischer-Tiné & J. Tschurenev (eds.), *A History of Alcohol and Drugs in Modern South Asia. Intoxicating Affairs*, London: Routledge, 2014, pp. 65-89; D. Arnold, *Colonizing the Body: State Medicine and Epidemic Disease in Nineteenth-Century India*, Berkeley: University of California Press, 1993, pp. 11-24.
2. Larsen, *Dansk-Ostindiske Personalier og Data*, entry 'Quentius, Johann Friedrich Lebrecht'.
3. CNH, Wallich letters, Extract af Depechen fra det Kongelige Raad i Frederichsnagore, 27 December 1805: 'at ville forsyne Stedet med en kundig, erfaren og examineret Doctor'.
4. CNH, Wallich letters, Secret Council Serampore to Commerce kollegiet, 27 December 1805.

5. CNH, Wallich letters, Wallich to the Surgical Academy, 15 September 1806.
6. CNH, Wallich letters, index, p. 7.
7. CNH, Wallich letters, Wallich to the Surgical Academy, 15 September 1806.
8. CNH, Wallich letters, Wallich to Christian VII of Denmark, 23 September 1806.
9. Wallich reassembled these testimonies in his own hand into a single document. One copy is among the Wallich letters in Calcutta, and it is likely that he handed another copy to the decision-makers at the Surgical Academy. CNH, Wallich letters, copies of testimonies, Vahl 11 July 1804, Schumacher 17 September 1806, Viborg 22 September 1806, Hornemann 25 September 1806, Holbøll 28 September 1806.
10. L. Bobé, Article 'Conrad Georg Friederich Elias v. Schmidt-Phiseldeck', in Carl Frederik Bricka (ed.), *Dansk Biografisk Leksikon*, vol. 15, Copenhagen: Gyldendal, 1901, pp. 233ff; cf. also: Conrad Friedrich von Schmidt-Phiseldeck, *Ueber das jetzige Verhältnis der Jüdischen Nation zu dem christlichen Bürgervereine, und dessen künftige Umgestaltung*, Copenhagen: Gräbe, 1817.
11. Schmidt-Phiseldeck, *Ueber das jetzige Verhältniß*, p. 52.
12. CNH, Wallich letters, index, p. 3.
13. Ibid., p. 7.
14. CNH, Wallich letters, Danske Kancelli to Wallich, 11 October 1806.
15. Ibid., Commercekollegiet, Promemoria, 1 November 1806.
16. Ibid., Wallich to the Directors of the Asiatisk Kompagni, 4 November 1806.
17. Ibid., Factory of the Asiatisk Kompagni Serampore to Wallich, 19 November 1807.
18. Bricka, *Fonden ad Usus Publicus*, vol. 2, p. 113, 22 November 1806.
19. Ibid.
20. Ibid.
21. CNH, Wallich letters, Wallich to Commercecollegiet, 11 November 1806.
22. Ibid., Wulff Lazarus Wallich, 6 January 1807.
23. Ibid., Wulff Lazarus Wallich to Commercecollegiet, 18 March 1807.
24. CNH, Wallich letters, index, p. 13.
25. Ibid., p. 11.

26. RAK, Asiatisk Kompagni, Faktoriet i Frederiksnagore, Regnskabs-journaler, 2144, 14 November 1807.
27. CNH, Wallich letters, index, p. 13.
28. Ibid., Commercecollegiet to Wallich, 17 March 1807.
29. CNH, Wallich letters, index, p. 13.
30. CNH, Wallich letters, Wallich, March 1807.
31. RAK, Asiatisk Kompagni København, Skibsprotokoller, 752-3, Printzen af Augustenborg, 29 March 1807; CNH, Wallich letters, index, p. 13.
32. CNH, Wallich letters, Jacobson to Wallich, 29 March 1807.
33. CNH, Wallich letters, Jacobson to Wallich, 8 April 1807; RAK, Asiatisk Kompagni København, Skibsprotoller, 752-3, Printzen af Augustenborg, 31 March-3 April 1807.
34. Ibid., 14-18 April 1807.
35. J.H. Deuntzer, 'Af det Asiatiske Kompagnis Historie', *Nationaløkonomisk Tidsskrift*, vol. 46, 1908, p. 383.
36. This emerges indirectly: CNH, Wallich letters, Roxburgh to Wallich, 11 February 1810.
37. CNH, Wallich letters, index, p. 17.
38. RAK, Asiatisk Kompagni København, Skibsprotokoller, 752-3, Printzen af Augustenborg, Christensen to the management of Asiatisk Kompagni, 10 October 1807.
39. Ibid., 26 August to 8 September 1807.
40. Krieger, 'Der dänische Gesamtstaat', pp. 40ff.
41. RAK, Asiatisk Kompagni København, Skibsprotokoller, 752-3, Printzen af Augustenborg, Christensen to the management of Asiatisk Kompagni, October 1807.
42. Ibid., 8-9 October 1807.
43. On the general urban development of Tranquebar, see the special volume Tranquebar, Architectura, Arkitekturhistorisk Årsskrift, 9, 1987.
44. J. Gröschl, 'Missionaries of the Danish-Halle and English-Halle Mission in India 1706-1844', in A. Gross, Y. V. Kumaradoss and H. Liebau (eds.), *Halle and the Beginnings of Protestant Christianity in India*, vol. 3, Halle: Franckesche Stiftungen, 2006, p. 1516.
45. CNH, Wallich letters, John to Wallich, 17 October 1807.
46. Ibid.
47. CNH, Wallich letters, index, p. 15.
48. CNH, Wallich letters, Ruhde to Wallich, 16 October 1807: 'især i Ting som angaae vores fælles Videnskab'.

49. CNH, Wallich letters, Ruhde to Wallich, 16 October 1807.
50. RAK, Asiatisk Kompagni København, Skibsprotokoller, 752-3, Printzen af Augustenborg, 8–9 November 1807.
51. Ibid., Christensen to Asiatisk Kompagni, 18 November 1807.
52. Ibid., 16 November 1807.
53. CNH, Wallich letters, index, p. 17.

CHAPTER 4

Serampore

THE DANISH FLAG IN BENGAL

After a seven-months sea voyage, with only short stopovers, the young surgeon must have been relieved finally to have solid ground under his feet once again. The hot and humid plains of Bengal were, henceforth, to be his home and he was not to revisit Copenhagen and see his parents until more than two decades later. When Wallich reached Serampore, the Danish flag had been hoisted over the small colony for more than half a century. The settlement officially bore the name Frederiksnagore in honour of the former Danish King Frederik V.

Attracted by the treasures of Bengal, especially its textiles and opium, the trading posts of the Europeans were lined up like a string of pearls along the Hooghly, a branch of the Ganga River. The beginning had been made by the Portuguese in the sixteenth century,[1] but the ousting of the Portuguese by the Mughals in the 1630s had led to an opening of Bengal to other European trading nations. In 1633, the Dutch arrived, and three years later the British East India Company established a trading-settlement at Balasore on the southern periphery of that region (in today's Odisha).[2] The Danes also joined these endeavours, although their involvement initially showed a considerable degree of discontinuity. As early as 1625, a fleet of three Danish ships had reached the port of Pipli, situated to the north of Balasore, where some merchants were left behind to establish trade.[3] In 1636, they also took possession of a larger plot of land in Balasore, which is still known today as Dinamardinga (in which the name of Denmark is phonetically hidden). Such initial undertakings were, however, short-lived.

In 1698, only eight years after Job Charnock founded an English settlement in an obscure fishing village called Dihi Kolikata (modern-day Kolkata), the Danes established a small colony called Dannemarksnagore on the right bank of the Hooghly. This ended abruptly in 1714, when a Mughal army razed it to the ground.[4] The frequent interruptions of Danish involvement in Bengal are a clear indication of major administrative problems and a lack of capital.[5]

In the middle of the eighteenth century, Danish trade in Bengal entered calmer waters when it was monopolized by the Danish Asiatic Company, founded in 1732. This Company had entered the Chinese tea and porcelain trade with extraordinary success. To a certain extent, the income gained was reinvested in the lands around the Indian Ocean. In the 1750s, two small trading settlements were established on the Malabar coast of southern India and the Nicobar Islands between India and the Malay Peninsula were also taken over.[6]

In 1755, with the energetic assistance of the French, the Danes were granted a Mughal privilege which allowed them

Plate 4.1: Peter Anker, Serampore, watercolour, 1798.
(Museum of Cultural History, Oslo)

to trade freely throughout Bengal in exchange for the payment of customs duties. At the same time, about twenty-five kilometres north of Calcutta, a piece of land on the Hooghly was acquired beside the small village of Serampore, from which the Danish colony soon took its name. Two years later, following the Battle of Plassey, the British emerged as the major territorial power in Bengal after which the Danish territory became an enclave within the extensive sphere of influence of the British East India Company.[7]

In 1799, four English Baptist missionaries appeared in Serampore. Forbidden to settle in British territory, they were favourably received by the Danish colonial authorities and founded a large mission station on a site in the east of the village. One of the missionaries was the Rev. William Carey, the most intellectual scholar Serampore was ever to receive. Carey had originally been a shoemaker from Northamptonshire, but as an autodidact he had acquired a solid education in Christian theology and the classical languages and, immediately on his arrival in India he began to study both classical and modern Indian languages. The versatile missionary also had a passion for botany and together with his comrades, Carey founded a printing shop next to a small botanical garden.[8]

A later Baptist project was the founding of an educational institution under the title 'College for the Instruction of Asiatic and other Youth in Eastern Literature and European Science'. King Frederik VI agreed to this idea in 1821, and donated a temporary building for its activities. Six years later, the college itself was founded with a royal privilege—the third university in the Danish monarchy after Copenhagen and Kiel.[9]

Serampore experienced its greatest flowering in the decades before Denmark entered the Napoleonic Wars. Danish neutrality brought enormous profits to the pockets of local merchants through the exchange of goods, but also through the transfer of capital and illegal trade using Danish Sea passports. Two major construction projects were started only a few years before Wallich's arrival—the prison and court building (*catcherie*), and the St. Olav Church—buildings that still stand today.

Both were later to be connected with Wallich's life—as the Royal Surgeon he was responsible for the health of the prison inmates; and in the church his wedding was to take place.

For many years after the end of the devastating Napoleonic Wars, Serampore was still regarded as a jewel in colonial India. In the 1830s, the traveller Emma Roberts considered the town with its clean streets to be the best kept and most beautiful European settlement in India.[10] Even in 1845, when Serampore and Tranquebar were sold to the British, the Danish admiral Steen Bille was full of praise, 'With astonishment I looked at the beauty, cleanliness and order of small Serampore during my visit, as well as the contentment and prosperity that apparently reigned here'.[11] The small town was thus characterized by a solid, colonial comfort—an idyll within what could be seen as the turbulence of an 'exotic' Indian environment. Such an impression could, however, prove to be misleading, as Nathaniel Wallich was soon to discover.

AT WAR

When the *Prince of Augustenburg* was still moored off Diamond Harbour a mailbag was sent ahead to Serampore, in which the representatives of the Asiatic Company were given details of the cargo sent from Copenhagen. While the large quantity of iron was very welcome, this was far from the case for the food and drink, except for the 20,000 bottles of French wine.[12] The main complaint (as mentioned in the record book of Serampore) concerned the gin of which there were still large quantities in the warehouse from previous cargoes, and it would take time before it could be sold. The same applied to the cheeses, the despatch of which from the mother country could only have been arranged by someone unfamiliar with Indian conditions. A financial loss should have been more than foreseeable here, just as with the sale of the European salad oil, which was currently available in such abundance that the selling price to be achieved was hardly higher than that for an

Indian oil. The joy was greater when another message was found in the mailbag, the letter from the company directors with the news that the long-awaited Royal Surgeon was also travelling on the ship.[13]

A few days later Wallich arrived in person and was immediately appointed by the Danish chief Jacob Krefting to his new position as Royal Surgeon. The same day Caspar Top, the local head of the Asiatic Company, simultaneously appointed him as the Company's Surgeon.[14] Thus, the recently arrived man, like his predecessor Quentius, was a servant of two masters, which would provide him comfortably two regular sources of income.

Wallich had brought with him from Copenhagen personal letters of recommendation to the members of the European elite of Serampore.[15] These provide evidence of the great importance of intercontinental patronage networks in developing overseas careers many thousands of kilometres from home. A newcomer to India could usually not resort to personal or family contacts, and letters of introduction replaced direct personal advocacy to an even greater extent than in Europe itself.[16] As was soon to become apparent, however, these references ultimately served less to consolidate Wallich's reputation as the surgeon of Serampore, than to establish a regional and transregional communication network with which the doctor sought to further his natural history interests.

Wallich's monthly salary as Royal Surgeon was 31 Rd. besides which he received an additional 15 Rd. each month for his service as a Company doctor. The combined sum was rather more than the income of Ruhde, his counterpart in Tranquebar,[17] and put him in third place on the Danish payroll in Serampore after Chief Krefting and the second on the Council, Bernhard August Wickede.[18] Despite this, since he had to establish himself, and as the European standard of living in India was far from low, his salary in the first month was not sufficient, so he was forced to apply for a loan from the government in Serampore.[19] We don't know what he spent the money on, nor, do we know where exactly he lived but it can be assumed that he rented a room in one of the European houses in the heart of the town or else moved into rooms in the government complex.

During the first few weeks, Wallich became familiar with the small Indo-European society of Serampore. Even though Krefting was his direct superior, his friendship with Caspar Top would prove to be more stimulating and ultimately more significant. Top maintained close and long-standing contacts with William Roxburgh at the East India Company's Botanic Garden in Calcutta. Before his transfer to Serampore in the 1790s, the senior company merchant had been head of the Asiatic Company's enterprises in Tranquebar, while Roxburgh had at the same time made a similar move, having been in charge of a large experimental plantation at Samal Kota in the Godavari-Krishna delta. Both had business connections with each other.[20] Top was older and looked back on many years of experience in India; he soon developed an almost paternal relationship with the young surgeon.

Wallich also made contact with other Europeans in the town. He shared a passion for natural science with the businessman and entomologist Bernd Wilhelm Westermann whom he would remember decades later as an 'old and valued friend of mine'.[21] One of his closest contacts was William Carey, with whom Wallich regularly exchanged botanical information. As countless letters by Carey to Wallich display, they remained in close personal contact until Carey's death in 1834.[22]

Wallich never gave the impression that he intended to devote himself immediately and exclusively to medical practice; boxes with medicine brought from Copenhagen remained closed. Instead, all his efforts were directed towards making contact with Roxburgh as quickly as possible (certainly to the delight of his academic teachers in Copenhagen). After all, he had the letters of recommendation from Hornemann in Copenhagen and from John in Tranquebar, as well as local introductions from Caspar Top and Carey.

It was Carey who personally opened the gates to Roxburgh

William Roxburgh M.D. F.L.S

Superintendant of the Honble the East-India Company's
Botanic Garden at Calcutta,
Late Honorary Corresponding Member of the Society
for the Encouragement of Arts, Manufactures and Commerce.

Engraved by Charles Warren Esq.r from a Miniature
in the possession of M.rs Roxburgh.

Plate 4.2: William Roxburgh, copperplate
engraving, 1815.

for Wallich. Just three days after his arrival, the missionary took him on a visit to the Botanical Garden in Calcutta.[23] The fact that Wallich, who had only just received his letter of appointment as Royal Surgeon, left his new workplace so quickly shows clearly where his greatest interest lay from the start—for him medicine primarily served as a living. Instead, Wallich was to break through the tight corset of the office to devote himself to the wide field of botany.

The weeks passed quickly, and it was not until 3 January 1808 that Wallich found time to open the boxes he had brought with him from the royal pharmacy in Copenhagen. Despite the long journey and the warm climate, he found the medicines in excellent condition.[24] It can be assumed that he re-equipped the pharmacy in the government complex and perhaps, he also set up a surgery there and carried out his first treatments of the sick.

In the meantime, Denmark and Britain had been at war with each other for four months. When news of this reached Bengal in the late January 1808, a bitter shock must have passed through the small Danish community in Serampore. For decades, the Danes had been closely linked to the British colonial economy in nearby Calcutta and a disturbance of the delicate transfer of money and goods between the two places could not but have had severe consequences for the local economy. On 28 January, things got serious. From Barrackpore on the opposite bank to Serampore, three companies of Indo-British Sepoy troops crossed the Hooghly, their commander demanded the immediate handover of the small colony. Since the Danes, with their forty or so Indian soldiers and a few cannons, had nothing with which to oppose the British, this demand was immediately granted. Equally drastic was the seizure of Danish ships at anchor—twelve vessels partly loaded with cargoes of valuable commercial goods had to be surrendered. The *Prince of Augustenburg* had already made her way back to Calcutta after her stay in Serampore, but on the same day, i.e. 28 January, she was captured by the British at Diamond Harbour. The Danish officials of Serampore were placed under arrest and were not allowed to leave the town; a British commissioner based in nearby Chinsurah took control of the small colony.[25]

This war unfolded its destructive effect, though without further fighting in Serampore. Trade collapsed completely and the Danish private merchants left the small colony. The British occupation drove Wallich's friend Westermann to ruin, but he was lucky in misfortune for in Dutch Batavia, where misery drove him, he found a rich lady. Later, as a wealthy man and owner of a sugar refinery, Westermann was able to settle in Copenhagen with one of Denmark's largest private natural history collections.[26]

The liberal attitude of the British Governor-General, Lord Minto, nevertheless ensured that informal personal relations between Serampore and the British in Calcutta remained largely intact during the long years of war. Less than a month after the occupation, the Danes regained their freedom of movement and enjoyed a small salary. From then on Wallich received 'subsistence money', though this was considerably less than his Danish salary.[27] By British grace the promising Royal Surgeon had become a 'Surgeon of Serampore'. Financially broken and with reduced social status, he was no longer a royal Danish civil servant, nor yet a permanent employee of the British East India Company, though as a doctor he still had his hands full.[28]

After the initial harsh surprise, the British occupying forces proceeded in a calm and relaxed manner, in Serampore as well as in Tranquebar. From time to time Wallich received letters from Ruhde, who reported that Danish law and Danish customs continued to apply in Tranquebar where Danish officers had even profited from the occupation with a sharp increase in their pay. Unlike his colleague in Serampore, Ruhde was fortunate not to be financially worse off than before.[29]

The difficult financial situation strengthened Wallich's pragmatic attitude towards money and we find him negotiating hard for his salary, travel grants and other gratuities in the decades that followed. But the war also brought forth drastic changes in other respects. His contact with his parents, teachers, and friends in his distant homeland severed almost completely for several years. While letters between Europe and the East Indies had taken around six months in peacetime, their journey was now greatly lengthened. A letter written by Hornemann in January 1809, for example, did not reach Serampore until 13 December 1810, almost two years later.[30] Personal communications within Bengal, therefore, became all the more important and nearby Calcutta offered a wealth of opportunities. Wallich was eventually to find a kind of substitute family through the natural history and botanical network that he built up in Bengal.

WILLIAM ROXBURGH

From the beginning William Roxburgh was at the centre of Wallich's life and work in India. In addition to a lively exchange of letters between Serampore and the botanical garden of Calcutta, personal encounters also served to strengthen this connection. While Carey had arranged the first personal visit to Roxburgh, Caspar Top would now play an important role. For him, the trip to the Garden situated at Shibpur south of Calcutta was sometimes a family undertaking. For example, when Top suggested a visit on 7 July 1808, on which he intended to take his daughter and her acquaintances, he wrote to Wallich and said that it would be a great pleasure if he were also to be one of the parties. It would be best for the group to set off in the afternoon to reach Calcutta in the evening. From there, after an overnight stay, the group was to continue its journey before dawn to arrive at the garden in the coolness of daybreak, when the whole magic of the Garden was seen to its best advantage. The peak of the rainy season was reached in July, so by visiting early in the morning it was possible to avoid having to stay outside during the heavy rains, which tended to fall at midday and in the afternoon. The return trip then depended on the tidal current of the Hooghly.[31]

Learning from Roxburgh, a Linnean with three decades of

experience in India, Wallich deepened his knowledge about the collection and description of plants. This exchange benefitted Roxburgh as well, to whom Wallich would frequently send pressed and dried plants from Serampore. Wallich also asked Roxburgh for advice on the making of plant drawings. Roxburgh subsequently sent an Indian plant draughtsman named Chunassi to Serampore. His advice was to 'Try him and pay him according to his ability'.[32] Wallich, therefore, learned to work with local artists and plant-collectors—a skill he would develop as we shall see, for example, in Nepal. Tirelessly he collected and dried plants, had them drawn or drew them himself.[33]

Wallich gained Roxburgh's trust and the contact paid off, for the prospect soon opened up for him to exchange his poorly paid job at Serampore for a position at the Botanic Garden. Since February 1809 Roxburgh had been working hard to obtain permission from the East India Company to enrol Wallich into the service of the Botanical Garden. Aware of the talent and devotion of his young protégé, Roxburgh intended to profit from it himself. It was not his intention to actually employ Wallich in the Garden itself, but to send him on journeys as a collector, not only of botanical material, but also of animals and geological samples. All this, as Roxburgh wrote to his superiors to solicit their approval, was intended to benefit the British in view of the great importance of India's natural resources—a clear indication that Roxburgh was aware of the enormous significance of natural science to the Company.[34]

Roxburgh duly received permission to take Wallich into service. This permission is something of a surprise and must testify to Wallich's networking skills since, as a Dane, he had officially been a prisoner of war of the East India Company. On the other hand, things were different in India from Europe and someone who might be an enemy in Europe did not necessarily have to be perceived as an enemy overseas (especially if he were Danish rather than French). Nevertheless, Wallich was far from being officially appointed as an employee of the British East India Company. The financial recompense was also to remain modest: in addition to his meagre salary from Serampore, Wallich was to receive only a small travel allowance during the planned expeditions. Nevertheless, he accepted the position offered to him with optimism.[35]

With a new and more attractive job in his pocket he set off for Shibpur at the beginning of the hot season, probably in April 1809, to prepare for his botanical missions.[36] It may be assumed that his work was satisfactory because soon Roxburgh tried to increase his salary. This, however, was rejected by the local administration and, even worse, Wallich's appointment became increasingly controversial.[37] Presumably, the colonial authorities soon became aware that after Wallich's departure, a doctor was now missing in Serampore. The British Commissioner for Serampore, Ernst, sent a request to Calcutta to cancel Wallich's assignment to the Botanic Garden as soon as possible. The prospect of permanent employment at the Garden proved to be in vain and his appointment did not last longer than two months. By July 1809, at the latest, Wallich was back in Serampore.[38]

Even though his stay with Roxburgh had been of short duration, he had gained one important skill—to speak and write fluently in English. Whereas his early correspondence was mainly in Danish, from now on he increasingly used English and with this his handwriting underwent a significant change. The austere style, influenced by the Danish cursive script, was replaced by bold handwriting that is not always easy to read. We may presume that with the change of his mode of communication, his view of the world also changed. The young surgeon from Copenhagen perhaps gradually transformed himself into a cosmopolitan.

SURGEON OF SERAMPORE

After the bitter setback at the Botanic Garden, the subsequent months at Serampore passed quietly, and a doctor's routine emerged. Time and again, however, letters with botanical interest would land on Wallich's desk. For example, Roxburgh once inquired about clove trees (now *Syzygium aromaticum*) that, unusually for Bengal, were said to grow somewhere near Serampore. Wallich found that these had existed, but that they had died some time before.[39] Roxburgh would invite him for short visits to his spacious house in the Garden beside the Hooghly River: 'When you have nothing to do, come and spend a day or two down here, to refresh your botanical memory',[40] he wrote.

Even though the research expeditions had been temporarily disrupted, medical work allowed some freedom for smaller botanical enterprises. A three-week expedition towards the northwest, which Wallich undertook in the dry season of 1810, stands out, about which he reported in detail to Hornemann. It was not easy for leave to be granted for such a comparatively long time and Wallich justified it to the British authorities by saying that he wanted to stay away from his practice for only three days to treat Europeans outside Serampore— this period was granted but he then extended it on his own authority.[41]

On 19 February he went about seven kilometres up the Hooghly River, then proceeded overland to the town of Burdwan where he made the planned medical visit. From there the surgeon conducted short trips to the surrounding area for eight days to botanize. He also visited the bed of the river Damodar, which at that time of the year was dry. Finally, he went further north into the hill country of Birbhum, then back eastwards, and again reached the Hooghly at the village of Katwa. Within three days he headed back to Serampore. He explained to Hornemann that the route he had chosen had not proved to be particularly advantageous from a botanical point of view—but a start had been made.[42]

His penchant for the world of plants and these occasional botanical excursions do not obscure the fact that he took his profession as a surgeon seriously and gradually built up a reputation as a gifted physician. He was always keen to expand his knowledge of local diseases and their treatment, which included some brave self-experimentation. On one occasion,

Plate 4.3: Charles D'Oyly, On the road to Serampore, *c.* 1830.
(Victoria Memorial Hall, Kolkata)

Roxburgh sent him several dried insects whose contact with the skin could lead to blistering. Wallich immediately prepared a paste from the ground-up animals, which he applied to his own skin. Between its application at noon and seven o'clock in the evening 'a very large and fine bladder had indeed formed', as he delightedly reported back to Roxburgh.[43]

Wallich's patients included both Indians and Europeans, and he was consulted not only by Danish officials still living in the area, but by Danish civilians and the Baptist missionaries.[44] A particularly intensive patient-doctor relationship developed with the missionary the Rev. William Ward, who suffered from severe stomach problems and other illnesses.[45] Wallich also had patients in British Barrackpore on the other side of the Hooghly,[46] and his reputation as a competent physician finally opened the gates to Calcutta, which promoted his social networking in the colonial metropolis.

Among his first contacts in the city was the English merchant George Cruttenden. Cruttenden had retired as a major in the Bengal Army and became a partner in the trading house of Downie, Cruttenden & Co, later Cruttenden & Mackillop.[47] There is no record of how Wallich first made contact with him, but it may have been through his Danish compatriot Jens Christian Wolff, who lived in Calcutta. Cruttenden recommended Wallich to other friends and decades later, the latter wrote with great respect about Cruttenden as an esteemed friend and described him as a 'most excellent man, who was so universally beloved by all—natives as well as Europeans'.[48]

Among Wallich's early British patients and patrons was the Rev. David Brown. Brown, who grew up in England, served for twenty-two years as a pastor in the Old Church in Calcutta, was founder of the local Auxiliary Bible Society and, for a time, director of the renowned College of Fort William. Since Brown lived with his large family in the village of Aldeen, very close to Serampore, it was almost inevitable that Wallich would sooner or later be called to his house as a doctor, and Brown would emerge as a cornerstone of Wallich's Bengal patronage network.[49] Brown, for his part, had excellent contacts with the colonial establishment in Calcutta, which was to be of use to Wallich in many ways. Brown, for instance, was a close friend of the colonial official William Byam Martin and of the Rev. Thomas Truebody Thomason, private chaplain to the Governor-General, Lord Moira.[50] In addition, one of Brown's daughters was married to the judge Robert Merttins Bird,[51] who would soon be involved in efforts to secure Wallich a permanent position with the East India Company.[52]

While medical care for high-ranking British civil servants contributed to colonial networks, the treatment of other Europeans and Indians in Serampore was a duty that Wallich fulfilled with no less dedication. This included the treatment of prisoners in the local jail, where he was responsible for the health of about one hundred inmates. Here, too, Wallich had a remarkable track record and, according to his superiors, the mortality rate under his care was below average.[53]

Wallich also showed a sense of responsibility towards the rest of the population, which included his plan to establish a 'Native Hospital'. In contrast to Serampore, Tranquebar already had such a hospital, with no fewer than 21 couches and 13 beds.[54] In 1810, Wallich approached the British Commissioner with his own project; Ernst approved of it and encouraged him to turn the idea into reality as quickly as possible. There was no time to lose, and Ernst also promised Wallich funds to pay for the employment of an Indian doctor.[55] Wallich then made detailed proposals and requested money for the purchase of a building and regular allocations for its maintenance. However, Ernst's successor, Gordon Forbes, who was appointed only shortly later, had reservations about the planned hospital and immediately made cuts. It was now said that only a small amount could be spent and that finance to purchase a building would be impossible. Forbes also referred to the possibility of financial support from the missionaries. This was disappointing, and the project was only realized long after Wallich had left Serampore.[56]

It was not only diseases that brought Wallich patients; accidents also occurred, and he was there to help. On one occasion in the middle of the hot season he was called to the Hooghly near Brown's house to examine the lifeless bodies of twenty Indians lying on the shore who had capsized. His attempts at resuscitation failed and a few days later, while on his way to see a patient, Wallich was drawn back to the scene by an appalling stench. He found the bodies of the dead laid out on bamboo litters and exposed to the scorching sun. Such a laying out was not unusual, because the water of the Ganga (and thus also of the Hooghly) is considered holy by the Hindus. Corpses were, therefore, often laid out on the bank as an offering to 'Mother Ganga'.[57] Wallich was aware of the health risk posed by decomposing corpses and ordered the immediate removal of the bodies.[58]

Documents preserved from the years after 1808 give the impression that, despite the war, the British occupation of Serampore and with still poor career prospects, Wallich had gradually found his feet in his assigned role. With a great sense of responsibility, he pursued his task as a doctor without ever losing sight of his great passion, botany. At the same time, he built up a communication network that included excellent contacts with the colonial elite of Calcutta. The working days of the man, now almost thirty years old, were undoubtedly long, and he was still unmarried.

JULIANA MARIE

The months between May 1811 and August 1812 were to change Wallich's life, and at the same time to lead him into his first serious personal crisis. There were few unmarried European women in colonial India, which would lead to curiosities such as the 'fishing fleet'—women who might have been unable to find a husband at home arriving from Europe in ships. In small Serampore, the choice might not have been wide, and Nathaniel's affection fell upon Juliana Marie Hals, a Norwegian then only thirteen years old. In colonial India, such a low age was no obstacle to marriage, just as countless European men ended up marrying significantly older widows.

Juliana Marie's mother Caroline Franziska Bie was born in Norway. Somehow Caroline's father had received permission to emigrate to India with his wife and daughter, to his brother Ole Bie the then Governor of Serampore. Here Caroline grew up and met the Dane Christopher Hals whom she married in 1793. On 10 September of the following year, somewhere on a journey in northern India, their first daughter Sophie Amalie was born, and, on 19 September 1797, Juliana Marie followed.[59]

How Juliana Marie and Nathaniel met and came together must remain a matter of speculation. In any case the liaison meant a more or less stable economic position for the adolescent girl; their engagement was announced on 30 May 1811. The forthcoming wedding forced Wallich to look for a financial basis better suited to support his future family. Boldly, and without much hope, he applied for an appointment as an Assistant Surgeon with the East India Company.[60] Wallich's local network at least offered scope for a small pay rise and he was by now assisted by a local doctor.[61]

Wallich, furthermore, established contacts with the venerable Asiatic Society to enhance his career. The Asiatic Society had been founded in Calcutta in 1784 by Sir William Jones as a forum for debates on the cultures, languages and the history of India. The knowledge generated not only served the purpose of intellectual discourse, but also contributed to strengthen colonial rule. Even though ancient India was certainly not one of Wallich's primary passions, it offered an opportunity to make lasting contact with influential personalities, so he decided to become an Orientalist and to study the ancient Indian languages, perhaps with a view to further improving his situation. It was this that would lead to the establishment of the Society's 'Asiatick Museum'. The idea to develop this interest in ancient India may have come to him in the Rev. David Brown's house, where Thomason, Bird and Martin regularly met as eager amateur-Indologists. Thomason and Martin were already members of the Asiatic Society,[62] then under the presidency of Judge Henry Thomas Colebrooke, undoubtedly the world's foremost expert on ancient India then.[63] Wallich himself was proposed for admission to the Society by the missionary the Rev. Joshua Marshman on 3 October 1810 and was immediately accepted.

The minutes of the meetings of the Asiatic Society, which were held every two to three months, give the impression that Wallich was initially able to attend the meetings only irregularly, but that he was able to make use of the contacts now offered to him.[64] By 1811, he already had a small collection of Sanskrit manuscripts which he had copied himself from the collections of Carey, Colebrooke and the Asiatic Society. He was particularly interested in texts with a medical and botanical content.[65] In this Wallich was in good company, for Sir William Jones had already demanded that the description of plants in ancient Indian texts should be studied to gain the most comprehensive knowledge possible of Indian flora.[66]

At the Asiatic Society, Wallich notably formed a friendship with its vice-president Dr John Fleming who held a leading position on the Bengal medical establishment and could, therefore, be useful for his future career.[67] However, Fleming was also known for his botanical expertise. In 1810 he had published a catalogue of plants in *Asiatick Researches*, the journal of the Asiatic Society, under the title 'A Catalogue of Indian Medical Plants and Drugs, with their Names in the Hindustani and Sanskrit Language', which combined his linguistic and botanical research.[68] Some years earlier Fleming had served as acting Superintendent of the Botanic Garden during a European leave for William Roxburgh.[69]

In the following years, Fleming repeatedly supported Wallich's endeavours for professional advancement, specifically for a position within the East India Company's medical establishment. Thus, about four months after Wallich had become a member of the Society, Fleming wrote a letter of recommendation to the local administration in Calcutta, highlighting the misfortune that had befallen the Dane with the occupation of Serampore by the British as a particular cause of hardship.[70] This sounds like a moral appeal, as it was the British who had robbed Wallich of his job in Serampore. Fleming went on to say that he knew Wallich personally and that his recruitment would be of the greatest benefit to the Company's medical service. In his more than forty years of work, he said, he had rarely met anyone with such outstanding human and professional qualities. Wallich's expertise in natural history was praised and Fleming pointed out that, especially in India, such knowledge was of great benefit: 'There is not a wider field for botanical and mineralogical pursuits than in these provinces or in which a person conversant in that sciences could render his knowledge of greater utility to the public'.[71] Such an appointment could be made only in London, but was prevented by the ongoing war, as Fleming was written to: 'We are at War with Denmark and such a nomination is illegal'.[72] Not a good prospect for a starting family.

Exactly one year after the engagement, the wedding to Juliana Marie Hals took place in a Christian ceremony on 30 May 1812.[73] The busy Wallich had married a woman who had barely grown out of childhood. Whether the two had much to say to each other, or whether it was more of a marriage of convenience, is hard to tell. There is also no record of the cause of Juliana's death on 1 August 1812, in the middle of the rainy season, at the shockingly early age of fourteen. One year after her death, a memorial was unveiled in St. Olav's church, when the missionary Ward preached the sermon.[74] The modest plaque was made in Calcutta by the sculptor Philip Hunt and the lines of the epitaph convey the sorrow of the young widower:

Sacred / To the Memory / of Juliana Maria Wallich. / She was born 19 September 1797 / and married 30 May 1812 / to N. Wallich. / She died 1 August 1812 / Farewell but not for ever. / How unavailing her blooming youth. / The spotless innocence of her character. / The universal esteem she enjoyed. / The fondness of her affectionate Husband / to arrest the arm of death. / All, all is changeable, beneath / the unchangeable GOD. / Behold, He taketh away, who can hinder him. / Who shall say unto him. What doest thou. / Job. IX., 12 / I was dumb, I opened not my mouth. / because *Thou* didst it. Psal. XXXIX. 9.

While the plaque in St. Olav's still reminds us of Juliana's short life, her gravestone, which could still be seen in the Danish cemetery at Serampore in the 1920's, has now disappeared.[75]

A TRIP TO MAURITIUS

The years Wallich had already spent in India gradually began to leave their mark and he had long suffered from physical ailments, especially from dysentery. The consequences of emaciating diarrhoea had already led him to a desire for recuperation before the wedding. Hill stations as health-resorts for Europeans did not yet exist in India and sea voyages to the home country were hardly possible due to their long duration. The only option was to look for a suitable area with a healthier climate in the Indian Ocean region, which had in the past usually meant South Africa. By 1810, however, an alternative had emerged that was closer to the subcontinent and at

SACRED
To the Memory
of
JULIANA MARIA WALLICH
She was born Sept: 19ᵗʰ 1797
and married May 30ᵗʰ 1812
to N. WALLICH.
She died August 1ˢᵗ 1812

Farewell but not for ever!

How unavailing her blooming youth.
The spotlefs innocence of her character.
The universal esteem she enjoyed.
The fondnefs of her affectionate Husband
to arrest the arm of death.

All, all is changeable, beneath
The unchangeable GOD.
Behold, He taketh away, who can hinder him
Who shall say unto him, What doest thou?
Job ix. 12.
I was dumb, I opened not my mouth,
because *Thou* didst it. Psal. xxxix. 9.

Philip Hunt Scˡ
Calcut

Plate 4.4: Juliana Marie Wallich's epitaph in St. Olav's
Church, Serampore. (Simon Rastén, Copenhagen)

least as pleasant and beneficial to health: Mauritius. For, like
Serampore, the Île de France, as the island in the Indian Ocean
was called by the French, had fallen to the British during the
Napoleonic Wars.

It is not unlikely that the idea to visit Mauritius originated
with Roxburgh as the island had, since the seventeenth century, been a paradise for botanical research.[76] In order to allow
the voyage and, above all, to obtain a free passage on a ship, it
was necessary to obtain letters of recommendation or medical certificates from as high-ranking officials as possible. While
Juliana Marie was still alive Wallich had already contacted
the British surgeon of Barrackpore, who certified that he was
in poor health. But it was his contacts in Calcutta that proved
to be decisive and his good friend from the the Asiatic Society,
John Fleming, eventually issued a certificate, which confirmed
Wallich's dismal health and suggested that he undertake a sea

voyage.[77] Not a word was said in the relevant documents about Wallich's young fiancé. It would have been unusual, if not impossible, to take her to the island, and accordingly she, like many other European women in India, would have been destined to wait at home for the return of her husband-to-be.

In July 1812, only a short time before the death of Juliana, there seems to have been some movement in the matter. Wallich did not yet have written confirmation, but he must have received some verbal encouragement as he now increasingly tried to get the letters of recommendation that he wanted to take to Mauritius. Five days before Juliana's death, Roxburgh wrote such a document, which was to open the doors to influential botanists on the island.[78]

Barely two weeks after Juliana Marie's death, the plans became more concrete. His friend David Brown from Aldeen issued a letter of recommendation to the British Governor of Mauritius, Robert Farquhar.[79] On 15 August 1812, the official confirmation finally came through and Commissioner Forbes informed Wallich that the Governor-General in Calcutta had granted his request.[80]

However, as Wallich himself later noted, it was not the Governor-General himself, but his Secretary Neil Benjamin Edmonstone who granted the sick leave. Edmonstone, a member of the Asiatic Society already since 1791, had first been in the service of the East India Company as a Persian translator, before being appointed professor of Persian at Fort William College in Calcutta. In 1801 he was promoted to Secretary of the Foreign Affairs Department and eight years later he became Senior Secretary. At that time, he, therefore, had direct access to the Governor-General. According to Wallich, Edmonstone not only arranged for the free sea-voyage, but also gave Wallich a letter of recommendation to Farquhar. Much later Wallich wrote, 'In India as well as at home Mr Edmonstone continued to be my generous patron and friend to the day of his death'.

The approval of the trip speaks for itself, for Wallich's official title was still merely 'Surgeon of Serampore'.[81] As a Dane, he was completely at the mercy of the British East India Company, without being directly in its service. Accordingly, it was solely due to his good personal contacts with high-ranking decision-makers, and perhaps also to his reputation as a talented doctor and naturalist, that he was eventually allowed to go on sick leave. Little is known about the trip to Mauritius, which was to be the last act of his four and a half years of work as a Serampore doctor. However, there is no doubt that this was not only for recuperation, but that Wallich also (perhaps even primarily) sought to conduct botanical studies on the mountainous island with its rich flora.[82]

Arriving in Mauritius, probably in September 1812, Wallich contacted the Northern Irish doctor Charles Telfair who, as secretary to the Governor, was well acquainted with the island.[83] In Telfair, Wallich also found an eager botanist who gave him twelve further letters of introduction for his travels across the island. But he hardly needed these because many doors opened up for him practically of their own accord,[84] as he crossed the whole of Mauritius collecting countless plants, including mosses and ferns, which he dried. Of this herbarium material, he sent a large part to Fleming and others to Sir Joseph Banks, the President of the Royal Society in London. This may have been the first occasion when Wallich came to the attention of the mighty Banks and thus did Wallich astutely start the use of the global dispatch of herbarium specimens as a means of expanding and consolidating his network of communication and patronage. From his journey to Mauritius this network, therefore, came to include London.[85]

While in Mauritius, Wallich's patron and friend Caspar Top died in Serampore.[86] There had also been a radical change at the Calcutta Botanic Garden; after thirty-seven years in South Asia the great William Roxburgh felt exhausted and ill, though at this point it wasn't to be a final farewell. Roxburgh had only applied for a sick leave, which he wanted to spend either at the Cape or on St. Helena. Henry Thomas Colebrooke, whom Wallich knew from the meetings of the Asiatic Society, would in the meantime act as Superintendent. With his wife, three of his numerous children and two Indian servants, Roxburgh left India. A short stay at St. Helena did not bring any recovery to his health and it may have been at this point that Roxburgh decided to retire from India and settle permanently in Britain.[87]

NOTES

1. S. Arasaratnam, *Maritime India in the Seventeenth Century*, Delhi: Oxford University Press, 1994, pp. 149-54.
2. Ibid., p. 154
3. M. Krieger, *Kaufleute, Seeräuber und Diplomaten. Der dänische Handel auf dem Indischen Ozean (1620-1868)*, Cologne, Weimar & Vienna: Böhlau, 1998, pp. 82f.
4. RAK, Ostindisk Kompagni, 2034b, Bengalske Dokumenter, 1674-1778, 146; Krieger, *Kaufleute, Seeräuber und Diplomaten*, pp. 121-4.
5. Krieger, *Kaufleute, Seeräuber und Diplomaten*, p. 28.
6. Ibid., pp. 149ff.
7. M. Krieger, 'Serampore around 1800', in Thomas Riis (ed.), *Urbanization in the Oldenburg Monarchy, 1500-1800*, Kiel: Ludwig, 2012, pp. 68ff.
8. S. Dasgupta, *Awakening: The Story of the Bengal Renaissance*, Noida-London: Random House, 2011, pp. 78-81.
9. E. Gøbel, 'Det Seramporske Collegium. Skoler og College i Serampore 1800–1845', in B. Riis Larsen (ed.), *Skole Kirke Arkiv*, Odense: Syddansk Universitetsforlag, 2004, pp. 27-39.
10. E. W. Herbert, *Flora's Empire: British Gardens in India*, Philadelphia: University of Pennsylvania Press, 2011, p. 87.
11. S. Bille, *Bericht über die Reise der Corvette Galathea um die Welt in den Jahren 1845, 46 und 47* , vol. 1, Copenhagen & Leipzig: Reitzel, Lorck, 1852, pp. 125f.
12. RAK, Asiatisk Kompagni, Faktorierne i Frederiksnagore og Patna, 2031, Protocol of Resolution, 14 November 1807: 'Ved at igiennemgaae Facturen bleve vi eÿ synderlig vel til Mode'.
13. Ibid.
14. Ibid., 19 November 1807.
15. CNH, Wallich letters, Government of Serampore, 19 November 1807.

16. For general information see S. Mentz, *The English Gentleman Merchant at Work: Madras and the City of London 1660–1740*, Copenhagen: Museum Tusculanum Press, 2005, in particular Chapter 6.

17. RAK, Asiatisk Kompagni, Faktorierne i Frederiksnagore og Patna, 2031, Resolutionsprotokoller, 19 November 1807; BL IOR, F/265/5862, Revenues at Serampore; Larsen, *Ostindiske Personalier og Data*, entry: 'Ruhde, Anton Wilhelm Friedrich'. Larsen states that in 1805 the annual salary was 429 Rd.

18. BL IOR, F/265/5862, Revenues at Serampore.

19. CNH, Wallich letters, Wallich to Government in Serampore, draft, 30 November 1807; RAK, Asiatisk Kompagni, Faktoriet i Frederiksnagore, Regnskabsjournaler, 2144, 31 July 1808.

20. CNH, Wallich letters, index, p. 19: 'He was . . . a most worthy and universally reputed old man, and my dear patron and friend to the time of his death'; Larsen, *Ostindiske Personalier og Data*, entry 'Top, Caspar.'

21. CNH, Wallich letters, index, p. 79: 'an old and valued friend of mine'.

22. Arnold, *Plant Capitalism and Company Science*, p. 907.

23. CNH, Wallich letters, index, pp. 19ff.

24. CNH, Wallich letters, index, p. 11.

25. A. Rasch, *Dansk-Ostindien 1777-1845*, 2nd edn., Copenhagen: Fremad, 1967, pp. 197ff.; J. Clark Marshman, *The Life and Times of Carey, Marshman, and Ward: Embracing the History of the Serampore Mission*, vol. 1, London: Longman, Brown, Green, Longmans & Roberts, 1859 (rep. Serampore, 2005), pp. 381f.

26. CNH, Wallich letters, index, p. 79.

27. CNH, Wallich letters, index, pp. 17ff; BL IOR, F/265/5862, Revenues at Serampore; CNH, Wallich letters, index, p. 19; ibid., Krefting to Wallich, 14 March 1808.

28. Holmsted was a physician who had been hired in Copenhagen in 1807 on the private East Indiaman 'Admiral Chapman' of the company Duntzfeldt & Co. and reached Calcutta half a year later. With the outbreak of war in India, the 'Admiral Chapman' had also been confiscated. Holmsted was stranded in Calcutta and from there went to Serampore. He stayed there only for a short time, returned to Europe during the war and after the conclusion of the Kiel Peace Treaty undertook two further journeys from Copenhagen to the East Indies. Holmsted died on 16 August 1820 at the age of 42. See:

Larsen, Ostindiske Personalier og Data, entry 'Holmsted, Frederik Christian'; Feldbæk, India Trade under the Danish Flag, p. 228f.
29. CNH, Wallich letters, Ruhde to Wallich, 11 November 1808.
30. CNH, Wallich letters, index, p. 21.
31. CNH, Wallich letters, Top to Wallich, 7 July 1808.
32. CNH, Wallich letters, Roxburgh to Wallich, 3 October 1808.
33. For example: CNH, Wallich letters, Roxburgh to Wallich, 27 July 1812.
34. Bastin, *Letters*, pp. 2, 40 (note 8); CNH, Wallich letters, Roxburgh to Government, 1 February 1809.
35. CNH, Wallich letters, Government to Roxburgh, 10 March 1809; CNH, Wallich letters, index, p. 21.
36. Ibid., index, p. 21.
37. Ibid., Governor General to Roxburgh, 24 April 1809.
38. Ibid., index, pp. 21ff.
39. Ibid., Roxburgh to Wallich, 10 October 1809.
40. Ibid., Roxburgh to Wallich, 2 September 1809.
41. SNM, Letters from Wallich I, 1, Wallich to Hornemann, 10 March 1810.
42. Ibid.
43. CNH, Wallich letters, Roxburgh to Wallich, 2 September 1809.
44. Ibid., Roxburgh to Wallich, 2 August 1809.
45. Ibid., Ward to Wallich, 30 April 1814; ibid., 24 June 1814.
46. Ibid., index, p. 29, 'where in fact I had a great deal of practice'.
47. Dhrubajyoti Banerjea, *European Calcutta. Images and Recollections of a Bygone Era*, 3rd edn., New Delhi, 2008, p. 116.
48. Christian Kampen, *Min Wolffske familie*, manuscript, n.d., pp. 19ff.; CNH, Wallich letters, index, p. 39; ibid., p. 79.
49. CNH, Wallich letters, index, p. 25.
50. P. Thankappan Nair (ed.), *Proceedings of the Asiatic Society*, vol. 2, Calcutta: The Asiatic Society, 1995, pp. 633f., 674f.; CNH, Wallich letters, index, p. 25.
51. CNH, Wallich letters, index, p. 25.
52. BL IOR, L/Mil/9/366/148, Wallich, Nathaniel, 1814.
53. CNH, Wallich letters, Bie, 25 October 1813.
54. RAK, Det Kgl. Ostind. Guvernement i Tranquebar, 1378h, Rapport fra Overdragelses Kommission af 10. Juli 1816, List Danish Valuation of Public Property taken at Tranquebar, 1808.
55. CNH, Wallich letters, Ernst to Wallich, 1 October 1810.
56. Ibid., Forbes to Wallich, 19 November 1810.

57. Dasgupta, *Awakening*, p. 77.
58. CNH, Wallich letters, Wallich to Judge & Magistrate 24 Parganas, 26 May 1812.
59. Ibid., p. 238.
60. BL IOR, L/Mil/9/366/146, Wallich, Nathaniel, 1814: 'That your Petitioner has applied himself with great Diligence to the Study and Practice of Surgery and is desirous of being appointed an Assistant Surgeon on the Bengal Establishment'.
61. CNH, Wallich letters, index, p. 27.
62. Nair, *Proceedings*, vol. 2, pp. 633f., 674f.
63. Ibid., pp. 576f.
64. Ibid., passim
65. CNH, Wallich letters, index, p. 27.
66. Some of those manuscripts are today kept in the Royal Library of Copenhagen. See H. Buescher, *Catalogue of Sanskrit Manuscripts*, Copenhagen: NIAS, 2011, pp. XV-XIX; R. Desmond, *The European Discovery of the Indian Flora*, Oxford: Oxford University Press, 1992, p. 54.
67. Desmond, *European Discovery*, p. 53.
68. Nair, *Proceedings*, vol. 2, p. 592.
69. CNH, Wallich letters, index, p. 1.
70. BL IOR, L/Mil/9/366/148, Wallich, Nathaniel, 1814, Fleming to Government, 25 November 1811: 'Dr. W. was sent out some years ago by the Danish Company as Surgeon to their settlement at Serampore, but on his arrival he found the place had been taken possession by this Government'.
71. Ibid.
72. CNH, Wallich letters, Bird to Wallich, 7 April 1814.
73. MS, L. Bie, *Periodiske Annotationer paa Serampore i Bengalen 1809-22* (manuscript); see also: ibid., in *Personalhistorisk Tidsskrift*, vol. 9, no. 4,52/1931, pp. 102-14.
74. William Ward, *Sermon Preached on the 1st of August, 1813, in the Settlement Church at Serampore on Occasion of the Erection of a Monument to the Memory of the Lady of N. Wallich*, Serampore, 1813.
75. A. Krarup Nielsen, *En Østerlandsfærd*, Copenhagen, 1923, p. 97.
76. T. Robinson, *William Roxburgh, The Founding Father of Indian Botany*, Chichester: Phillimore, 2008, pp. 107, 117.
77. CNH, Wallich letters, Fleming, 31 August 1811.
78. Ibid., index, p. 19.
79. Ibid., p. 31.

80. Nair, *Proceedings*, vol. 2, p. 586; CNH, Wallich letters, index, p. 31; ibid., Forbes to Wallich, 25 August 1812.

81. Ibid., Fleming, 31 August 1811.

82. Various plants collected by him reached Calcutta via Serampore and later found their way into the herbarium of the East India Company which includes over 180 specimens from Mauritius. See A Numerical List of Dried Specimens of Plants in the East India Company's Museum, collected under the superintendence of Dr Wallich of the Company's Botanic Garden at Calcutta, online version of the Royal Botanic Garden Edinburgh, http://wallich. rbge.info/, e.g. no. 14-15, 21, 33, 42, 46.1, 82.

83. M. S. Rivière, 'From Belfast to Mauritius: Charles Telfair (1778-1833), Naturalist and a Product of the Irish Enlightenment', *Eighteenth Century Ireland. Iris an dá chultúr*, vol. 2, 2006, pp. 134f.

84. CNH, Wallich letters, index, p. 35: 'I found that the universal hospitality of that sweet island rendered them unnecessary!'.

85. Ibid.

86. Ibid., Colebrooke to Wallich, 27 April 1813; ibid., index, p. 19.

87. Robinson, *William Roxburgh*, pp. 73f.

CHAPTER 5

Calcutta

A HOUSE IN ESPLANADE ROW

As of now the small, British-occupied, Danish colony of Serampore held little attraction for Nathaniel Wallich. The regular exchanges with the missionaries Carey, Marshman, and Ward were only small consolations compared with the opportunities that awaited him if he moved to the colonial metropolis of Calcutta. Following Roxburgh's retreat, carousel of personnel at the botanical garden had been turning. Even if the Superintendent's position was still beyond reach, Wallich had made a name for himself at the Botanic Garden and he was ready to seize every opportunity that presented itself there, no matter how small. Nevertheless, it was his medical skills that, at least for the time being, represented the only capital that could possibly be converted into a livelihood. The decision seriously to consider settling in Calcutta as a freelance doctor may have been made by Wallich after his return from Mauritius. In this, however, he received support from his friend George Cruttenden, who investigated possibilities with the British authorities and arranged for further important contacts.[1]

Krefting, who was still in office as head of the Danish administration under the authority of Commissioner Gordon Forbes, regretted the plans, but in the end could not prevail against Wallich's influential friends.[2] On 21 September 1813, Forbes announced that the British government in Calcutta had agreed to his request.[3] Wallich was relieved and informed Cruttenden of the joyful news only one day later. However, the joy was not to remain undiminished for long because his successor, Kennedy by name, had to arrive in Serampore before Wallich could leave, and Kennedy did not want to, or could not, start work there as early as hoped. Wallich showed himself rather quickly annoyed and it seems that there was an angry exchange of letters between the pair.[4] The assumption remains that Wallich moved to Calcutta some time in November or early December, leaving behind in Serampore the grave of his young wife Juliana Marie and memories of a difficult time.

Wallich now had to think about his future place of residence. Just as today, living space was scarce in Calcutta and especially in the so-called 'White Town', and renting a suitable residence was not affordable to everyone. Living in shared flats (*chummings*) was common among single male Europeans, and Wallich received an offer to share in the rent of a house but declined.[5] Undoubtedly, the desire for his own household was due not only to the need for a certain discretion in running a medical practice, but also expressed a desire for a genteel lifestyle such as he had come to know from his powerful friends. He, therefore, took his own apartment at 17 Esplanade Row where, within three months, he succeeded in establishing a flourishing and profitable private medical practice.[6]

Thus, Wallich was established in the middle of the European quarter, the centre from which not only Bengal was governed, but also the political heart for the whole of British India. Located in the immediate vicinity of the Governor-General's residence, Esplanade Row was one of the grandest residential areas. The buildings occupied only the northern side, with views across a large water basin (*tank*) to the extensive Maidan, the favoured park for evening walks, and horse and carriage-rides. A stroll to the west led to Chandpal Ghat, a landing spot on the Hooghly from which a cooling, day-time breeze often blew along the houses.

In the years when Wallich came to know and appreciate Calcutta, the city was a permanent construction site. In 1808 the building of the Asiatic Society was completed on the corner between Chowringhee and Burial Ground Road (today Mother Teresa Sarani).[7] Perhaps, the most ambitious construction project was the Town Hall, completed in 1814, shortly after Wallich's relocation.[8] The garden suburbs south of the Maidan had long since been developed with the building of spacious residencies, especially Alipur with the rococo palace of the Belvedere. At that time, still surrounded by dense jungle, the large cemetery, today's South Park Street Cemetery, lay to the east of Chowringhee. Those who didn't make it back to Europe (or those who perhaps did not want to) found their final resting place there among huge, neo-classical funerary monuments, one of the tallest of which commemorates Sir William Jones, founder of the Asiatic Society. The earthly remains of Robert Kyd, founder of the Botanic Garden, rested in an earlier burial ground on the opposite side of the street.[9] North of European Calcutta lay the no less magnificent Indian city with its bazaars and palaces. There, among others, lived the great families of Tagore and Deb, the wealthy local economic and educational elite who would also influence Wallich's path in India.

Calcutta was also the intellectual centre of British India. Besides the Asiatic Society, there was the College of Fort William, which had been founded under Governor-General Lord Wellesley in 1800. Conceived as an 'Oxford of the East', it was intended to prepare employees of the East India Company for their work in India. In addition to European knowledge, languages such as Arabic, Persian and Sanskrit were taught.[10]

THE ASIATICK MUSEUM

Wallich quickly made the transition from the tranquillity of Serampore, and his presence in Calcutta is evident from his much more regular attendance at meetings of the Asiatic Society. It was probably little more than a quarter of an hour's walk that took him along Chowringhee from his home and practice on Esplanade Row to the societies' premises on Burial Ground Road. From now on, he would hardly ever miss a meeting and he soon belonged to the nucleus, an approximately ten-member circle of the society that by now had about 250 members.[11]

Colebrooke was undoubtedly one of the most original and intellectual minds of the Society. Wallich would also later write of his great respect for the talented secretary, Horace Hayman Wilson.[12] Originally from London, Wilson was a Calcutta-based member of the Bengal medical establishment, had been elected a member of the Society in 1810 and served as its secretary from 1811 to 1832. After leaving India Wilson became professor of Sanskrit at the University of Oxford.[13]

At this time there was no such thing as 'professional' Orientalists and members of the Society were what are now termed 'amateurs', whose professions were commonly military, administrative, medical or in commerce, which often took them 'out of station', especially during the dry season. Oriental studies were understood as a serious intellectual pursuit, which served to add to knowledge, but also provided an occasion for social networking. Devotees of Orientalist studies remained, however, in a small minority and many leading protagonists of colonial rule postulated an alleged cultural dominance of the West and regarded dealing with India's cultural riches as a waste of money and time.[14]

The published minutes give a good impression of the wide range of topics discussed at meetings of the Society. Most of the essays, which were either presented personally or sent from abroad and read out, related to ancient India—again and again they dealt with antiquities discovered during travels, coins and the diversity of ancient and modern Indian languages. But, as envisaged by the founder Sir William Jones, natural history subjects were also treated.[15]

It may be assumed that Wallich took an active part in the discussions of this circle of European men (women were not present and Indians only as servants) and formulated his own thoughts. By the time of the second meeting he attended, after his move to Calcutta, he came up with an epoch-making idea that had results visible to this day—the founding of a museum. For many years, the Society had accumulated not only books and ancient manuscripts, but also archaeological and natural history objects. Even though Jones had not originally thought of a museum, the establishment of one for the Society's collections became more and more desirable and urgent. Such an institution had already been considered as early as 1796 but was postponed as the Society lacked suitable premises and the idea was put in cold storage for almost two decades.[16]

With Colebrooke, Wilson, Carey and Marshman among others present, Wallich presented his concept for a museum on 2 February 1814. The proposal clearly shows that he hardly considered himself an 'Oriental Scholar', but primarily as a naturalist. He explained to those present:

The vast regions which are comprised within the sphere of the Asiatick Society's views exhibit an inexhaustible and perhaps unparalleled treasury of the most wonderful and interesting productions of nature. The far greater portion of these have hitherto escaped the notice of Naturalists, or has been imperfectly, or what is much worse, erroneously described. The deplorable neglect to which the Natural History of this country has been exposed is very striking and must principally be attributed to the total want in India of that grand desideratum a public museum.[17]

The lack of a museum was, therefore, blamed for the backward state of natural-history research in India. Even if a few natural history specimens had already found their way into the collection of the Asiatic Society, the emphasis Wallich demanded was completely new and unusual. It reflected the spirit of Roxburgh, who wanted to increase the agricultural production of the country and to improve nutritional standards by exploring its riches.[18]

With a museum as a nucleus, the natural treasures of India could not only be explored but communicated to a wider public. Were such an institution to exist under the umbrella of the Asiatic Society, with expertise to preserve and display the harvests of their efforts and to make them accessible for comparative research? Wallich was convinced that men from all over the country would be prepared to send specimens.[19] While expertise would be needed to protect the exhibits from insects and the harmful Indian climate, such an undertaking would not be unduly costly. Finally, he offered his own services and generously presented his own private collection as a donation.[20]

Wallich's concept for the museum is remarkable, not least as there was no comparable model in India on which he could have based it. The question of the origin of his idea leads back to Denmark where, in the years since 1800, Copenhagen had experienced an intense debate about archaeological finds—their conservation and display. In April 1806 a small book by Rasmus Nyerup was published under a title that can be translated as 'An overview of the patriotic antiquities and how they can be placed in a future national museum. A proposal'.[21] Everywhere on his travels, Nyerup wrote, he had encountered material evidence of Danish prehistory and early history, but at the same time ignorance on the part of the local population and a lack of possibilities for the preservation of such specimens. The general carelessness towards antiquities might be countered by founding a central museum to which such items could be sent and where they could be permanently preserved.[22]

Wallich may not have developed the idea of founding his 'Asiatick Museum' from Nyerup's writing alone, and perhaps the British Museum also played a role as a model, nevertheless, Wallich's reference to Nyerup's observations is striking. As in Europe, throughout India there were interested individuals who collected objects relevant to research and public interest; everywhere, however, there was a lack of possibilities and knowledge to preserve them locally. Only a comparison of such objects would advance science, Wallich said, which could only be achieved by a museum in a central location.[23] At this point Wallich formulated for the first time the method that would shape his botanical research for decades to come: the systematic integration of a network of collectors (including women) in the periphery of the state, the bringing together of collected objects at the centre and the dispatch of objects towards the global transfer of knowledge.

The further progress of both museum projects, in Copenhagen and Calcutta, displays other similarities. Soon after the publication of Nyerup's text, the first donations were received and finally, with the installation of some rune stones in the attic of the Trinity Church of Copenhagen in the middle of February 1807, the first Danish national museum was founded.[24] It was a month and a half later that Wallich would board the *Prince of Augustenburg* to take him to the Danish East Indies. The fact that the young surgeon, from a cultured background, was most probably aware of this ambitious project in Copenhagen is suggested by the striking similarity with his own museum project seven years later.

Wallich's proposal met with approval of the Society and that very same evening a remarkable decision was taken. In view of the lack of a public collection, those present decided to follow his suggestion and to found an 'Asiatick Museum'.[25] In this way an institution came into being that would celebrate its bicentenary in 2014. If the decision of 2 February was aimed at giving a certain preference to the field of natural history, despite the significance of archaeological objects, this clearly bears Wallich's signature.[26] This new paradigm represented a considerable expansion of the programmatic approach of the Asiatic Society, which, until then, had dealt with India primarily through linguistic and archaeological studies. Now all that was missing was a capable director. Most of the members who would have been sufficiently qualified were busy through various offices and other occupations. It is not surprising, therefore, that the choice quickly fell on Wallich, the young Danish doctor who ran a lucrative private practice in Esplanade Row and who had brought himself to the Society's notice.[27]

The formal foundation of the museum was followed by the printing of a leaflet in which the public were asked to submit exhibits.[28] The advertising campaign was successful and in the following year Wallich was able to boast an impressive list of patrons, including Lady Loudon, wife of the Governor-General Lord Moira, the Surveyor General Colin Mackenzie, Rev. William Carey, the painter Robert Home, Colebrooke, and Wilson. The great Scottish surgeon and naturalist Francis Buchanan, at that time engaged in a major statistical survey of Bengal, sent statues of the Buddha from the ruins of Rajagriha (Rajgir) in northern India.[29] Wallich himself presented zoological objects, including skulls of an elephant, buffalo and rhino, two shark jaws, the shell of a river turtle, monkey skulls and a kangaroo skull from Australia.[30]

It must have taken Wallich some effort to sift through the exhibits and classify them. As the new museum director, however, he simultaneously raised the profile of the new institution by his organizational skills. Coins, copper plates, sculptures and other archaeological objects were given to the Asiatic Society's library; natural history ones were retained so that Wallich's museum became solely one of natural history and was only later complemented with substantial archaeological collections—as is still to be seen, and which was undoubtedly the original intention of the initiator.[31]

Wallich remained director of the Asiatick Museum until 1817, when a growing workload at the Botanic Garden forced him to resign from this post.[32] But the museum continued to flourish and in 1878, two decades after Wallich's death, the by now impressive collection of natural history and world-class art moved into a new, spacious building on Chowringhee with four wings enclosing a green and colonnaded courtyard, under the name of the Imperial Museum—today's Indian Museum. The great success of the Asiatick Museum constituted Wallich's entry-ticket to the colonial society of Calcutta and contributed to his final acceptance into the Company service.

ASSISTANT SURGEON

While Wallich made a name for himself and developed his career in Calcutta, his native country experienced one of the most serious crises in its history. Denmark was increasingly driven into insolvency by the high burden of war and in 1813 experienced the near collapse of its public finances. Norway, which was practically cut off from the vital supply of grain from Denmark by the loss of the Danish fleet was in an even worse state, but, thanks to the courageous intervention of Sir Joseph Banks, it had been possible to keep Danish Iceland and Greenland out of the war. On 14 January 1814, Denmark signed the Treaty of Kiel with Britain and Sweden, because of which Denmark had to cede Norway to Sweden. However, the overseas colonies occupied by the British, including Tranquebar and Serampore, were to be returned to the Danish crown.[33]

Wallich was informed about these events only irregularly. His cousin Ludvig Levin Jacobson's letters were full of details and information, but due to the war, were rare. With relief, the 'antipode', as Wallich was called by Jacobson, probably received a letter in November 1815 informing him that everyone at home was well. Hannah, Wallich's mother had aged, but Wulff Lazarus, his father, had hardly changed over the years.[34] Nathaniel's brother Arnold, with whom Jacobson had lived in Paris for some time, was also reported to be satisfied and happy.[35]

About three months after the conclusion of the Treaty of Kiel, news pertaining the end of hostilities between Britain and Denmark reached India.[36] Once again, the Danish flag was hoisted over Serampore and Tranquebar. In the meantime, virtually everyone in Calcutta must have known that Wallich regarded his private practice as only temporary and was in fact seeking employment as an Assistant Surgeon with the Honourable East India Company. Life as a physician, but able to undertake scientific research represented the fulfilment of his highest aims. As he would remember much later:

There is I firmly believe no country upon earth, which affords such inexhaustible treasures of natural production as India does; nor is there perhaps any service, that can boast of more favourable opportunities for pursuing research in all branches of Natural History, than the Honourable Company's Medical Establishment.[37]

Officers could make observations wherever they happened to be stationed, which collectively would allow insights into the vast diversity of natural treasures of the different regions.

'There is not one among my brethren of the profession, who has not made botany a part of his academic studies', he recollected,[38] and at this period it was naturalist Assistant Surgeons who were the major contributors to scientific progress in British India.

With the Treaty of Kiel, Danes were no longer enemies, so the way was paved for their potential Company service. The fact that everything went comparatively smoothly and rapidly was due to the fact that some of Nathaniel's powerful friends had already been working for him for some time. Above all, his acquaintance with the judge Robert Merttins Bird proved of particular importance. Bird was a member of the Asiatic Society, but Wallich had probably met him earlier at Brown's house in Aldeen. Bird was acquainted with George Smith, who for many years served in London as one of the powerful directors of the East India Company. Probably already around 1812 Bird had written to Smith praising Wallich as 'a warm and true-hearted man'.[39] On 10 May 1814 Wallich's appointment was finally made in London as an Assistant Surgeon with the East India Company, together with Frederick Corbyn, the Honourable Francis Sempill, and Thomas Casey.[40] He was accepted into the Company's medical establishment, which had already produced several outstanding natural scientists.[41]

It soon, however, became apparent that, while the self-confident and sometimes bold young man had made friends, he had also antagonized others and that the appointment was not to everyone's liking. If the appointment could not be prevented, some ill-disposed members of the Bengal medical establishment successfully tried to keep him out of Calcutta. Decades later, Wallich recorded with bitterness: 'friends having exerted themselves to get rid of me at Calcutta'.[42] It was decided that Wallich should first take up a position as a civilian doctor in the remote province of Birbhum, more than 250 kilometres from Calcutta, the place where he had undertaken his first botanical expedition several years earlier.[43]

Events turned out differently, for the East India Company was on the verge of war against neighbouring Nepal, and skilled doctors were to prove more necessary during the bloody fighting in the Himalayan state than in a remote province of Bengal.[44] Moreover, in the eyes of Francis Buchanan, the sending of the talented naturalist to Nepal would kill two birds with one stone: Wallich would not only look after the sick and wounded, but would also be able to collect plants *en passant* and help to explore the almost unknown flora of the Himalaya. One of the instructions written by Buchanan, who had been to Nepal himself in 1802-3, expressly stipulated that Wallich should collect natural history objects and produce descriptions and drawings.[45] One of the aims was to answer the question as to which Nepalese plants might potentially be used commercially in India.[46] In colonial South Asia, war meant more than a fight for territory and always involved the acquirement of knowledge as an instrument of imperial expansion.

NOTES

1. CNH, Wallich letters, index, p. 47: 'As this most excellent and dear friend had been mainly instrumental to my leaving Serampore and settling as a private practitioner in Calcutta, he was anxious to secure some appointment to me there, now that I had gone into the service'.
2. Ibid. Cruttenden to Wallich, without date, 1813.
3. Ibid., Forbes to Wallich, 21 September 1813; ibid., index, p. 41.
4. Ibid., Cruttenden to Wallich, 9 October 1813.
5. Ibid., Cruttenden to Wallich, 23 September 1813.
6. Ibid., Bird to Wallich, 7 April 1814: 'I am happy to hear from all quarters of your increasing practice in Calcutta'.
7. Indian Museum (ed.), *The Indian Museum 1814-1914*, Calcutta: Baptist Mission Press, 1914, rep. Calcutta, 2004, p. 1.
8. D. L. Nilina, *Calcutta: Built Heritage Today—An INTACH Guide*, Calcutta: INTACH, 2006, p. 124.
9. Holmes and Co. (ed.), *The Bengal Obituary; or, a Record to Perpetuate the Memory of Departed*, London & Calcutta: W. Thacker & Co., 1851, p. 99.
10. Dasgupta, *Awakening*, pp. 52ff.; Rosane Rocher and Ludo Rocher,

The Making of Western Indology: Henry Thomas Colebrooke and the East India Company, London & New York: Routledge, 2012, p. 64.

11. R. Mitra, *History of the Society: Centenary Review of the Asiatic Society of Bengal 1784–1884*, part 1, Calcutta: The Asiatic Society, 1885, rep. 1986, p. 83.

12. Wallich letters, index, 'He was the greatest Sanskrit scholar of his time, combining a variety of attainments as general linguist, historian, chemist, accountant, numismatist, actor and musician'.

13. Nair, Proceedings, vol. 2, p. 686.

14. Ch. Allen, *The Prisoner of Kathmandu: Brian Hodgson in Nepal, 1820–43*, New Delhi: Speaking Tiger, 2016, p. 17.

15. Nair, *Proceedings*, vol. 2, passim.

16. Ibid., pp. 119–22.

17. Ibid. p. 467; CNH, Wallich letters, Wallich to Wilson, 2 February 1814.

18. CNH, Wallich letters, Minute of the Governor General, 1 June 1805.

19. Nair, *Proceedings*, vol. 2, p. 467; CNH, Wallich letters, Wallich to Wilson, 2 February 1814: 'The means of getting access to animals, plants and minerals are here innumerable and comparatively easier than in many other parts of the globe. A number of gentlemen who travel or reside in the interior of India would, I am warranted to say, be happy to exert themselves if a repository existed under the auspices of the society, where specimens could be deposited and preserved, and where they would admit of a closer and more attentive examination and comparison than what possibly could be bestowed upon them on the spot where they are found'.

20. Nair, *Proceedings*, vol. 2, p. 467; CNH, Wallich letters, Wallich to Wilson, 2 February 1814.

21. R. Nyerup, *Oversigt over Fædrelandets Mindesmærker fra Oldtiden*, Copenhagen, 1806.

22. J. Jensen, *Thomsens Museum. Historien om Nationalmuseet*, Copenhagen: Gyldendal, 1992, p. 18.

23. Ibid.

24. Ibid., p. 19.

25. Nair, *Proceedings*, vol. 2, p. 471.

26. Ibid.: 'It is, however, in the departments of Science that a Museum in this country would be found most specially serviceable, and the facility of its accumulation is proportionable to the extent of its utility. In Natural History, Botany, Anatomy, Chemistry, Mineralogy

and other branches, a collection would accumulate rapidly if once commenced; and from the first moment of its accumulation would furnish additional matter in the stock of knowledge.'

27. Nair, *Proceedings*, vol. 2, pp. 471f.
28. CNH, Wallich letters, Asiatic Society, July 1814.
29. Ibid., Buchanan to Wallich, 18 October, 1814.
30. Nair, *Proceedings*, vol. 2, pp. 138-40.
31. Mitra, *History of the Society*, pp. 34f.
32. Nair, *Proceedings*, vol. 2, p. 597.
33. M. Bregnsbo, 'Der Friedensvertrag und seine Unterzeichnung in Kiel am 14, Januar 1814', in S. Kinzler (ed.), Der *Kieler Frieden 1814. Ein Schicksalsjahr für den Norden*, Neumünster: Wachholtz 2013, pp. 47-57.
34. CNH, Wallich letters, Jacobson to Wallich, 28 December 1814.
35. Ibid.
36. Ibid., Bird to Wallich, 7 April 1814.
37. Ibid., Bird to Adam, 8 October 1825.
38. Ibid., Wallich to Adam, 8 October 1825.
39. Ibid., Bird to Wallich, 10 September 1813.
40. Bastin, 'Letters of Sir Stamford Raffles', p. 54.
41. D. Grey Crawford, *A History of the Indian Medical Service 1600-1913*, 2 vols., London: W. Thacker, 1914, vol. 1, pp. 197-222, vol. 2, pp. 139-61; H. Fischer-Tiné, *Pidgin-Knowledge. Wissen und Kolonialismus*, Zurich & Berlin: Diaphanes, 2013, pp. 29-40.
42. CNH, Wallich letters, index, p. 57.
43. Ibid.
44. On the war in Nepal, see: B. Dat Sanwal, *Nepal and the East India Company*, (no place of publication), 1965, pp. 156-87.
45. CNH, Wallich letters, instruction to Wallich 1814: 'As a large proportion of the substances used by the native physicians of India is the produce of different parts of the territory of Nepal, Dr Wallich will especially direct his attention to the description of these substances'.
46. Ibid.

CHAPTER 6

The Botanic Garden

COLONIAL BOTANY

Since the early European trade voyages to India, botanical interests had travelled with them. At first amazement at the lush, unknown plant world may have been the driving force behind a more intensive study of South Asian flora. Botany was a popular pastime for a significant number of merchants, missionaries and Company servants, in whose spare time plants could be collected and dried, to create herbaria at little expense. In the course of time Indian plants were gradually brought within the realm of European knowledge, given Latin names, integrated into botanical systems, and researched for their commercial usefulness or healing properties.

After the pioneering attempts of the Portuguese in the sixteenth century, the Dutch followed. The most outstanding work of the period was undoubtedly the *Hortus Indicus Mala-baricus* initiated by Hendrik Adriaan van Reede tot Drakenstein. With the growing influence of the British in the eighteenth century, Madras became a centre of botanical research. Having started his career in Tranquebar, Johann Gerhard Koenig, a missionary Physician from German Halle, in 1778 became the first full-time naturalist of the East India Company, on its Madras establishment. But from the 1780s Calcutta would replace Madras as the major centre for botanical research,[1] a considerable part of which (as in other fields of natural history) was now carried out by Company surgeons.[2]

With British territorial expansion in India after Plassey, botany was increasingly placed in the service of imperial statehood and economic development. It was generally believed that research into the native flora, but also the transfer of crops, would lead to an increase in agricultural production and thus also in exports from the colonies.[3] The major focus was on forests, because timber was of great importance for the rapidly growing cities in the maritime periphery of India as well as for shipbuilding.

In 1786, the practical economic interest led Colonel Robert Kyd, Secretary to the Military Board, to propose to the Governor-General in Calcutta the establishment of an acclimatisation garden, in which foreign plants could be prepared for commercial cultivation in India. As he correctly recognized, the indigenous population frequently lived under the threat of famine, and the systematic cultivation of alternative crops, such as the sago and date palms, could help to redress this problem. Even more important was the introduction of exportable agricultural products and medicinal plants, with which the balance of trade of British India could be improved. As examples Kyd mentioned a broad spectrum of species including cotton, indigo, tobacco, coffee, tea, sandalwood, pepper, asafoetida, copal, camphor, nutmeg, cloves, sarsaparilla, gum lacquer and ipecac.[4]

The Governor-General had, with his approval, passed on Kyd's idea to the Company directors in London. The encouragement of Sir Joseph Banks did the rest, and the Court of Directors gave its approval, but urged the greatest possible thrift.[5] Near the village of Shibpur, on the western bank of the Hooghly River a few kilometres south of Calcutta 'The Honourable East India Company's Botanic Garden' was created. In the British colonial world, the only precedent for such an institution was the garden founded in 1765 on the Caribbean Island of St Vincent.[6]

In 1793 Robert Kyd, its originator and first honorary director, died and in the same year the botanical garden received a full-time Superintendent, William Roxburgh.[7] Roxburgh was one of several talented natural scientists who had studied medicine at the University of Edinburgh. Even as an undergraduate, he had benefitted from socialising in the intellectual and social network of the Scottish Enlightenment and natural history research.[8] On a voyage as a ship's doctor, the young surgeon left the ship in early 1776 in Chinese Canton to seek his fortune in the East Indies. As it turned out, Roxburgh would prove to be successful as a plantation entrepreneur in India, but his lasting reputation is as a natural scientist.[9] Arriving at Shibpur as the new Superintendent, he soon brought his large family with him. Since Roxburgh wanted to live in the Garden itself, rather than in nearby Calcutta, he built a stately villa with money from the Government, today's 'Roxburgh House' next to the Central National Herbarium.[10]

Under its first salaried Superintendent, the garden developed into one of the leading institutions within a network of increasingly globalized botanical research. The number of plant species grown increased under his aegis from 300 to about 3,500.[11] At the same time the Garden developed into an imperial institution that, through its study of the Indian flora, was to strengthen control over the colony's natural resources and, thus, contribute to the stability of imperial structures. It was years of his dedicated work that gave the Botanic Garden the shape and reputation that Wallich was to inherit and develop further.[12] However, the tireless collecting, preparing, documenting, publishing and shipping of plants with a staff of Indian and European employees could not hide the fact that Roxburgh was in an ailing condition. In 1798, he went on his first sick leave to the Cape of Good Hope.[13]

Even at this point a struggle for the position as Roxburgh's successor commenced, but he was to remain in office for another decade and a half. As early as 1806, Francis Buchanan had been nominated Roxburgh's successor by the Court of Directors in London. Like Roxburgh, Buchanan had studied medicine in Edinburgh before serving for ten years as a ship's surgeon on British East Indiamen, eventually being admitted to the Bengal medical service in 1794. From the beginning he also showed a deep interest in natural history in the tradition of the Scottish Enlightenment, and almost immediately began his research on behalf of the Indian government, starting in

Burma. His outstanding statistical survey of Mysore followed in 1800-1801 after which he took part in a British embassy to Nepal as a doctor and naturalist. His longest survey was that of Bengal from 1807 to 1814 but, remarkably, Buchanan's considerable research achievements did not lead to much by way of progress for his career. He was promoted only once, and only in 1807 rose from the rank of Assistant Surgeon to Surgeon.[14]

As already mentioned, Roxburgh took a longer sick leave at the beginning of 1813, but finally retired permanently to Great Britain via St. Helena, and died in Edinburgh two years later. It was initially unclear as to whether he would return, and since a permanent appointment to the Superintendentship could in any case only be decided in London, the government in Calcutta was looking only for a temporary replacement. The post of acting Superintendent was well remunerated and correspondingly attractive, but there were few suitable candidates in India.

In the meantime, Roxburgh's nominated successor Buchanan (later Buchanan Hamilton) had himself resigned due to his lack of movement up the career ladder and had begun to transfer his modest assets to Europe with a view to retirement in Scotland. In the meanwhile, however, he was still fully occupied with his survey of Bengal. With Roxburgh's continued absence the choice now fell on the judge and Orientalist Henry Thomas Colebrooke. Though highly respected, Colebrooke had been removed from his government post due to disapproval of his taxation policy for Bengal. A suitable position had to be found for him and he was given the acting Superintendence of the Botanic Garden while he waited for an opportunity to travel home.

Colebrooke's tenure was brief as in November 1814 he resigned, and left India for London the following month.[15] The Government once again had to look for a candidate, which was offered to Buchanan a second time despite his already expressed desire to leave India. It was the post Buchanan had once longed for, but it came almost a decade too late and, like

Colebrooke, he agreed to accept, only to take his leave just a few months later.[16] A third time within two years, the question of a successor was raised and again the decision made in Calcutta could only be of a temporary nature. However, a new potential candidate had in the meanwhile become acceptable—someone well connected within the colonial elite of Calcutta and, since the peace concluded with Denmark, in the position of an Assistant Surgeon on the Bengal establishment.

ACTING SUPERINTENDENT

Due to a lack of other candidates, the Bengal government finally had to acknowledge that Wallich alone was eligible as an acting Superintendent. Even if he did not have the intellectual breadth of Colebrooke or Buchanan, with his Asiatic Museum he had proved that he had organizational talent, could work hard, and had good contacts. With minor research expeditions under his belt and several years of correspondence with Roxburgh and Carey he had also proved that he was knowledgeable about the botany of Bengal.

Wallich once again benefited from his influential patrons in Calcutta, and Colebrooke, who knew him well from the Asiatic Society, had warmly recommended the young Dane to the Calcutta administration. It was only gradually, however, that Wallich himself came to know about the upcoming promotion. His direct superior, surgeon Robert Leny, must first have had a conversation with him around 20 December 1814, but according to his own statement he was extremely surprised and asked Buchanan about the matter.[17] On 25 December George Nugent, a member of the Government, issued the order that Wallich should not be allowed to go to Nepal, as had been proposed, but should instead make himself available in Calcutta.[18]

To keep him near Calcutta, until his appointment could be finalized, Wallich now was to be sent to the Sangor Road roadstead south of the city. His official task was the medical inspection of private merchant ships on their way to Calcutta from the Bay of Bengal.[19] Facing prospects of further advancement he cannot have taken this task too seriously. In January 1815, for example, Wallich received orders to visit the *Countess of Loudon* lying on the Hooghly, but at the time he was on his way to botanize somewhere in the countryside. It was not until three weeks later that he found the order in the office of his friend Cruttenden in Calcutta, by which time another doctor had already been sent to the ship.[20] The fact that such an obvious breach of duty apparently had no consequences for Wallich indicates how closely networked he was with the colonial powers of British Calcutta in those months. The doors to his further career had been wide open since the Kiel Peace Treaty, and the year 1815 was finally to bring him not only professional success, but also private fulfilment.

It would soon become clear that Wallich was in a particularly privileged position. While he was preparing himself for his new task, the British troops he was supposed to have accompanied had penetrated far into Nepal, into a bloody war that met with fierce resistance from the Nepali armed forces. His colleague and friend, Fred Corbyn, was there and reported in long letters about the cruel everyday life and the fact that he himself had only narrowly escaped death.[21]

On 10 February 1815, Wallich was officially appointed as acting Superintendent of the East India Company's Botanic Garden.[22] The appointment was well received and recognized by the colonial elites. Colin Mackenzie, Surveyor General of India, eminent collector and Orientalist, was pleased and expressed his hope that the position at the Garden would become a permanent one.[23] Much of appreciation also came from Tranquebar, from the missionary Johann Peter Rottler who, more than anyone else, was aware of the direct connection between the end of the Napoleonic Wars and the beginning of Wallich's career. Almost prophetically he wrote: 'We have again great news from Europe which may be of great consequence. God preserve the peace, and may he grant you life and true happiness'.[24]

Only his former colleague Ruhde displayed a degree of envy. While Wallich could hope for a professional career and social advancement in the British colonial metropolis, the fate of the Danish possessions in East India following the end of the Napoleonic Wars, in his words was, uncertain. Ruhde complained to the missionary Klein, that he considered it an injustice that his former colleague had left the Danish service.[25]

Wallich now had a regular income and resided in the spacious Roxburgh House facing the river Hooghly; but since his appointment remained temporary, his situation remained precarious. At any time, he could have been replaced by a Superintendent sent from London and would have had to go to the war in Nepal. Meanwhile, the administration granted him the considerable allowance of 750 rupees per month.[26] Though generous, it was only half of the regular salary that the Court of Directors had approved for the holder of the permanent position of Superintendent.[27] For comparison, a gardener at the Botanic Garden had at this period to be satisfied with three rupees a month.[28]

When he took over the garden at Shibpur it had a size of about 120 hectares.[29] It consisted of four different compartments, each of which was reserved for particular plant families, in addition to a teak plantation, a Linnaean garden, and an orchard.[30] The new Superintendent immediately reviewed the staff available to him. To his regret, he had to note that the number of permanent employees had, for reasons of economy, been halved from 200 to 100 in 1806, while an additional 76 prisoners had been employed instead. The waters of the Hooghly gnawed at the embankment, which had made it necessary to re-assign workers who were now unavailable to work elsewhere in the Garden. Accordingly, as early as March 1815, he applied for the hire of additional gardeners and an increase in the number of prisoners.[31] The response of the Government was as brief as it was negative: additional prisoners could not be made available at present under any circumstances. Wallich soon realized that the botanical garden was not yet a strategic focal point for a frugal colonial Government and even if a 'green imperialism' already existed it was not yet a major priority.[32]

The fact that the acting Superintendent did not always find the time to take care of the Garden with full attention was due to two fierce conflicts that occupied his immediate attention. Straight after taking office, he was drawn into a dispute between Buchanan and the Governor-General, Lord Moira. Buchanan was still in Calcutta when it became known that he intended to take numerous plant and animal drawings, commissioned by himself and his colleagues, back to Britain. Lord Moira, however, believed the drawings were the property of the Government in Calcutta and that they should remain there.[33] By this time, Wallich had already been appointed but had not yet officially taken over the office from his predecessor—a situation that put him in a delicate position vis-à-vis both parties. The government unceremoniously took possession of Buchanan's drawings and placed them under Wallich's care. Despite his affection for Buchanan, he could only bow to the facts.[34]

Buchanan's intervention in another personnel matter, obviously initiated by Wallich himself, turned out to be equally problematic. In July 1815, the new acting Superintendent dismissed the head nurseryman and chief draughtsman John Roxburgh, an illegitimate son of William Roxburgh, who had inherited a love of botany from his father. John had stayed in the Cape Colony between 1799 and 1804 to collect plants to send to his father. After his return to India, in addition to the post of head nurseryman, he was appointed by his father as chief draughtsman in charge of the Garden's group of Indian artists.[35] Despite his achievements Wallich accused John Roxburgh of unreliability while receiving a high salary; he was also alleged to have beaten a servant.[36] It may be assumed that Wallich perhaps wanted to get rid of a possible competitor or someone who could at least weaken his position. That the dismissal was of a certain explosiveness becomes clear from the fact that Wallich mentions the dismissal of a 'nurseryman' in a letter to Hornemann, but wisely concealed that his name was Roxburgh.[37]

SOPHIA

Despite these minor impediments, life was running along a smoother course and the newly appointed Superintendent was once again able to devote attention to private affairs. At the beginning of 1815 it was known among Calcutta society that Wallich was looking for a wife. For two and a half years the mortal remains of Juliana Marie had rested in the cemetery in Serampore and a second marriage would now not only strengthen his integration into local society but might also produce hoped-for offspring.

Wallich, who was busy taking over the Garden, asked some of his friends to help him in his search. Francis Sempill, a confidant and colleague in the medical service, asked around. He knew where the few young European women who were still available were most likely to be found and recommended that his friend look around among the ladies promenading along Chowringhee: 'I hope your visits are not too frequent', he cautiously advised.[38] A young lady metaphorically described by Sempill as a 'blushing rose bush' might be particularly 'worth the attention of any botanist',[39] and with his by now improved career prospects Wallich himself was highly eligible.

The lady in view was to eighteen-year-old Sophia Collings, the younger daughter of an English colonel, born in Patna.[40] The rose met the botanist's taste, and some time later Sempill was pleased to note that Sophia and Nathaniel were promised to one other and added teasingly: 'It is now your own fault if you are not happy'.[41] Rumours of the love affair quickly spread among their acquaintances. Some companions, like Fred Corbyn who was still deployed in the war against Nepal, might have felt a pang of envy.[42] The wedding took place unusually quickly, on 18 March 1815, in Calcutta.[43] That the wedding ceremony of the Jewish Wallich again was a Christian one shows that he had by now been fully assimilated into British colonial society. In this the legacy of his secular enlightened parental home is clearly visible.

On 16 November a son was born who, two months later,

was baptised as George Charles and was later to follow his father's footsteps as a surgeon and naturalist. Two and a half years later a daughter followed, but she did not survive her first year.[44] Eight months after her death, a second daughter was baptized at Dum Dum near Calcutta, under the name Hannah Sarah,[45] with whom Nathaniel would have a particularly close relationship throughout his life.

The marriage with Sophia would last for almost four decades, until Nathaniel's death and she survived him by a further two. In all the couple had seven children, but two of them died in infancy. The mutual affection soon found expression in two portraits, which the popular painter George Chinnery painted for them, but the whereabouts of these is unfortunately not known.[46] Sophia, not only developed love and trust towards her husband, but always identified herself with the great project of his life, the Botanic Garden. Years later, along with daughter Hannah and another newborn child in the dusty lowlands of northern India, she would long to return to the place she regarded as her home: 'I wish I was in my charming loving Botanic Garden out of which I never feel comfortable nor happy. I believe I shall never quit it again'.[47]

In mid-1815, after several years of personal crisis, Nathaniel was in good shape again—a quiet happiness had entered his troubled life. The war in the native country was now in the past, he had an attractive young wife, was in good health and was acting Superintendent of the respected Botanic Garden of Calcutta.[48]

THE NETWORK

From Wallich's home on Esplanade Row, and later from the Botanic Garden, a communication network emerged that gradually became increasingly dense. It included personal local contacts and correspondence within India, as well as connections with Denmark and Britain. From the very beginning Wallich understood communication as a give and take. For the dispatch of information and plants, he expected something in return, but he also understood the use of intermediaries and the value of patronage, and finally he was himself in a position to offer support to people within the network. Since a large part of the communication is likely to have been oral, many of its aspects must remain closed to us.

Wallich maintained tight contacts with the Danish colonies in India especially Serampore with the Baptist missionaries. In Tranquebar, it was his former colleague Ruhde who, despite his resentment, expressed the wish to get in touch with Wallich again in October 1815.[49] Stranded Danish compatriots also enjoyed support in Shibpur, for example, the Wallich couple was worried about an old acquaintance from Copenhagen named Ewers. He had been in French service during the Napoleonic Wars, had got into personal difficulties and one day appeared at the Botanic Garden. A letter from Ewers is preserved, in which he expresses his exuberant gratitude for support given over some unspecified matter.[50]

Much more significant was the fact that after the end of the war contact with the mother country once again became more regular. From his desk in the Roxburgh House, Wallich must, now and then, have noticed with pleasure when a proud East Indiaman under the Danish flag was carried upstream towards Serampore on the incoming tide. Thanks to local contacts, he also knew at short notice when a Danish vessel was to lift anchor from Serampore and set off for home. Letters were quickly written and boxes with herbarium material put together, which could easily be put on board as it passed the Garden.[51]

Wallich's old teacher Hornemann was at the centre of the professional links with Denmark. He not only provided Wallich with up-to-date information from home, but also arranged further contacts in Denmark. In February 1815, for example, Wallich wrote that he considered it to be a patriotic duty to send rare plants home.[52] The royal gardener Holbøll, with whom he had earned his first spurs in practical horticulture, also benefited from shipments from Calcutta.[53]

The imperial centre played an increasingly important role—

for Wallich, as a servant of the East India Company, this meant London. Many contacts were made possible by the support and protection of influential patrons. First and foremost, he intended to attract more attention of Sir Joseph Banks, who since its establishment, had observed the development of the Botanic Garden in Calcutta with interest and who was able to forward many a career through his connections with the highest London circles. Wallich, despite the plant specimens sent to Banks from Mauritius, yet had no direct contact with him and to do so used his friend Thomas Hardwicke. Hardwicke was an army officer and fellow member of the Asiatic Society, who cultivated his passion for zoology on extensive journeys through India and was a correspondent of Banks.[54] He had returned to Calcutta from a long absence in Mauritius in late September 1815 and learned of Colebrooke's and Buchanan's departure as well as of the appointment of Wallich, whose activities he followed closely. As he wrote to Banks at the end of October, he was highly satisfied with Wallich's performance: 'He appears to be a man highly qualified for the charge he has', his work held great promise and Hardwicke predicted that, 'I make no doubt you will soon know more about Dr Wallich'.[55]

Hardwicke also opened up to Wallich a completely new group of correspondents in Britain—women with serious interests in botany and horticulture. This was initially perceived as a matter of establishing contact with Banks, but in the course of time Wallich's connections with Diana Beaumont came to be of importance in its own right. Diana was the wife of Thomas Richard Beaumont, a member of the House of Commons, who had brought a considerable fortune from her father's inheritance into the marriage and maintained a large garden with a magnificent conservatory at Bretton Hall in Yorkshire. The couple also spent much time in London, where they were in touch not only with Banks, but with the patron of science Aylmer Bourke Lambert and the board of directors of the East India Company.[56] It was Hardwicke who made the introduction to Mrs Beaumont, and as early as December

1815 Wallich sent her living plants and seeds.[57] The system worked smoothly as can be seen from a letter by Diana that expresses her intention to send seeds to Calcutta in return: 'I shall request my gardener this autumn to collect all seeds that he thinks will be acceptable to you, for the Botanical Garden at Calcutta, which I have mentioned to the India Directors, and requested they would send them out to you, this offered me the opportunity of mentioning your views and offering my strongest recommendation, which I have also done to Sir Joseph Banks, and to Mr Lambert, and have every reason to hope it will be attended to'.[58]

However, Wallich also took his own initiative. One day several boxes were packed for departure to London addressed to Robert Brown, librarian and close confidant of Banks. With this dispatch, Wallich not only consolidated his access to Banks, but also established a decades-long exchange of letters with Brown himself.[59]

In order to obtain interesting plants for shipment to Europe Wallich had to maintain and expand the Garden's existing contacts across the vast Indian hinterland. The system of communication through plants, already established by Roxburgh, was now developed to perfection and an ever increasing number of specimens flowed into the Botanic Garden from various parts of India—from the Himalaya to the far south, as well as from the immediate vicinity of Calcutta.[60] Wallich made himself indispensable as an intermediary between plant collectors in India and other parts of the world, thus strengthening patterns of global botanical exchange.[61] In addition, the acting Superintendent immediately set about developing the Garden itself, which in his eyes had been neglected after Roxburgh's departure. He increased its area by eleven hectares and founded an agricultural experimental farm.[62] In the first few months he also described the plants in the garden and had many of them drawn.[63]

By the time he took up office, however, it must have been clear to Wallich that a reputation as an internationally renowned scientist could not be founded on plant shipments and the expansion of the garden alone, and that a certain amount of publication activity would also be required. Wallich's earliest identifiable publication soon appeared, an eleven-page paper, illustrated with four plates, entitled 'Description of two new Species of Sarcolobus, and some other Indian Plants', in the twelfth volume of *Asiatick Researches* in 1816. *Sarcolobus globosus*, first described only a few years earlier, occurs in various regions of Asia, including the mangrove forests of Bengal and is a shrub whose shoots and leaves have been and are still used medicinally.[64] Even before receiving the printed copies, Wallich proudly sent a handwritten version of the text to Hornemann, and he ensured that a printed copy reached Sir Joseph Banks via Hardwicke.[65] In order to illustrate his *Sarcolobus* paper with copper engravings, he needed a professional engraver who was also well-versed in the field of plant depiction. His contact with the missionaries in Serampore, however, proved disappointing and he came to the conclusion that good prints could simply not be produced in India.[66] Carey, therefore, proposed to train a 'clever young man' himself and offered to teach him everything he himself knew in the field of printing.[67] The project was successful, and the first four copperplate engravings illustrate Wallich's first paper.[68]

Wallich, however, had a larger project in mind. The illustrations were to constitute the first issue of a botanical compendium scheduled to be published in several fascicles of 25 illustrations each under the title *Tentamen Florae Asiaticae Illustratae*. The plan to describe and publish large numbers of Indian plants with their native names took up an idea already suggested and begun by Sir William Jones, but which Roxburgh had not managed to develop.[69] Wallich wrote to Hornemann that he was aware of the great difficulties of producing a high-quality work in India—heaven only knew whether the intended publication would ever be positively received by reviewers.[70]

The Tentamen was threatened with failure from the very beginning because of the high costs of paper and printing, which Wallich had to raise from his own resources and which he was sure would never be compensated for by sale proceeds.[71] The project dragged on, but in December 1817 he succeeded in sending the six finished sheets of the first issue to Hornemann.[72]

BOTANIST ON DEMAND

It was soon clear that professional success could prove fragile. Already, when appointed acting Superintendent, Wallich had complained to Buchanan about the uncertainty of life: 'What I dread is this eternal instability of employment which renders a man's endeavours, let his exertions be, however, strong, vain and fruitless'.[73] Since the beginning of his career Wallich had to deal with competitors who challenged his professional advancement. In Copenhagen his opponent had been Schmidt-Phiseldeck's candidate; in Calcutta his opponent was James Hare.

Like Wallich, Hare was a surgeon. He had studied in Edinburgh where he obtained a Doctor of Medicine in 1796 and had a deep interest in India. A member of the Asiatic Society from 1799, he had been appointed as an Assistant Surgeon in 1801 and promoted to Surgeon thirteen years later.[74] Long before Wallich's career began, Hare had pointed out the great importance of natural history research for the colonial state. In 1808, he had proposed the formation of a committee within the Asiatic Society to promote relevant studies.[75] Hare showed himself at home in the field of botany, and as he and Wallich had similar goals it was precisely this similarity that made them rivals. Hare had a higher rank as Surgeon and, according to tradition, should have been given priority in the temporary management of the Botanic Garden already by beginning of 1815. It was only Hare's poor health that had prevented his, rather than Wallich's, appointment. The only hope was that with Hare's illness and possible return to England, the matter would eventually resolve itself.[76] Meanwhile, among his friends, Wallich tried to polarize opinion against Hare.[77]

Hare's state of health, however, improved considerably from April 1815.[78] For a while it seemed as if he was to be put in charge of a gunpowder factory, but then things got serious for Wallich.[79] His temporary employment as a Superintendent came to an end on 11 December 1815, having lasted less than ten months. The reasons that led to his replacement can no longer be clearly determined, but in the end, it was probably Hare's improved health and higher rank that tipped the scales. However, as will be seen, there were probably other, social, factors at play as Hare's eponymous uncle was a senior Calcutta doctor and, since December 1814, Hare himself had been personal physician to the Governor-General, Lord Moira.

Wallich felt disappointed with his return to the rank of an ordinary Assistant Surgeon and, more particularly, the loss of his enhanced salary as acting Superintendent. In the face of economic challenges, which also resulted from his publishing activities, he and his young family found themselves in a financially precarious situation. To show the government his difficult situation and perhaps to make it willing to compromise, Wallich sat down at his desk on 19 January 1816 to write a five-page letter. In it he described in detail, and not without self-praise, his achievements at the Botanic Garden. He claimed that, beyond question, he had maintained the garden better than it ever had been. As one of his most important achievements he stressed the sending of many plants to other parts of the world, and especially to well-known British institutions. He had also significantly expanded the seed collection and put its organization on a scientific basis. He also pointed out possible future difficulties in adequately feeding his family while at the same time continuing his scientific work. As evidence of the latter, he supplemented the letter with printed matter and several engravings—presumably samples from his planned botanical work.[80] Wallich could not then have known that steps for his benefit were already working for him in London.

NOTES

1. Isaac Henry Burkill, *Chapters on the History of Botany in India*, Calcutta: Botanical Survey of India, 1965, pp. 4-14.
2. Fischer-Tiné, *Pidgin-Knowledge*, pp. 29-40.
3. Desmond, *European Discovery*, p. 53.
4. Grove, *Green Imperialism*, pp. 332-8.
5. Desmond, *European Discovery*, p. 57; Harrison, 'Calcutta Botanic Garden', p. 236.
6. Grove, *Green Imperialism*, p. 281.
7. Desmond, *European Discovery*, p. 60.
8. Robinson, *William Roxburgh*, pp. 7-10.
9. Ibid., pp. 21f.
10. Ibid., pp. 44ff.
11. Harrison, *Calcutta Botanic Garden*, p. 237.
12. Ibid., p. 235.
13. Robinson, *William Roxburgh*, pp. 55ff.
14. M. Vicziany, 'Imperialism, Botany and Statistics in Early Nineteenth-Century India. The Surveys of Francis Buchanan (1762-1829)', *Modern Asian Studies*, vol. 20, 1986, pp. 632-8, 643ff.
15. Rocher & Rocher, *Making of Western Indology*, pp. 125-31.
16. Vicziany, 'Imperialism, Botany and Statistics', p. 656.
17. Ibid.
18. Ibid.
19. Cf. for example CNH, Wallich letters, inspection of the 'General Hewitt', 20 January 1815.
20. CNH, Wallich letters, order dated 25 January 1815.
21. Ibid., Corbyn to Wallich, 25 January 1815.
22. CNH, Wallich letters, Wallich to Wood, 31 August 1816.
23. Ibid., Mackenzie to Wallich, 11 August 1815: 'to get your situation recommended home in such manner may secure the ultimate approval by the Court of Directors'.
24. Ibid., Rottler to Wallich, 21 July 1815.
25. Ibid., Klein to Wallich, 30 July 1815.
26. BL IOR, F/4/513/12340, Extract Public Letter from Bengal, 7 October 1815.
27. CNH, Wallich letters, N.N., 9 May 1815.
28. BL IOR, F/4/513/12340, Extract Bengal Public Proceedings, Wallich to Trotter, 10 April 1815.
29. Desmond, *European Discovery*, p. 83.

30. Ibid., p. 81; CNH, Wallich letters, Wallich to Governor-General, 19 January 1816.
31. BL IOR, F/4/513/12340, Extract Bengal Public Proceedings, 13 March 1815.
32. Ibid., Trotter to Wallich, 30 March 1815.
33. Desmond, *European Discovery*, pp. 78f.
34. CNH, Wallich letters, Wallich to Trotter, 26 February 1815.
35. Desmond, *European Discovery*, pp. 81f.
36. Ibid., p. 82; Robinson, *William Roxburgh*, p. 67; SNM, Breve fra Wallich, I, 3, Wallich to Hornemann, 10 February 1816.
37. SNM, Letters from Wallich, I, 3, Wallich to Hornemann, 10 February 1816; on John Roxburgh in general see Robinson, *William Roxburgh*, pp. 63-7.
38. CNH, Wallich letters, Sempill to Wallich, 17 January 1815.
39. Ibid.
40. Family Search.org (retrieved: 10 October 2016); Carøe, *Den Danske Lægestand*, p. 218; *The Asiatic Annual Register . . . for the Year 1801*, London, 1802, p. 103.
41. CNH, Wallich letters, Sempill to Wallich, 16 April 1815.
42. Ibid., Corbyn to Wallich, 11 March 1815: 'I intend becoming a candidate among the fair sex'.
43. BL IOOC, N/1/9, p. 256, see indiafamily.bl.uk (retrieved 21 October 2013).
44. BL IOR, N/1/10, p. 581, see indiafamily.bl.uk (retrieved 21 October 2013); CNH, Wallich letters, Cruttenden to Wallich, c. 16 November 1815.
45. BL IOOC, N/1/10, p. 581, see indiafamily.bl.uk (retrieved 21 October 2013).
46. Landsarkivet for Sjælland, QA-035, Engelholm Gods, 1811-52, Wolff family private archive, correspondence 29-8, Wallich to Benjamin Wolff, 27 January 1821.
47. Ibid., Sophia Wallich to Benjamin Wolff, 29 December 1820.
48. CNH, Wallich letters, Rottler to Wallich, 21 July 1815.
49. CNH, Wallich letters, Ruhde to Wallich, 8 October 1815.
50. Ibid., index, p. 55: 'F.W. Ewers, an old acquaintance from Copenhagen, had been in the French Service during the war'.
51. SNM, Letters from Wallich, I, 8, Wallich to Hornemann, 29 November 1817.
52. Ibid., I, 2, Wallich to Hornemann, 2 February 1815.
53. Ibid., I, 3, Wallich to Hornemann, 10 February 1816.

54. N. Chambers (ed.), *The Indian and Pacific Correspondence of Sir Joseph Banks*, vol. 8, London: Pickering & Chatto, 2014, pp. 375f.

55. Hardwicke to Banks, 30 October 1815, in: Chambers, Indian and Pacific Correspondence, p. 142.

56. Diana Beaumont, www.dukesfield.org.uk (retrieved: 5 April 2017).

57. CNH, Wallich letters, Diana Beaumont to Wallich, 24 June 1816.

58. Ibid.

59. Mägdefrau, *Geschichte der Botanik*, p. 81.

60. For example CNH, Wallich letters, Steward to Wallich, 20 June 1815, about a consignment of plants from Burabazar, today a district of Calcutta.

61. Ibid., Rottler to Wallich, 27 July 1815.

62. Ibid., Wallich, 19 January 1816.

63. Ibid.

64. N. Wallich, 'Two New Species of *Sarcolobus*, and some other Indian Plants', *Asiatic Researches*, vol. 12, 1816, pp. 566ff.

65. SNM, Letters from Wallich, I, 3, Wallich to Hornemann, 10 February 1816; Hardwicke to Banks, 12 January 1816, in Chambers, *Indian and Pacific Correspondence*, p. 153.

66. 'It may be done in this country but never well done, there is not a good engraver in this country.' CNH, Wallich letters, Lawson to Wallich, 29 June 1815.

67. SNM, Letters from Wallich, I, 3, Wallich to Hornemann, 10 February 1816.

68. Wallich, 'Two New Species'; Hardwicke to Banks, 12 January 1816, in Chambers, Indian and Pacific Correspondence, p. 153.

69. Desmond, *European Discovery*, p. 54.

70. SNM, Letters from Wallich, I, 3, Wallich to Hornemann, 10 February 1816.

71. CNH, Wallich letters, Wallich, 19 January 1819.

72. Ibid., 4 December 1817.

73. Wallich to Buchanan, 25 February 1815, cited from Desmond, *European Discovery*, p. 81.

74. Nair, *Proceedings*, vol. 2, p. 605.

75. Ibid., p. 238.

76. CNH, Wallich letters, Sempill to Wallich, 20 May 1815: 'I long to hear of Hare going home, as you may be then certain of getting full charge, which you should have had at first, and he can never enjoy good health in this country'.

77. Ibid., Corbyn to Wallich, 11 March 1815.

78. Ibid., Leny to Wallich, 21 April 1815.

79. Hardwicke to Banks, 30 October 1815, in Chambers, *Indian and Pacific Correspondence*, p. 142.

80. CNH, Wallich letters, Wallich to Charles Milner Ricketts, 19 January 1816.

CHAPTER 7

Superintendent

PATRONAGE

The loss of his temporary position at the Calcutta Botanic Garden hit Wallich deeply. At first there was no choice other than to accept the subordinate position offered to him as Hare's assistant and to live on the 300 rupees per month due to him in the rank of an Assistant Surgeon. At least he was able to continue to live in Roxburgh House, as Hare himself, to be close to Lord Moira, lived near the summer residence of the Governor-General at Barrackpore and visited the Botanic Garden only irregularly. *De facto*, therefore, Wallich was still in charge. Soon there were renewed provocations between the two, in which Lord Moira was finally involved on Hare's side.[1] The fact that Hare reinstated John Roxburgh, previously dismissed by Wallich, as chief gardener probably did nothing to ease the situation. After the situation had become unbearable for both sides, Wallich resigned his position,[2] and, as he wrote to Joseph Williamson in Liverpool, felt exploited: 'Circumstances have obliged me to decline accepting a subordinate situation at the Botanic Garden near Calcutta, which while it comprised the whole duties of a superintendent, would not have allowed me to continue a very expensive work of Indian plants'.[3] He had effectively to perform the duties of Superintendent under Hare but had been officially demoted to a subordinate position as his assistant.

Presumably, sometime in April or May 1816, Wallich moved back with his family to Esplanade Row to resume his flourishing private medical practice, in addition to his work for the Company as an Assistant Surgeon. The rules of the

Medical Board gave him the freedom to do so, which he, doubtless, exploited through his good contacts with Calcutta's European elites. He soon expressed a certain bitter satisfaction to Hornemann that he could now earn 1,000 rupees a month—which indicates that his passion for a substantial income came next only to that for botany.[4] This did nothing, however, to diminish his drive to continue his success in the field of botany: he still owned a herbarium and continued to dispatch plants to many countries. In mid-1817, for example, two boxes were sent to Hornemann, one containing plants from the Botanic Garden, the other sent by William Carey from Serampore.[5]

Hare's state of health deteriorated once again, so that at the end of 1816 he was forced to return to Britain. For a fifth time an acting Superintendent had to be found. Wallich's short-term hopes were quickly dashed, as his attacks against Hare had made him unpopular with the Governor-General who now, to Wallich's great disappointment, had Thomas Casey appointed as director—the same Casey who had been appointed as Assistant Surgeon at the same time as Wallich and who, in the meantime, had won the favour of the Governor-General and his wife.[6]

What Wallich did not suspect in those dark moments was the fact that his withdrawal was only to be temporary. His carefully established network of patrons gradually began to prove its worth and behind the scenes in London, Banks was working on his comeback.[7] Immediately after the dismissal, Wallich had written a letter to his predecessor Francis Buchanan, by now living in Britain, asking for support in his precarious situation. Wallich probably hoped for Buchanan's intervention with the Court of Directors in London, but Buchanan was unable to do anything about it as he had already ended his career with the East India Company and, deeply disappointed, retreated to private life on his inherited property at Leny in Stirlingshire, Scotland.[8]

The situation with regard to Colebrooke was different. While Colebrooke did not aspire to any official role in the East India Company, he was highly regarded in England as a former member of the Calcutta government, and continued to maintain his scientific reputation through his Sanskrit research. He also lived at the political centre of London.[9] Here Wallich's friendship with Carey, who was more familiar with Colebrooke than himself, paid off. The missionary turned to the famous Sanskrit scholar with the request to present Wallich's case for reinstatement as Superintendent to the Court of Directors. Colebrooke's answer to Carey on 6 January 1817 was positive: 'I have no doubt that Dr Wallich has exerted himself to the utmost at the Botanic Garden. Natural History, particularly Botany, is his favourite discipline and he is certainly entitled to much consideration for what he has done. The[re] is no one better qualified for the charge of the Garden than himself'.[10] At the same time, however, Colebrooke admitted that he would not be surprised if the Court of Directors preferred to send an established botanist from England to Bengal. The appointment was still an open question.

Besides Colebrooke, Wallich also had support from his acquaintance from the Asiatic Society and from the Bengal Medical Board, John Fleming, who had retired to England in 1813 and was now a Member of Parliament.[11] The Court of Directors seems to have initially favoured the appointment of a botanist from Britain but, after enquiries had produced no result, Colebrooke's and Fleming's promotion of Wallich's case carried all the more weight.[12]

Through Hardwicke, Wallich also attempted to obtain the support of Banks. Hardwicke informed the President of the Royal Society of the insecurity of Wallich's situation and made it clear that he considered his protégé to be the best candidate as Superintendent.[13] But the exotic plants sent to Diana Beaumont also proved to have paid-off and she promised to appear with her husband before Banks, Lambert and the Court of Directors.[14]

Banks' pressure was, ultimately, the deciding factor and on 29 January 1817 a decision was made in London. On the basis of the certificates submitted to the Bengal Government, as well as its own enquiries, it was reassured that Wallich was uniquely qualified to manage the Botanic Garden, and the Government in Calcutta was instructed to appoint him as permanent Superintendent with immediate effect. In the event that the Government had already appointed another director, as was, in fact, the case with Casey, such an appointment was to be reversed.[15] Even better, Wallich's temporary appointment of two years earlier was simultaneously confirmed—a decision that was far from insignificant for his financial circumstances, as it granted him the full remuneration of a full-time Superintendent retroactively from his first term of office.[16]

The news reached Calcutta in July 1817. Full of euphoria, and with a healthy dose of self-confidence, Wallich immediately informed Hornemann, denouncing his opponents as the antagonists of the Roman goddess Flora.[17] Such a rapid rise within the Company hierarchy was unusual and Wallich had achieved in a short time what was usually possible only after decades. He knew whom he had to thank for the appointment, and the letter he wrote to Banks on 24 July 1817 sounds almost grovelling.[18] But Wallich's gratitude was expressed above all in the fact that, in Banks' last three years of life, ship after ship of the East India Company sailed laden with dried specimens that Banks incorporated into his herbarium, and living plants that he passed on to Kew Gardens. The arrival of a living musk deer and a turtle, sent back in the early 1820s, was something, however, that the famous participant in Cook's first circumnavigation did not live to see.[19]

Although he had every reason to be happy Wallich could not refrain from taking revenge on his competitor Dr Hare, who was by now back in Britain. During his tenure, Hare had commissioned Indian artists from Calcutta to make copies of the Roxburgh plant drawings in the Botanic Garden's collection, which he considered to be his own property. He had taken 573 complete ones with him, but a further 619 had been made after his departure. When Hare asked for the latter to be forwarded to him, they were immediately seized by Wallich, who argued that they had been made without the permission of the Government; moreover, the original drawings and bindings had been damaged in the copying process. The new Superintendent had the remaining copies sent to the library of the East India Company in London and Hare was allowed, after some negotiation, to keep the drawings already in his possession, though was forbidden to publish them.[20] Wallich won the conflict with Hare in the short term, but there were further negotiations and in 1826 the second batch (by now numbering 627) were eventually passed on to Hare.[21] There was more behind this story than merely a display of personal vanities for Wallich took his commitment to the Company and its property immensely seriously. During his long period of work at Shibpur, he would ensure that all materials coming into the Garden were considered to be Company property and that all plants and books dispatched around the globe were sent in the name of the Company.

Wallich's new position allowed a previously unknown continuity of his own research, provided financial security for his steadily growing family and the freedom to develop new interests and perspectives. This was helped by the fact that in the early days the Company interfered little with his running of the Garden, allowing him largely a free hand.

Wallich had reached the zenith of his career at the age of only thirty-one; from now on his major effort was aimed at enhancing his scientific reputation and extending his botanical network. This proved to be difficult, especially in the early days, as routine matters took up a large part of his working time. He complained to Hornemann that he hardly had time to write longer letters—something of an understatement considering the constantly growing correspondence.[22]

THE CORRESPONDENCE

Wallich spent almost exactly three years based at the Botanic Garden between his permanent appointment and the beginning of his extensive travels. During this time, he perfected his practice of the exchange of letters, plants, and books into a sleekly running system. The capital he had to offer was not only in the form of plants, but also information in written form. Correspondents felt particularly flattered when Wallich named a recently discovered plant after them and often responded with gifts of books. While he is by no means to be credited with the invention of a global network of scholars, what was distinctive and new about his system was the systematic placement of the Botanical Garden as an interface between the Himalayan foothills on the one hand and Europe on the other. This mountainous region was now integrated into a global botanical communication system in an unprecedented way.

In those first three years, from 1817 to 1820, Wallich received almost 800 letters, whose authors and places of origin show a pattern that reflect his intentions and both strategy and methodology for communication. Due to the high cost of postage, and long delivery times, the number of letters arriving from Europe tended to be lower than ones from Indian locations. Internal communication within Calcutta, with friends and supporters and official exchanges with Company officials, continued to play a major part: Close contact was kept with his friend Colonel Hardwicke (61 letters between July 1817 and June 1820), and with his Indian confidant Ram Comul Sen (24). From the small number of their letters, major communication with his friends Corbyn (6) and Horace Hayman Wilson (5) seems likely to have been mainly oral. Contact with the Danish colonies was maintained at a rather low level with Rottler (5) and Klein (3), and only the correspondence with Carey at Serampore (17) was more frequent. It was only now, however, that the connections with the southern slopes of the Himalayas were strengthened.

Between Cooch Behar in the east and Kumaon in the west, Wallich maintained contacts with military and civilian Company officials, who sent him plants and information. To ensure a high standard, Wallich instructed his correspondents as to the data he required and, in some cases, provided them with professional Indian plant collectors from the Botanic Garden. This emerges from the extensive correspondence with Robert

Colquhoun (41), William Spencer Webb (35), George Govan (21), Alexander Gerard (19), and David Scott (17). It was at this time that the exchange of letters with Nepal developed, especially with the Honourable Edward Gardner (100) and Robert Stuart (45), to be explored in the next chapter.

In Cooch Behar, which lies immediately south of Bhutan, he had a correspondent in the person of David Scott. Scott was the representative of the Governor-General in the northeastern border region of Bengal and was admitted to the Asiatic Society in 1819. He knew the foothills of the Himalaya adjacent to Bhutan in detail and not only sent Wallich information about his explorations but asked him to forward letters to his correspondents in Europe, especially to Colebrooke.[23] Time and again Scott sent plants, roots and seeds to Calcutta.[24]

From Kumaon, to the west of Nepal, Wallich was regularly supplied with plants and seeds by Captain William Spencer Webb, who was making surveys there. Webb also sent samples of local woods, including the wild Himalayan pear, chestnut, walnut, evergreen oak, white Himalayan oak and rhododendrons.[25] He also provided valuable information about medicinal rhubarb and various types of grain and by way of gratitude Wallich named the Western Himalayan fir *Pinus webbiana* (now known as *Abies spectabilis*) for him.[26]

From Calcutta, Webb received a copy of Humboldt's 1816 *Mémoires sur les Montaignes de l'Inde* in which the German natural philosopher wrote, among other things, about the snow-line in the Himalayas. Webb, who at the same time was working on fossils and their possible significance for the deciphering of the Earth's history, undertook on his own initiative a translation of this publication into English. Though not entirely satisfied with it he sent it for discussion before the Asiatic Society,[27] where Wallich presented the translation, with comments, at the meeting of 11 February 1818.[28] The transcripts of the debate were returned to Humboldt who, decades later, used them in his seminal work *Cosmos*.[29] Sir Robert Colquhoun, commander of the British troops in Almora in the western Himalayas, also sent valuable material to Shibpur.[30] It was not without pride that Wallich could report to Colebrooke: 'We have latterly had enormous quantities . . . of rare plants from Nepal, Sylhet, Saharanpore, Almora, etc'.[31]

Correspondence with Britain was much as it had been before 1817 and Wallich maintained an exchange of letters with his two predecessors Colebrooke (7) and Buchanan (7), as well as with Diana Beaumont (5). The communication with Banks was rather one-sided. While 20 letters were sent by Wallich, only three letters from Banks are known. Though Banks was still well disposed towards him, in the last years of his life he was severely restricted by increasing health problems.[32] On 3 November 1818, Wallich was accepted as a Fellow of the Linnean Society of London, which, under the aegis of James Edward Smith, administered and kept alive the Linnaean heritage and, with the royal gardens at Kew, increasingly perceived itself as a communication hub for a global botany.[33]

While the sources do not allow any statement about Wallich's private correspondence with his own family, professional contacts with Denmark were maintained through Hornemann (11) and, to a lesser degree, through his cousin Jacobson (4). Correspondence with Holbøll (2) and other contacts from his student days played only a minor role. It was undoubtedly Hornemann who profited most from the connection with India, and with almost every letter Wallich sent living plants or one or more boxes of roots, seeds or herbarium material to Copenhagen—some to Hornemann himself, others to Holbøll. For this purpose, he entrusted plants to the care of the captains or supercargoes of the Danish East Indiamen passing the Garden, such as the *Ludvig* at the end of 1819, or the *Kronprind-sessen* at the beginning of 1820.[34]

Wallich also made use of his expertise as an Orientalist to expand professional contacts with his home city of Copen-hagen, and to generate a sense of mutual cooperation. At the end of 1818 an impressive shipment of books and manuscripts in classical and modern Indian languages, as well as in Persian, Arabic, and Chinese, reached the Copenhagen University

Library as a donation. Wallich had acquired these works largely from other institutions, in which 158 volumes were donations from the Government in Calcutta and 39 from the mission in Serampore. In addition, there were 18 volumes of Bible translations into various Indian languages for the Danish Bible Society donated by two Bible societies in Calcutta; and finally, there were 65 printed volumes from Wallich's own library and about 37 manuscripts collected by himself.[35]

Among the printed works were original texts and translations, but also commentaries and grammars, such as the first volume of the *Grammar of the Sanscrit Language* by his friend Colebrooke, *The Ramayana of Valmeecki, in the original Sanskrit*, edited and with a commentary by Carey and Marshman, and Jones' famous edition of *Sacontala, or the fatal Ring, an Indian Drama* by Kalidas, printed in Calcutta as early as 1789. A large portion of the books and manuscripts, however, were medical. Wallich addressed the shipment to his father Wulff Lazarus, who delivered them to the university.[36]

The donation was of considerable benefit to the Copenhagen University Library and greatly strengthened its oriental collection, as many of the works had not previously been available in Denmark. But the gift also found recognition beyond the university and a complete list was published in the journal *Dansk Litteratur-Tidende*, in which tribute to Wallich's extraordinary merits was paid.[37] Two years later, Rasmus Nyerup, the man who a decade and a half earlier had suggested the establishment of a Danish National Museum, published an annotated catalogue of a selection of the books.[38] Further book shipments followed, for example a copy of *Asiatick Researches*, which Wallich sent to the Danish Academy of Sciences, for which the famous natural scientist Hans Christian Ørsted wrote a letter of gratitude.[39] In return, a no less remarkable donation of books in Old Norse language was sent to the College of Fort William and in this way works by the Icelandic historian Snorri Sturluson and an Icelandic-Danish dictionary somewhat surprisingly found their way to India.[40]

It was not only books and manuscripts that were received

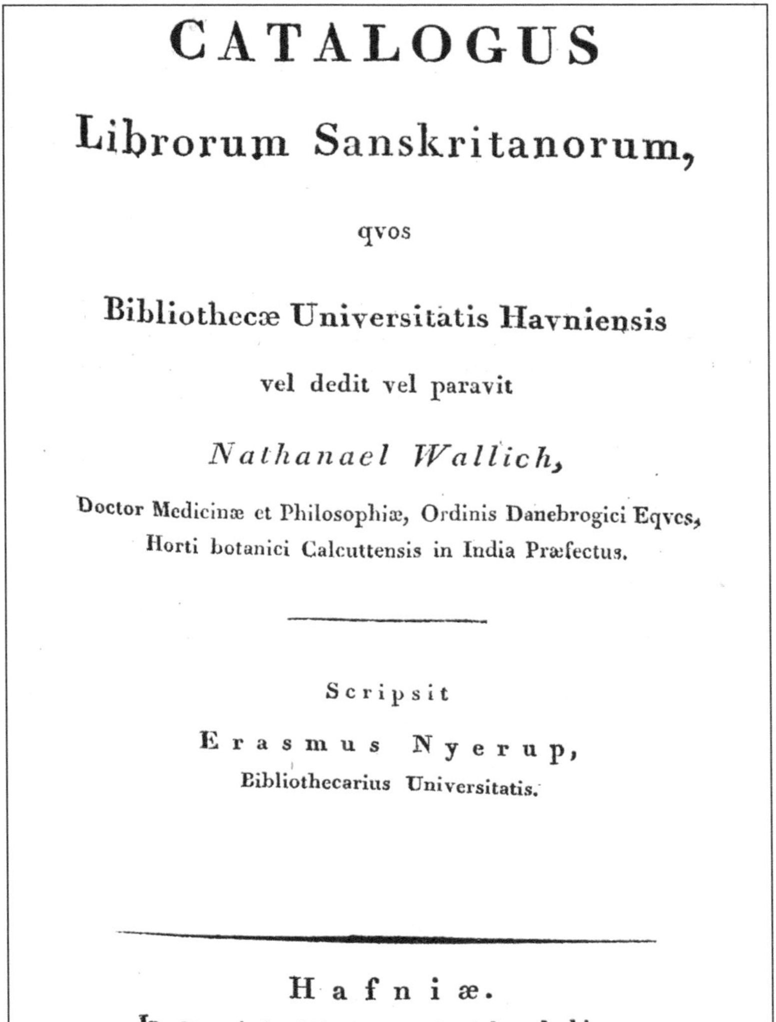

CATALOGUS

Librorum Sanskritanorum,

qvos

Bibliothecæ Universitatis Havniensis

vel dedit vel paravit

Nathanael Wallich,

Doctor Medicinæ et Philosophiæ, Ordinis Danebrogici Eqves,
Horti botanici Calcuttensis in India Præfectus.

———————

Scripsit

Erasmus Nyerup,

Bibliothecarius Universitatis.

———————

Hafniæ.

In commissis librariæ Gyldendalianæ.
Excudit Johannes Thiele.

1 8 2 1.

Figure 7.1: The catalogue of Wallich's dispatch of 'Oriental' books
and manuscripts to Copenhagen, edited by Rasmus Nyerup, 1821.
(University Library, Kiel)

from Wallich in Copenhagen, but also countless herbarium specimens and other natural history objects. Wallich's patrons campaigned for their distant countryman to be honoured, which was achieved in 1819 when King Frederick VI made him a Knight of the Order of the Danebrog—one of the highest honours of the Danish monarchy.[41] Crown Prince Christian Frederik, who was deeply interested in natural science, expressed his appreciation two years later in a personal letter, for which Wallich thanked him with a detailed account of his travels and activities.[42] Though until now Wallich had no direct connections in Germany, his botanical explorations and his mediation between India and Europe were well-known there, and on 1 April 1820, he was appointed as a member of the Academia Leopoldina, under the cognomen 'Reede', in memory of his famous Dutch predecessor in the East Indies.[43]

Wallich's fellow countryman Rasmus Rask looked with resentment at Wallich's specatular rise in status. Rask was one of the most original linguists of his day and, in search of a common original Nordic language, had embarked on a journey to Iceland. He later tried to reconstruct a proto-European-Indian language that he called the 'Thracian language', for which he undertook a journey over several years via Russia and Persia to India and Ceylon. There he wanted to collect manuscripts and, in this way, strengthen his reputation in Copenhagen. That Wallich denied him the fame of being the first to send texts from South Asia to Denmark, was revealed in a letter from Nyerup, while Rask was on his way to Russia in which Nyerup also reported Wallich's admission to the Danebrog Order. Rask, who was plagued by depression and financial constraints, did eventually succeeded in acquiring some manuscripts in India himself. In April 1821, he travelled to Serampore, and then on to Calcutta, but did not find Wallich there as by this time he was on his expedition to Nepal.[44]

In addition to maintaining contacts with Denmark, Wallich's attention was also increasingly drawn to France. Remarkable and new were his connections with several French botanists who discovered in India a promising field of research. Letters were written to Pierre-Médard Diard (13), Alfred Duvaucel (6), Jean-Baptiste Leschenault de la Tour (8) Jean-Louis-Auguste Loiseleur-Deslongchamps (4), François Victor Mérat de Vaumartoise (3) and André Thouin (3). Wallich wrote to Banks that he also had an exchange with the famous naturalist and zoologist Georges Cuvier.[45] Word of Wallich's accomplishments spread and finally he was no longer compelled to make his own contacts entirely through his own efforts. One of those who now approached him was the renowned botanist Augustin-Pyramus de Candolle of Geneva.[46]

THE GLOBAL TRANSFER OF PLANTS

Wallich kept few herbarium specimens from his early collections, as most he sent to botanists in Europe. In the days before the advent of air conditioning and modern conservation methods, a herbarium in India often proved to be perishable, as Roxburgh had concluded earlier. By this time, Wallich said that there was as little left of the collection he had gathered in Rio de Janeiro so many years earlier as there was of the one subsequently assembled in Serampore. Both collections had been largely destroyed by the rigours of climate and insects, and it was only his Mauritius specimens that had survived.[47]

A large part of the plant material he amassed since joining the Garden, or was sent in by his collectors and correspondents, now was kept in Calcutta. This formed the basis for the huge East India Company herbarium which Wallich took back to London in 1828 or sent on ahead to India House. These were later documented in the 'Wallich Catalogue' when he distributed the East India Company herbarium. Meanwhile, he sent plants, plant lists, and explanatory letters to Europe in considerable quantity. This was not always herbaceous material of modest dimensions and weight. Botanical specimens of considerable size sometimes also made the journey to Europe, such as palm leaves or the trunks of tree ferns several metres long.[48] Shipping on a large scale was expensive and put the Botanic Garden under considerable financial pressure, which Wallich tried to redress with countless letters to the colonial authorities and requests for funds.[49]

Wallich put a great deal of thought into the question of how living plants were to get from India to Europe safely during a sea-voyage that usually took about six months. In a letter to Hornemann dated 30 November 1817 he provided a set of 'state of the art' instructions for the transport of plants on long sea-voyages. First of all, a trustworthy person had to be found who would take responsibility for the care of the plants on board the East Indiaman—no easy matter. These were best packed in boxes on deck in a place where, ideally, they were shaded from direct sunlight. There they would be surrounded either by earth or by sand mixed with grated charcoal.[50] Additional seeds could be sown in the earth in the hope that these would germinate on the journey to Europe, and thus, increase the botanical harvest. The type of box mentioned may have been the transport crate developed by Roxburgh, which had feet to prevent salt water from soaking up into it and a metal grid to prevent any grazing animal that might be on board from taking a nibble of the valuable greenery when the wooden lid was opened.[51] As he further explained, should the plants ever come into contact with salt water, they must be washed. Salt, always the greatest danger, could also reach the plants when cleaning the deck with seawater. Living plants, however, require moisture and in the event of rain the boxes were to be opened until the soil was sufficiently moist, but in dry weather it would be difficult even for an attentive observer to notice when the plants required water. Shoots that grew strongly above the original plant were to be removed.[52] Finally, documents had to be obtained to ensure that living plants were not kept for longer than a bare minimum on arrival at a European customs house.[53]

Gradually, uniform standards for the shipment of living plants developed. From 1829 transport by sea was hugely improved with the development of the so-called 'Wardian Case', a sealed, glazed container like a miniature greenhouse developed by Nathaniel Ward.[54] Precautions also had to be taken when transporting seeds. These should be stored in a dry place and care should also be taken to ensure that this was in a closed room with adequate air circulation (and not in the hold with other goods). Under no circumstances should they be exposed to excessive heat.[55]

Despite these precautions, intercontinental shipments proved to be vulnerable, as demonstrated by the loss of letters and herbarium material and the demise of living plants, which could be due not only to poor transport conditions but on occasion to shipwreck, fire and piracy. One was never sure whether a correspondent on the other side of the world had written or sent something, or whether a valuable delivery had not reached its destination. For this reason, the following letter always referred to the previous shipment, and the recipient always mentioned when he had received a letter or a delivery in his or her reply. With dismay Wallich noted the loss of the 'Paragon' in 1819, with which he had expected mail from Europe.[56]

RAM COMUL SEN

Wallich's system of communication and plant shipment could never have worked smoothly without the cooperation of highly qualified and educated Indian partners. Indians served Wallich not only as draftsmen and gardeners, but also as plant collectors, advisors and confidants. One of the most important of these was Ram Comul (or Indianized Ramkamal) Sen.

Sen, who came from a family from rural Bengal, had a remarkable *curriculum vitae*. In the service of European colonial authorities, he was not only able to achieve considerable wealth and prestige, but actively to participate in the intellectual life of Calcutta. Sen had been sent by his father to Calcutta around 1800 to learn English and to make a career. There he acquired considerable knowledge and language skills and over the years rose from a simple employee to the position of chief Indian accountant of the Bank of Bengal. He also held various administrative positions at educational and research institutions, including the Asiatic Society, the College of Fort William, and the Sanskrit College. Despite a huge workload Sen found leisure for intellectual activity. He compiled two Bengali textbooks and published an English-Bangla dictionary and a treatise on European medicine in Bangla.[57] Sen always maintained a traditional Hindu outlook, as can be seen from his agitation against the efforts of Indian liberals and the British authorities to end the practice of the burning of widows (*sati*).[58] While Wallich had hardly any contact with Bengali liberals, he had strong connections with conservatives such as Sen and, later, with Radhakanta Deb.

For the whole period of Wallich's tenure at the Botanic Garden, Sen occupied an important role of an intermediary not only between Indians, but also for members of the European elite. While much of the exchange between the two is likely to have been oral, their correspondence is also one of the most frequent and long-lasting. A total of 88 letters written by Ram Comul are recorded between 1815 and 1843, although only a handful of these have survived. Over this long period a close familiarity and openness developed between Sen and Nathaniel, which allowed criticism on the Indian part.[59]

The letters bear eloquent witness to the many functions that Sen performed for Wallich. In the Botanic Garden he took care of building materials for repair work, was responsible for financial transactions in Wallich's name and arranged for printed books to be sent to Europe,[60] for which it is to be assumed that he received remuneration. But Sen certainly also received payment in kind, in the form of plants, which could be traded by him in return for favours from others.[61] Sen simultaneously undertook his own research trips for the Asiatic Society and for Wallich's Asiatick Museum.[62]

Wallich also developed close links with Calcutta's Agricultural and Horticultural Society, founded under the inspiration of William Carey in 1820. In contrast to the European-dominated Asiatic Society, this developed into a significant platform of exchange between Europeans and Bengalis, including Sen, and the entrepreneur and social reformer Dwarkanath Tagore.[63]

Wallich had a keen eye for other skills offered by Indian staff and rapidly recognized the talent of a Brahmin working at the Botanic Garden, Bharat Singh. In 1802, Singh had accompanied Francis Buchanan on his expedition to Nepal and stayed on in his service during the Bengal Survey. With Buchanan's return to Europe, Wallich continued to employ Singh as a plant collector and to send him on research expeditions into the virtually impassable mangrove swamps of the Sundarbans.[64] Singh was later to become of importance for his collecting activities on Wallich's own visit to Nepal.

The number of employees grew steadily. Long-term relationships of trust developed, as with the chief draughtsman Vishnuprasad, who had worked at the Garden since 1815.[65] Wallich would eventually employ twenty plant draughtsmen, but even these were unable to cope with the enormous work of documentation. It was not only government thriftiness that prevented him from hiring more artists, but by this time botanical artists in and around Calcutta were in short supply.[66]

The principle of flexibility also proved its worth to the Garden employees and in recognition of special merit. Wallich arranged for pay rises for deserving individuals, including the chief gardener Karim Khan, who had worked there since Kyd's time. He also praised Sheikh Mooty to the government in warm tones, even if with a certain colonial condescension: 'The knowledge of the treatment and cultivation of plants, his acquaintance with the system and what is more surprising, with the natural classification are such, as would do honour to any European gardener'.[67]

Following the earlier suggestion of the Serampore missionaries to find a 'clever young man' and train him as an engraver, Wallich came up with the idea to raise 'clever and healthy boys' from the orphanage school in Calcutta into potential gardeners. As he wrote to the government, such young men would initially be useful workers in the Botanic Garden but would later be able to enter the private service of Europeans. The proposal was approved, but Wallich could not find suitable boys. From the free school, however, he recruited four young men such as Henry Bruce and William Gomez, who developed into gifted plant-collectors.[68]

RAFFLES AND JACK

At the beginning of his career, Wallich had profited greatly from patronage. With his permanent appointment, he was now able to continue the tradition by supporting other naturalists in their professional advancement. This was especially true in the case of William Jack, who, in return, gave Wallich a first insight into the botanical riches of Southeast Asia. Born in Aberdeen, Jack embarked on medical studies in his hometown at the age of fourteen and, in the good Scottish tradition, began botanising at an early age. After his exams in London, friends arranged for his appointment as an Assistant Surgeon with the East India Company, and in 1813 he left for Calcutta,[69] He must have arrived in the very days when Wallich was making intensive efforts to move himself from Serampore to Calcutta.

Jack's initial service took him to the war in Nepal, where he contracted a serious lung disease that, seven years later, was to cost him his life in a ship off Sumatra. For several years, he stayed in various garrisons in northern India, and it was only in 1818 that he first contacted Wallich by letter. As he wrote to his parents, he hoped that an exchange with Wallich would bring him into line with the latest state of botanical research, since he had previously botanised without professional contacts and was insufficiently familiar with Roxburgh's material. In the hope of making Wallich receptive to further communications, he sent him seeds and also a description of a *Lobelia* he had discovered in Nepal. A quick and friendly reply confirmed that it was indeed a previously unknown plant.[70]

Even from a distance Wallich recognised Jack's talents and showed himself anxious to help the young man, his junior by ten years. He successfully proposed Jack for membership of the Asiatic Society and mentioned his name in one of his articles in *Asiatick Researches*.[71] Jack finally received permission to travel to Calcutta and in August 1818 was invited to stay permanently at the Botanic Garden and undertake research there. It is to be assumed that Wallich himself had been able to push through such an offer by the colonial authorities due to Jack's poor health, which probably limited his ability to perform his duties as an Assistant Surgeon. Having arrived in Calcutta, Jack used the Garden to relax and to work on his botanical discoveries.[72] His stay there, however, was to be short as he was soon to embark on a great journey into the unknown. Sir Stamford Raffles, Resident of the British trading post at Bencoolen on Sumatra, was looking for a capable botanist and a personal physician for himself and his wife, and it was in Wallich's house in the Calcutta Botanic Garden that the paths of the colonial administrator and the junior surgeon-naturalist were to cross.

Raffles, a talented naturalist, had been Lieutenant-Governor of the British-occupied island of Java during the Napoleonic Wars from 1811 to 1816. While there he had recognized and drawn on the services of talented scientists, including the American doctor Thomas Horsfield, who was already in Java working for the Dutch authorities. An unexpected and fortuitous arrival in 1815 was that of Joseph Arnold, returning from a trip to Australia as a ship's doctor. Stranded in Batavia, Arnold stayed and botanised with Raffles before returning to England taking with him plants from Raffles for Sir Joseph Banks.

The political fate of the formerly Dutch-controlled island of Java was always uncertain, depending on the outcome of settlements following the Napoleonic Wars. There had been accusations of extravagance over Raffles's administration of the island, so he was appointed to the much less prestigious post of Resident of Bencoolen on the southwest coast of Sumatra. This remote base threatened to be a check on the career of the ambitious Raffles, so instead of immediately accepting the new post he returned to England in 1816 where he maintained contact with Banks and published his *History of Java*. The following year he prepared to leave for Bencoolen via Batavia, taking Arnold back with him as personal physician and naturalist. Arnold died after only four months in

Bencoolen,[73] but his friendship with Raffles was to attain immortality in the name of the giant-flowered parasitic plant *Rafflesia arnoldi*, which they found on a joint excursion in 1818.[74]

During a visit to Calcutta from Bencoolen in October 1818, Raffles must have told Wallich of his search for a successor to Arnold and they soon came to an agreement. Jack wrote in a letter to his parents of their meeting with Raffles 'during which Dr Wallich and I had a long conversation with him, the result of which has been my agreeing to accompany him to Sumatra, and his promising to forward my views, and in particular, to afford me every facility for exploring the Natural History of this island'.[75] Wallich, for his part, must have hoped for new botanical knowledge from this hitherto unknown region and would be not disappointed in Jack's efforts.[76] He reported to Colebrooke that Jack had 'now got a Situation as personal Surgeon to Sir S. Raffles (though he belongs to the Bengal Medical Establishment), and has, thus, the very finest opportunity for pursuing his botanical researches on which he is exceedingly clever'.[77]

Raffles had not undertaken the journey from Bencoolen to Calcutta solely with the aim of engaging a new naturalist and personal physician, he was also on a political mission. The strategically thinking man was driven by the idea of founding a British port at the southern tip of the Straits of Malacca, with which he undoubtedly wanted to further his own career.[78] Apart from a brief interruption during the Napoleonic Wars, the two main shipping routes from the Indian Ocean to China— the Straits of Malacca and the Sunda Strait—had long been under Dutch control.[79] With a new British base, East India Company trade with China, and at the same time the eastern flank of British India, could be protected more effectively.

With the blessing of the Government, Raffles set off from Calcutta to Johore on the Straits of Malacca and on 28 January 1819 reached the island of Singapore, the former Tumasik, as yet unclaimed by a European power. He agreed on a contract with the local ruler, which enabled the establishment of a British settlement.[80] The acquisition was approved by the Government in India and later by the Court of Directors in London, and under the first governor Colonel William Farquhar the settlement flourished at an astonishing rate. As early as 1821, it is said that around 5,000 people lived in Singapore, most of them Malay, about a fifth of them Chinese immigrants, in addition to Buginese, Indians, Arabs, Armenians, Europeans and Anglo-Indians.[81] For Raffles himself, however, everyday life quickly returned and in March 1819 he resumed his service in the somewhat run-down Bencoolen, with only a second brief visit to Singapore in June 1819.[82]

While Raffles was trying to establish a foothold in Singapore, he had left Jack on the island of Penang (then called Prince of Wales Island), located at the northern end of the Straits of Malacca, and ruled by the British since 1786.[83] The flora of Penang was already relatively well known. Between 1802 and 1804, the surgeon William Hunter had botanized there and had commissioned a Chinese artist to illustrate a selection of its plants. Even though the Flora did not appear in print until later, several sets of copies of the botanical drawings were made and circulated, one of which came into the hands of John Fleming. It is not unlikely that Fleming and Wallich had pored over the drawings in Calcutta, which may have persuaded Raffles to drop Jack off in Penang.[84]

While on Penang, Jack botanized and reported regularly to Wallich. In his first, very long, letter he wrote almost ecstatically about the abundance of the flora and the crops cultivated there, such as nutmeg, cloves, pineapple, and mango. Full of pride, he also reported on plants not yet identified there, such as a lotus that he thought different from the Indian species and a blackberry species found on the Malay Peninsula.[85] Jack also kept Wallich informed about the progress of Raffles' negotiations in Singapore.[86]

Raffles, after his success in Singapore, hoped for the office of Governor-General but was unable to assert himself either in India or in London. The disappointment was deep and it motivated him, together with his family and Jack, to devote himself even more to natural science at his country estate of

Pematang Balam in what Jack sardonically called 'ultima Thule'.[87] To Raffles' and Wallich's dismay Jack's health deteriorated dramatically there and in one of his last letters to Wallich he wrote: 'At present I am literally doing nothing, being neither very well nor in good spirits'.[88] Jack died on 15 September 1822 on board the ship *Canton* in the port of Bencoolen, possibly a belated casualty of the war in Nepal.[89] Wallich was never to forget his brilliant young protege and had a monument erected for him in his Botanical Garden that stands to this day.

YOUR LORDSHIP'S MEMORIALIST

Wallich's entire attention continued to be focused on the development of the Botanical Garden as an internationally renowned institution. This included strenuous efforts to maintain and develop its library. Among his predecessors, book ownership had been largely a private matter, but gradually the East India Company had started to make regular donations of books from London for use by the Superintendent. In 1819, Wallich proposed the establishment of a public library at the Botanic Garden, as the libraries at the College of Fort William and the Asiatic Society were too far away for easy consultation. The government did not want to make a decision, so turned to the Court of Directors in which Wallich hoped for Colebrooke's support in return for fossils from Nepal.[90] The result was that the Board of Directors approved the substantial annual sum of £200 for the next ten years, for the purchase of books.[91] Many new publications, but also some classical works including those of Linnaeus, still testify to Wallich's skill in building up a botanical reference library.

Up to now Wallich had published rather little of his own work. With the death of Roxburgh in Edinburgh in February 1815, the question of the publication of his *Flora Indica* had been raised as a matter of some importance. Colebrooke suggested that Roxburgh's manuscript, of which there were copies both in India (with William Carey) and Britain (with Robert

Brown), should be edited and published in London.[92] When there was little sign of this happening Carey, unsurprisingly, grew impatient and asked Wallich to help to edit the copy of the manuscript entrusted to him by Roxburgh.

As the work had been compiled several decades earlier, Wallich chose to supplement Roxburgh's work with descriptions of additional plants found by himself.[93] The first two volumes, edited jointly by Wallich and Carey, appeared in Serampore in 1820 and 1824 under the title *Flora Indica; or Descriptions of Indian Plants, by the late William Roxburgh, edited by William Carey, to which are added descriptions of plants recently discovered by Nathaniel Wallich.*[94] Wallich sent a few copies of the first volume to his father as early as the beginning of 1820 with the request to pass one of them on to Hornemann.[95] The third volume, scheduled for 1825, was never to see the light of the day. Instead, in 1832, while Wallich was in Europe and working on his own *magnum opus*, Carey himself edited a three-volume, complete edition, without the Wallichian additions.[96]

In addition to all these tasks, Wallich may have found a free-minute here and there to think about himself and his profession—or rather his vocation. Even when he was appointed as Superintendent, he made no secret of his self-image as that of a practical naturalist. Of central importance to him was his own collecting trips to the remotest areas, which clearly distinguished him from his predecessors. Thus, he had written to Hornemann that in his eyes it was of vital importance, that the Garden's director personally undertook research trips, but also that the government should share this view and support him. The primary aim must be to bring as many of India's hitherto unknown botanical treasures into the care of the Garden as possible.[97] In this sense Wallich became part of an increasingly mobile imperial rule; what has been called an 'Itinerant Empire'.[98]

Correspondingly, Wallich's letters to Hornemann did not express any theory-based research programme that went beyond collecting and Wallich's rather traditional adherence to Linnaeus' sexual system of classification. He, thus, perceived himself as 'Your Lordship's Memorialist' as he once signed himself off in a letter to the Governor-General in Calcutta.[99] Here, perhaps, is to be seen an echo of Johann Gottfried Herder's dictum of a dichotomy between 'collector' and 'theorist', with Wallich defining himself as the former.[100] Even if Wallich thought globally as a communicator, his scientific self-image was far removed from the globally conceived, theory-based, natural philosophy of a Humboldt.[101]

NOTES

1. Desmond, *European Discovery*, p. 82.
2. Ibid., pp. 81f.
3. CNH, Wallich letters, Wallich to Williamson, February 1817.
4. SNM, Letters from Wallich, I, 5, Wallich to Hornemann, 13 May 1817.
5. Ibid.
6. CNH, Wallich letters, index, p. 47.
7. Harrison, *Calcutta Botanic Garden*, p. 237.
8. CNH, Wallich letters, Buchanan to Wallich, 4 February 1817.
9. Rocher & Rocher, *Making of Western Indology*, p. 131.
10. CNH, Wallich letters, Colebrooke to Carey, 6 January 1817.
11. Ibid., Colebrooke to Carey, 13 January 1817; Nair, *Proceedings*, vol. 2, p. 592.
12. CNH, Wallich letters, Colebrooke to Carey, 13 January 1817.
13. Hardwicke to Banks, 15 May 1816, in Chambers, *Indian and Pacific Correspondence*, p. 159.
14. CNH, Wallich letters, Diana Beaumont to Wallich, 24 June 1816.
15. Ibid.; Extract Public Letter to Bengal, 13 February 1817; H. B. Carter, *Sir Joseph Banks 1743-1820*, London: British Museum, 1988, p. 484.
16. BL IOR, F/4/513/12340, Extract Public Letter to Bengal, 13 February 1817.
17. SNM, Letters from Wallich, I, 6, Wallich to Hornemann, 28 September 1817.
18. Wallich to Banks, 24 July 1817, in Chambers, *Indian and Pacific Correspondence*, p. 191.
19. Carter, *Sir Joseph Banks*, pp. 484f.

20. Desmond, *European Discovery*, p. 83.
21. BL IOR Ms Eur F303/4 25 August 1826—of these almost 500 are now in the collection of the Royal Botanic Garden Edinburgh, though it is not known when or how they reached there. Kind notice by Henry Noltie.
22. SNM, Letters from Wallich, I, 9, Wallich to Hornemann, 1 July 1818.
23. CNH, Wallich letters, Wallich to Colebrooke, 20 April 1819.
24. Cf. inter alia: CNH, Wallich letters, Scott to Wallich, 29 September 1819; ibid., 2 February 1820; ibid., 12 May 1820.
25. Ibid., 18 September 1818.
26. Ibid., 25 January 1819.
27. Ibid.
28. Nair, *Proceedings*, vol. 3.1, p. 281.
29. A. von Humboldt, *Kosmos. Versuch einer physischen Weltbeschreibung*, vol. 1, Stuttgart & Augsburg: Cotta, 1845, pp. 41ff.
30. BL IOR, F/4/621/15534, Bengal Public Letter, Wallich to Lushington, 25 December 1818.
31. CNH, Wallich letters, Wallich to Colebrooke, 20 April 1819.
32. See Chambers, *Indian and Pacific Correspondence*, passim.
33. R. de Candolle & A. Radcliffe-Smith, 'Nathaniel Wallich, MD, PhD, FRS, FLS, FRGS, (1786-1854) and the Herbarium of the Honorable East India Company, and their relation to the de Candolles of Geneva and the Great Prodromus', *Botanical Journal of the Linnean Society*, vol. 83, 1981, p. 326.
34. SNM, Letters from Wallich, I, 13, Wallich to Hornemann, 16 January 1820.
35. Cf. Buescher, *Catalogue*, passim.
36. Dansk Litteratur-Tidende for Aaret 1819, Copenhagen, 1819, pp. 105ff.
37. Ibid. pp. 105-12, 121-8, 135-44, 153-7.
38. R. Nyerup, *Catalogus Librorum Sanskritanorum, quos Bibliothecae Universitatis Havniensis vel dedit vel paravit Nathaniel Wallich, Doctor Medicinae et Philosophias, Ordinis Danebrogii Eques, Horti botanici Calcuttensis in India Praefectus. Scripsit Erasmus Nyerup, Bibliothecarius Universitatis*, Copenhagen: Gyldendal, 1821. The manuscripts were later included in the collection of the 'Codices Indici et Iranici Bibliothecae Universitatis Havniensis'. See Buescher, *Catalogue*, p. xvii.
39. CNH, Wallich letters, Ørsted to Wallich, 16 December 1821.

40. Ibid.
41. BL IOR, F/4/751/20525, Bengal Political Letter, 29 March 1820.
42. SNM, Letters from Wallich, II, 38, Wallich to Crown Prince Christian Frederik, 1 July 1823.
43. CNH, Wallich letters, Leopoldina, 1 April 1820.
44. Cf. e.g. CNH Wallich letters, Rask to Wallich, 8 April 1821; ibid., 24 June 1821.
45. Wallich to Banks, 6 January 1818, in Chambers, *Indian and Pacific Correspondence*, p. 217.
46. SNM, Letters from, I, 15, Wallich to Hornemann, 12 April 1820.
47. SNM, Letters from Wallich, I, 2, Wallich to Hornemann, 2 February 1815.
48. CNH, Wallich letters, Wallich to Colebrooke, 15 July 1821.
49. Harrison, *Calcutta Botanic Garden*, p. 238.
50. SNM, Letters from Wallich, I, 11, Wallich to Hornemann, 1 January 1819.
51. Robinson, *William Roxburgh*, p. 89; SNM, Letters from Wallich, I, 9, Wallich to Hornemann, 1 July 1818.
52. SNM, Letters from Wallich, I, 8, Wallich to Hornemann, 30 November 1817.
53. CNH, Wallich letters, Diana Beaumont to Wallich, 24 July 1816.
54. R. Desmond, *Sir Joseph Dalton Hooker: Traveller and Plant Collector*, 2nd ed., Woodbridge, Suffolk: Antique Collectors' Club, 2006, pp. 167f.
55. CNH, Wallich letters, Wallich to Colebrooke, 20 April 1819.
56. Ibid.
57. P. K. Ray, *Dewan Ram Comul Sen and His Times*, Calcutta, 1990, pp. ii., 2ff.
58. Ibid., preface.
59. Ibid., 1 November 1825.
60. For example: CNH, Wallich letters, Sen to Wallich, 17 January 1815; ibid., 20 September 1817; ibid., 5 July 1820; ibid., 17 January 1825; ibid., 5 October 1825; ibid., 12 October 1825; ibid., 1 November 1825; ibid., 27 January 1826.
61. For example: ibid., 5 October 1825; ibid., 12 October 1825.
62. Ibid., 17 January 1815.
63. Agricultural and Horticultural Society Calcutta, archive, Proceedings, vol. 1, passim.
64. BL IOR, F/4/621/15534, Bengal Public Letters, Wallich to Government, 25 September 1817.

65. Ibid. p. 238f.
66. Harrison, *Calcutta Botanic Garden*, p. 238.
67. Desmond, *European Discovery*, p. 85.
68. BL IOR, F/4/621/15534, Bengal Public Letter, Wallich to Lushington, 25 December 1818; kind note by Mark Watson, Edinburgh
69. I. H. Burkill, 'William Jack's Letters to Nathaniel Wallich', *Journal of the Malayan Branch of the Royal Asiatic Society*, vol 73, 1916, pp. 147f.
70. Ibid., pp. 148f.
71. Ibid., p. 149; Nair, *Proceedings*, vol. 3,2, p. 1965.
72. Burkill, 'William Jack's Letters to Nathaniel Wallich', p. 149.
73. Ibid., pp. 29-33.
74. Noltie, *Raffle's Ark Redrawn*, pp. 31f.
75. See Burkill, 'Letters', p. 149.
76. C.E. Wurtzburg, *Raffles of the Eastern Isles*, London: Hodder & Stoughton, 1954, p. 468.
77. CNH, Wallich letters, Wallich to Colebrooke, 20 April 1819.
78. Noltie, *Raffle's* Ark Redrawn, p. 35.
79. T.T. Yong, 'Early Entrepôt Portal. Trade & Founding of Singapore', in A. Lau & L. Lau (eds.), *Maritime Heritage of Singapore*, Singapore: Suntree Media, 2005, p. 81.
80. T. Frasch, 'Autonomie im Griff des Kolonialismus. Südostasien', in M. Mann (ed.), *Die Welt im 19. Jahrhundert*, Vienna: Mandelbaum, 2009, pp. 159f.
81. Yong, 'Early Entrepôt Portal', p. 84.
82. Noltie, *Raffles' Ark Redrawn*, p. 37.
83. Burkill, 'William Jack's Letters to Nathaniel Wallich', p. 151.
84. Noltie, *Raffles' Ark Redrawn*, p. 27.
85. Jack to Wallich, 14 January 1819, in Burkill, 'William Jack's Letters to Nathaniel Wallich,' pp. 151-60.
86. Jack to Wallich, 15 March 1819, in ibid., pp. 168-72.
87. Noltie, *Raffles' Ark Redrawn*, pp. 38ff.; Jack to Wallich, 19 August 1819, in Burkill, 'William Jack's Letters to Nathaniel Wallich', p. 181.
88. Jack to Wallich, 26 October 1821, in ibid., p. 238.
89. Jack to Wallich, 12 February 1819, in ibid., p. 161.
90. CNH, Wallich letters, Wallich to Colebrooke, 15 July 1821.
91. Desmond, *European Discovery*, p. 84.
92. Rocher & Rocher, *The Making of Western Indology*, p. 144.
93. SNM, Letters from Wallich, I, 14, Wallich to Hornemann, 12 April 1820.
94. Chambers, *Indian and Pacific Correspondence*, p. 77, footnote 1.

95. SNM, Letters from Wallich, I, 14, Wallich to Hornemann, 12 April 1820.
96. Chambers, *Indian and Pacific Correspondence*, p. 127, footnote 2.
97. SNM, Letters from Wallich, I, 2, Wallich to Hornemann, 2 February 1815.
98. Arnold, *The Tropics and the Travelling Gaze*, pp. 16-21.
99. CNH, Wallich letters, Wallich,19 January 1816.
100. J. G. Herder, 'Persepolis. Eine Muthmassung', in B. Suphan (ed.), *Herders Sämmtliche Werke*, vol. 15, Berlin: Weidmann, 1851, pp. 571f.
101. Mägdefrau, *Geschichte der Botanik*, p. 78.

CHAPTER 8

Nepal

BHARAT SINGH AND FRANCIS DE SILVA

One country, in particular, exerted a virtually irresistible attraction—a barely accessible land hidden between the foothills and the world's highest mountains on the border with Tibet, the Himalayas. That country was Nepal, one of the so-called 'frontier states' directly bordering British India, which increasingly came under the control of the East India Company during the first half of the nineteenth century.[1] The numerous states of Nepal had been united in 1768 under Prithvi Narayan Shah of the Gorkha Kingdom and had since expanded towards India. In the loosely defined border area on the edge of the Indian lowlands a dangerous conflict was looming and in 1814 the Anglo-Nepal War broke out, which ended almost two years later with the Treaty of Sagauli, in which Nepal had to cede the western provinces of Kumaon and Garhwal, as well as part of the lowlands in the south, and Sikkim to the east. The treaty permitted the establishment of a permanent Residency near the capital Kathmandu, in order to observe political developments and, if necessary, to influence them. The distrust of the Nepal Durbar towards the British had been great ever since, and the British Resident was severely restricted in his freedom of movement. The Nepali government tolerated neither his direct contact with the monarch nor with the population, a situation that relaxed only slightly over the years.[2]

Nepal comprises several distinct natural zones between the subtropical lowlands known as the Tarai on the southern border with India and the 8,000 metre peaks under perpetual snow on the northern border with Tibet. Between these, is a mountainous region with altitudes of between three and six thousand metres. This is crossed by valleys, mostly running in an east-west direction, of which the Kathmandu Valley, often referred to in contemporary sources as the 'Valley of Nepaul', is the most important. Like India, the climate is monsoonal, even if temperatures are significantly lower than in the plains of the Ganga.[3]

To botanists at the beginning of the nineteenth century, Nepal was a country of dreams and desires, where unknown treasures were waiting to be discovered. Even on the slopes of the three-thousand metre peaks around the Kathmandu Valley an abundance of ferns, rhododendrons and orchids attracted attention. Wallich's predecessor Francis Buchanan had already undertaken the country's first significant botanical exploration in 1802-3. After a difficult journey through the Tarai and the foothills of the Himalayas, Buchanan and his travelling companions had reached Kathmandu with its almost European climate.[4] The mistrust of the Nepali authorities already restricted the British naturalist to the immediate surroundings of the capital.[5] To compensate for his lack of freedom of movement, Buchanan hired Indian and Nepali plant collectors who were able to move around more freely and who explored remote valleys and high mountains on his behalf, collecting and describing plants.[6] Buchanan noted that the flora of Nepal was more similar to that of Europe or Japan than to that of India—a remarkably prescient observation before the publication of Humboldt's *Ideas for a Geography of Plants*.[7] As most of Buchanan's remarkable botanical work was to remain unpublished, the most important result of his year-long stay was his 1819 book *An Account of the Kingdom of Nepal and of the Territories Annexed to this Dominion by the House of Gorkha*.[8]

Already at the beginning of his career as an Assistant Surgeon, Wallich had come into indirect contact with the hidden country as his superiors had planned to send him there as a surgeon with the British troops at the end of 1814. Even after it had become clear that he would be spared the need to tend sick and wounded soldiers, a decade-long passion had taken root.

Nobody made Nepal more familiar to Wallich than the Honourable Edward Gardner, from whom more than 160 letters have been preserved in the Wallich correspondence. Gardner was the first permanent British Resident and other than a break of nearly a year, held the office for a total of fourteen years from 1816.[9] Under his aegis the building complex of the British Residency was erected on an extensive plot of land just to the north of Kathmandu, in today's Lainchaur district. Gardner was not only a talented diplomat but also botanically inclined.[10]

It was due to chance that Wallich first had the opportunity in 1817 to send two plant collectors from the Botanic Garden to the Himalayan state. In that year, some members of the Nepal Durbar visited Calcutta and, thanks to his good connections, Wallich was able to establish contact with them and recommend to their attention the benefits of botanical exploration. In the form of a Sunday excursion, the courtiers visited the Botanic Garden, where Wallich convinced them to take two plant collectors back on their return journey and to ensure their unlimited freedom of movement in the country. Wallich had understood the unique opportunity offered to him, which would allow him to obtain herbarium material directly from Nepal. He already had two suitable candidates ready: his protégé Bharat Singh, and Francis de Silva.[11] De Silva was a so-called 'Portuguese', presumably an Indian Catholic or an Anglo-Indian, who had already been employed at the Botanic Garden for nine years as assistant to a Chinese gardener.[12]

Wallich once again convinced the government and, only one day after the request was made, permission was granted to dispatch the two collectors to Nepal, with an additional salary for the trip. That the decision was made so unusually quickly indicates the importance that the British colonial authorities attached to the natural history exploration of that frontier state, perhaps precisely because direct political influence was impossible.[13] Here is an early example of a policy that later became apparent in other regions as British influence expanded, such as in Burma, Awadh, Assam, and the Nilgiri

Hills. Under the guise of a search for natural resources, primarily wood, botanists followed the troops of the East India Company on foot, if, indeed, they did not precede them.

Singh and de Silva immediately set off on the journey with the Nepali delegation, while Wallich also sent plants with them for the King of Nepal.[14] Arriving in Kathmandu they were taken under the care of Gardner, who looked after and instructed them. They immediately began to hunt for plants and returned regularly to the Residency richly laden with herbarium specimens and seeds, to deliver their treasures for onward transport to Calcutta. The plants were sent overland to the Indian border, from where they were transported on river boats to the Botanic Garden. The precious material was not, however, left to anonymous skippers, but was accompanied by a local supervisor (*madum*).[15]

In this way, a wealth of plant specimens had already accumulated at the Botanic Garden by mid-1818, which made it impossible for Wallich to describe it in detail in its entirety, as reported to his mentor Hornemann.[16] But this was only the beginning because over the following two years the treasures were to increase even further.[17] From Shibpur a considerable part of the harvest from Nepal was sent to Britain—to Banks, Lambert, Colebrooke, William Jackson Hooker and James Edward Smith. He asked Lambert to send duplicates to Hornemann and Augustin-Pyramus de Candolle. Some of the material also went to the Court of Directors in London for the museum and library in East India House. Lambert, a patron of science with an extensive private herbarium, commissioned his librarian David Don to evaluate and publish the Nepal material of Buchanan and that sent by Wallich, which included the specimens received from Gardner.[18]

In 1819, Gardner was absent during a secondment to Bundelkhand in northern India. During this time the Assistant Resident Robert Stuart took over responsibility for the Residency and the care of the two collectors. Wallich reported to Colebrooke with satisfaction that Stuart also sent plants, seeds, and roots to Calcutta on every regular mail day, and

Plate 8.1: Charles D'Oyly, Edward Gardner,
drawing, *c.*1819. (British Library, London)

would also arrange for an additional transport by carrier
(*banghi*) twice a week.[19] Stuart was also responsible for securing permission from the Nepal Durbar for Wallich's visit in
1820-1, but died in March, nine months before Wallich arrived.
Stuart's successor was to be the young Brian Houghton Hodgson, who had been driven to Nepal by ill-health. During his
long stay in Nepal, Hodgson would emerge as one of the
leading scholars of Buddhism and of Himalayan natural history
(especially zoology), with whom Wallich corresponded over
several decades.[20]

Gardner used his stay in India for a visit to Calcutta, where
he briefly met Wallich for the first time. Wallich was greatly
impressed by the gracious nature of this 'charming man'.[21]
Gardner, for his part, was overwhelmed by the botanical
treasures whose transfer from Nepal he had himself arranged;
as Wallich wrote to Colebrooke: 'He has been gratified beyond

measure to see in the Garden the vast numbers of Nepal plants which we owe to his industry and liberality'.[22]

The collecting success of Singh and de Silva exceeded Wallich's greatest expectations so that, more than a year after they were sent out, he requested an extension of the mission for an indefinite period.[23] Before their field experience, he could not have been aware of the strains that would have to be overcome by the two collectors, due to the mountainous nature of the country and the unfamiliar climate. However, he always tried to get the best for his employees and realized that they deserved a higher salary, which he accordingly sought from the Government.[24] The request was approved, and the success encouraged him to consider sending collectors to other regions of India, particularly to Srinagar (in Garhwal) and to Almora.[25] Wallich's idea of cooperating closely with Indian plant collectors, and the trust this involved, had already proved its worth after only a short time.

CAMELLIA KISSI

It was through Nepal that Wallich came into contact for the first time with a plant that had been changing the world for some time—Chinese tea (*Camellia sinensis var. sinensis*). The leaves of the tea plant have played a steadily increasing role in the European consumer world since the eighteenth century, during which period they have changed from a luxury to a mass product. Whether in London, Amsterdam, Copenhagen or Hamburg, tea became universally known and loved, with cane sugar increasingly used as a sweetener. The tea that steamed in the cups of Europeans in the eighteenth century came exclusively from a type of camellia in China, and the Chinese kept its cultivation and processing a closely guarded secret. Since there was hardly any demand for European export goods to East Asia, tea was acquired mainly in exchange for precious metals and in this way, year after year, many tons of silver flowed from Europe to China.[26]

It was, therefore, not surprising that the economists and

politicians of certain European colonial powers finally asked themselves the question whether the tea plant could not grow just as well in their own tropical or subtropical colonies. This would enable the European states to reduce silver exports to the east. It quickly became clear that the tea debate arising in Europe was, ultimately, a botanical challenge.

As early as 1778, Sir Joseph Banks had suggested transferring Chinese tea plants to northern India. Following the Battle of Plassey, ever larger areas of South Asia had come under the direct rule of the East India Company, and enormous opportunities presented themselves not only to skim off the economic output of the Indians in the form of taxes, but also to use land for the production of export goods. Banks thought primarily of the transplantation of 'black' tea to India, without realizing that green and black tea came from the same plant and simply represented different forms of processing. The Chinese authorities were not willing to stand idly by and watch what is now termed as 'biopiracy', however the desire to grow tea in India gained momentum and would become a major preoccupation of Nathaniel Wallich.[27]

Banks' bold project first appeared to come to fruition in 1793 when the British envoy Lord Macartney took seeds and plants of tea to India from his diplomatic mission to China. It is unclear whether the plants survived, because hardly any living plant would prove more difficult to transport by sea over long distances and periods of time than the tea bush. Seeds did, however, sprout in the young Botanic Garden of Calcutta. A further transfer attempt in 1816 was a failure.[28]

Wallich inherited the tea question from Roxburgh, but for a long time it seemed that it was only a minor sideline. It was Edward Gardner who put him on the trail in 1818, but Wallich followed it only half-heartedly. Gardner had spotted a tea plant in the garden of a Kashmiri merchant residing in Kathmandu. The British Resident, always anxious to convey curiosities from the realm of flora to Calcutta, asked Wallich in September whether there was a tea plant in the Botanic Garden and must have received a negative answer.[29] Soon afterwards, specimens were sent to Calcutta, but Wallich seems to have taken little interest in them.[30]

In Wallich's eyes his communication with Gardner about tea had come to an end, which shows that in those early years he still had little feeling for the imperial-economic relevance of his botanical studies, and that he pursued botany primarily out of passion and as a quest for as many unknown plants as possible in the Linnaean tradition. Things were different with Gardner, who was increasingly interested in the potential economic uses of plants. He continued to take an interest in the beverage and wondered whether there were not natural occurrences of tea or related *Camellia* species in Nepal that could be used as a drink. During his research Gardner soon came across *Camellia kissi* on the slopes of the mountains of Shivapuri and Chandragiri.[31] *Camellia kissi* is a small tree that reaches a height of up to eight metres, with leaves that are very similar to those of the Chinese tea plant. It is found not only in Nepal, India and Bhutan, but also in Indochina regions, southern China and Taiwan. In the mountains of Nepal, it grows in many places at altitudes of between 900 and 2,100 meters and is known under various local names. Even today, its leaves are still steamed there, dried and then processed into a drink as an infusion.[32] In India, on the other hand, *Camellia kissi* is now considered to be a 'non-tea' and is not used commercially.[33]

The plant had first been collected in August 1802 by Francis Buchanan in the Kathmandu Valley. He first called it *Camellia tetrapetala* and later decided to make a specific name from 'Hengua', a Nepali name for the plant that he had recorded, but failed to publish this.[34] Buchanan's name was probably not known to Gardner and in any case he discovered another local name, 'Keesee'.[35] Wallich himself was to introduce Gardner's local name into botanical nomenclature, publishing it as *Camellia kissi* in *Asiatick Researches* in 1820, the name by which the plant is still known.[36]

Right from the start, Gardner was concerned with the question of whether this plant might be suitable as a commercially marketable drink like Chinese tea, and it was for this reason that he had sent a small box of its branches to Calcutta in November 1818. He asked Wallich for his opinion, who replied immediately, but disagreed with Gardner over its similarity to the Chinese species and correctly considered the Kissi plant to be a different species of *Camellia*.[37]

Gardner, however, seems not to have accepted Wallich's opinion and showed an astonishing persistence. Immediately after receiving the negative opinion he sent another sample of Kissi leaves, with other plants, to Calcutta via Sagauli, but this was lost and never arrived there.[38] At the same time he sent the plant collectors out to make unsparing efforts to find more specimens.[39] Gardner was aware that an infusion of Kissi leaves was used by the local population as a substitute for tea, and he now put it to the test: together with another Englishman, he procured more leaves and prepared an infusion from them that proved to be quite tasty. Even if the Nepali tea substitute were not to be equal to the high-quality Chinese teas in terms of aroma, it could still pass for an inferior tea suitable for consumption by the lower social classes in South Asia. Gardner advised Wallich to try it himself with good and, above all, completely dried leaves—'when they reach you, I beg you will call for some teapot and prepare a good quantity in the common way. With sugar and milk, the infusion is quite enjoyable'.[40]

From the beginning of December 1818, *Camellia kissi* occupied a prominent position in Gardner's letters and communicated an enthusiasm over his experiments to which Wallich finally responded. We do not know whether Wallich himself tasted the infusion but, in any case, he communicated the discovery to a wider public in Calcutta at a meeting of the Asiatic Society. After several brief reflections, he moved on to the most important topic of that meeting—tea and the Nepalese *Camellia*. Contrary to his initially rather sceptical assessment he now pointed out a certain similarity with the Chinese tea plant: 'It is so like the tea tree in its leaves and blossoms, as to be easily mistaken for it. The leaves on being dried have the peculiar fragrance of tea'.[41] Remarkably, he now formulated a prospect that one day *Camellia kissi* and the true Chinese tea bush might be introduced to the north of India, without developing this idea further.[42] He could not yet know that a plant closely related to Chinese tea occurred naturally in Assam.

As quickly as his interest in *Camellia kissi* had grown, this interest vanished again. Perhaps, he realized that knowledge about that plant was still too new to be worth further work with a view to its commercialization. Other, more exciting questions, perhaps landed on his desk, or he wanted to wait for his own expedition to Nepal. In any case, the topic disappears from the correspondence with Gardner, and Wallich did not see it as of interest to his European correspondents. In his letters to Hornemann, *Camellia kissi* is never mentioned and among the plants delivered to Copenhagen on 1 January 1819 there was neither a Nepalese *Camellia* nor a Chinese tea plant.[43]

TOWARDS THE HIMALAYA

Since mid-1817, Wallich had worked as Superintendent with no opportunity for a major expedition. He was, however, able to leave the garden from time to time and in April 1819 wrote to Colebrooke that: 'Since my latest dispatch I have had an opportunity of examining some of the lower ranges of the Bootan Hills, but in a very cursory manner.'[44] The burden of daily administration and the maintenance of the network weighed too heavily, as shown by the abundance of letters from this period. But in 1820 at last came an opportunity to see, in person, the land of his dreams. An entry permit, which would otherwise have been almost impossible to obtain, had come into view through Gardner's mediation with the Durbar in Kathmandu.[45]

On 8 April 1820, an application was made to the Government, with a detailed submission and bold demand for the financing of a one-year expedition to Nepal, to be led by Wallich himself, accompanied by draughtsmen, collectors, trainees and other officials. The main destination would be Kathmandu, from where he would head north towards the Himalaya. He also expressed his plan to inspect teak plantations *en route*. As reason to travel there in person, he said that while his Indian collectors were competent, they lacked the professional eye to undertake systematic research and a knowledge of current research questions. For these an expedition led by an expert was necessary.[46]

It may be assumed that Wallich had already held preliminary talks and that the application was the result of a longer negotiation process, because the answer was given after a mere six days. The finances of his travel companions were also approved.[47] This willingness is a testimony not only to Wallich's persuasiveness but might also be seen as an expression of British imperial ambitions, with botany playing an increasingly important role in the penetration of the frontier states. Three months of preparation were to pass before Wallich set off for Nepal on 10 July 1820 and he returned almost exactly eighteen months later.[48] On the outward journey he took his time to get to know the Ganga valley and to avoid crossing the dangerous Tarai during the rainy season.

In his few surviving private letters of the time, he shows himself to be a loving, caring family man who always wanted to have his family around him. His wife Sophia was pregnant again and Nathaniel was reluctant to part with her for a long time, so he decided to take with him Sophia and their daughter Hannah, who was not even one year old.[49] Five-year old George had been sent to his grandparents in Copenhagen a few months earlier on the Danish ship *Kronprindsessen*, taking with him the two portraits that George Chinnery had painted of his parents some years before.[50] Father and son met again eight years later, in London.

The fact that Sophia was willing to leave the comfortable Roxburgh House to accompany her husband across the northern plains of the subcontinent speaks of a deep bond between them. Nevertheless, Wallich must have been aware that a family trip to Kathmandu would undoubtedly be disallowed due to the restrictive foreign policy of the Nepali

a BUDGEROW

Plate 8.2: Budgarow. Wallich might have travelled with such
a boat along the Ganga river, lithography.
(Charles Allan, Camden)

authorities. But on Indian soil, in a town not far from the
Nepal border and only a few postal days away from Kathmandu, wife and daughter were to be left in safety.

The journey by river was more comfortable than overland,
because it was pleasantly cool on the water in a cabin on a
boat,[51] so with Sophia and Hannah, and a reference library, the
small expedition party was taken up the Ganga on the *Venus*.[52]
The group included, among others, the Indian draughtsmen
Gorachand, Vishnuprasad and Rajballabh, Jukho Khan Mali,
a gardener, as well as already-mentioned William Gomez,
an Indo-Portuguese, who had been trained in the Botanic
Garden. Gomez was later to accompany Wallich to London
in 1828.[53]

Around 10 August, the party reached Bhagalpur, and by the beginning of September, Patna came in sight. Instead of setting off directly from there to the nearby Nepal border, the group continued westwards on the Ganga towards Benares and Allahabad. In the beginning, the river journey was fast and comfortable, and they sailed upstream with a steady easterly wind. However, much earlier than expected, the wind suddenly veered to the west, which made further progress difficult and the 50 kilometres from Dinapur to Benares took eleven days. Early in the morning of 21 September the ship finally docked at Raj-Ghat in the holy city.[54] Wallich was fascinated by Benares and strolled around but did not find the time to visit the nearby European settlement that lay about three kilometres inland.[55] On 2 October the westernmost point of the journey was reached at Allahabad. During the outward journey Wallich wrote a detailed report, which he apparently intended to publish in Calcutta. At the beginning of October 1820, at least three folio booklets were completed, but these have not survived.[56]

The ladies enjoyed the trip, despite all the strains. From Allahabad, Nathaniel proudly reported to his compatriot Benjamin Wolff in Calcutta on the health of his little daughter Hannah: 'She is as fat as butter, and with all, the best tempered and healthiest infant that you can wish to meet with'.[57] The fact that he took his wife on the long journey suggests a relaxed attitude to her pregnancy and he met the everyday dangers of such travel with a certain equanimity. But Sophia was also well, with only a slight discomfort noticeable from time to time.[58] From Allahabad, the party soon turned back a little to the east reaching the city of Muzaffarpur sometime in the first half of November, from where it was not far to the border town of Sagauli. In Muzaffarpur, on 14 November 1820, Sophia gave birth to a son without any complications. A day later the proud father wrote to Gardner about the joyful event.[59] In the first days of December Wallich left his wife and children behind in the city and, with his small retinue, set off for Sagauli. Here, almost exactly five years earlier, a peace treaty had been concluded; and Kathmandu was now within reach. Gardner had sent a welcome party to accompany Wallich to the capital. Wallich was now in a hurry, and within two more weeks they reached Kathmandu. From the grounds of the British Residency at about 1,500 metres above sea-level, Nathaniel's eye probably wandered expectantly over the chain of mountains surrounding it. To the north were Gyauche (2,400 m) and Shivapuri (2,800 m); to the east Manichar (2,200 m) and Nagarkot (2,150 m); to the south Phulchowki (2850 m); and to the west Champadevi (2,450 m), Chandragiri (3,500 m) and Nagarjun (2,100 m). Soon after his arrival Wallich wrote enthusiastically to his friend Benjamin Wolff: 'My health is better than it ever was before, and except for the regret of being separated for such a length of time from my family. I never enjoyed life more fully'.[60] It was almost too cool and Wallich found the morning hours perishing.[61] It was above all the richness of the natural environment that left a deep impression on him: 'Take Napal in every sense—climate, productions, scenery—and above all others its everlasting Himaleh—and you will no doubt agree with me that it stands foremost in those respects among all the countries in the world. The Valley itself is undeservedly beautiful and has not its equal'.[62] In Kathmandu, he made the British Residency his headquarters, where he spent most of his time and met up again with Singh and de Silva, who continued to undertake expeditions on his behalf. For living and working he and his entourage had several rooms, and a warehouse on the premises at their disposal,[63] where plants were pressed, and seeds prepared.[64]

Wallich was well aware of the need for political sensitivity and the fact that his botanical expedition and the display of Western research and collecting methods might incur the suspicion of the Nepali authorities and were always in danger of being prohibited. For he was a *Firingi*, one of those casteless foreigners who could ritually defile the pious Nepali Hindus by touching alone, and whom the Durbar met with extreme reserve. It was, therefore, one of Wallich's primary objectives to allay such reservations as quickly and as far as possible. For such matters, he sought the advice of Gardner, who provided him with a written code of conduct that proved to be very effective in facilitating his aims. He also sought dialogue with the local authorities and finally enjoyed the goodwill of the Durbar.[65]

Wallich tried to gain the trust of the locals in different ways, including the use of his medical skills. On one occasion he treated a sick, high-ranking, member of the Nepal army, then sent him to Calcutta for further treatment. Medical practice, therefore, became a catalyst for intercultural communication. This paid-off and he finally also won the trust of the chief minister Bhimsen Thapa: 'Finally, the Minister, impressed no doubt with a perfect conviction of the purity of the objects in view regarding my mission, has repeatedly, not in private but in public invited me to return to Nepal whenever I pleased'.[66]

The trust of the Nepali government had its limits, of course, and the scope of Wallich's activities remained narrowly defined despite any expressions of mutual respect.[67] As they had with Buchanan twenty years earlier, the Nepali authorities prohibited Wallich from travelling further north and west to the Himalayan mountains. He was, however, able to send his Indian companions and the personnel recruited in Nepal to places like the Gossain Than region in the north.[68] Wallich and his companions collected thoroughly and when, 87 years later, the British botanist Isaac Henry Burkill visited the same places, he could hardly find a plant there that had not already been discovered and described.[69]

The botanical harvest turned out to be rich, despite all the difficulties, and political and organizational obstacles. Wallich was overwhelmed above all by the variety and size of the ferns—as he published in the German journal *Flora*: 'Nearly one-twelfth of the entire flora of Nepal consists of ferns and the same ratio (perhaps even more) is found in Jamaica. Many ferns are endemic'.[70] This statement gives the impression that in Nepal, Wallich began to consider ideas of plant geography. Thus, with respect to the flora, he did not see Nepal as an isolated area, but recognized that it had similarities with other continents. In the field of plants and insects he saw such links not only with China and Europe, but also with America.[71]

Besides ferns, Wallich also observed a large number of orchids, 'of which I have almost 100 species'. Countless other interesting plants were to be found within easy reach of the outskirts of Kathmandu.[72] At Shivapuri, he discovered plants of the previously unknown ginseng *Panax pseudoginseng* in full bloom. He also saw the lonely tea plant that Gardner had told him about in the garden of the Kashmiri merchant. In his study of plants, he used not only his own taxonomic knowledge and the literature brought with him, but also referred to the botanical research of his few predecessors in Nepal, attempting to identify the plants collected by Buchanan.[73]

Throughout the trip, Wallich was in close contact with his correspondents in Calcutta and beyond; he even received messages from Denmark. Again and again, he complained how sorry he was not to be able to write more often himself.[74] He limited himself, instead, to a smaller number of correspondingly long letters. In July 1821, four months before his planned departure for Calcutta, Wallich had time to reflect on what he had achieved in Nepal up to that point and to take stock of the situation. This found expression in two long letters that he sent at intervals of three days to Colebrooke in England and to Hornemann in Copenhagen.[75] Both contain substantial information on the flora of Nepal. Hornemann considered the letter addressed to him so significant that he published detailed excerpts of it in the *Tidsskrift for Naturvidenskaberne*, a journal he co-edited himself.[76] To Colebrooke Wallich summed up:

the treasures which I have collected, seeds, plants, roots, specimens, fruits, woods, drawings, are most splendid; . . . and my Store House & Rooms at the Residency have assumed an aspect, which would give You a tolerable idea of the forests and jungles from whence I have derived all these glories.[77]

While still in Nepal, Wallich worked on a manuscript on Nepalese ferns, a 'Filicologia Nepalensis'. The manuscript, which is extant, contains Latin descriptions of ferns, with the English commentaries of the place of discovery and comparisons with similar plants.[78] The manuscript was intended to be published under the title 'Tentamen de filicibus Nepalensibus sistens descriptiones et icones filicam in itinere Nepalensi Mauritii cognitis vel novi', in which he wanted to describe the Nepalese fern flora in comparison with that of India and Mauritius.[79] At the same time, the work was intended to serve 'as an introduction to the geographical spread of this family in the world,'[80] which implies a knowledge of Humboldt's work on plant geography. In fact, Wallich's first substantial work *Tentamen Florae Napalensis* contains no ferns. The first two fascicles of this unfinished work were published in Calcutta in 1824 and 1826 and include descriptions of 53 species of flowering plant and two gymnosperms. *Tentamen* is notable for his embracing of new technology—he had given up on etching as a reproductive method for his artists' drawings and the 50 plates are lithographic. In the work he commemorated the Danish royal gardener with the new genus *Holboellia*.[81]

While Nathaniel was hunting for botanical treasures in and around Kathmandu, Sophia waited with her two children in India, halfway between the Ganga and the Nepalese border. This was a lonely time for her, as expressed in two letters addressed to Benjamin Wolff. In these she appears a self-confident woman who made enormous physical and emotional sacrifices for her husband's sake and took an idealistic view of his botanical activities.[82] Wallich, for his part, was concerned about her well-being. He was well aware that his wife suffered from the winter cold; that she was bored and asked Benjamin Wolff to write her a few lines every now and then to cheer her up.[83]

In 1820 Sophia spent a quiet and lonely Christmas day in Muzaffarpur. She missed her husband, without whom she had little joy in this world other than the comfort provided by the presence of her children. She wrote to Wolff that she often thought of her home on the Hooghly and of the Botanic Garden, which she missed very much and would prefer never to leave again.[84] At the turn of the year she complained about low temperatures and the unpleasant morning and evening fog.[85] Nevertheless, she survived the winter with her two small children and on 20 March 1821 wrote that all three were well.[86] All the harder was the blow that was to fall on Sophia on 12 April. Her little son, just five months old, died. The death of infants was nothing unusual in colonial India and parents had to be prepared for it as hardly one in ten newborns of European parents survived their first year of life.[87] The mortal remains of the unnamed child were buried at Tirhut cemetery, where a gravestone with the following inscription could still be found around 1900:

The infant son of N. Wallich, Esq. M.D,
Born 14 November 1820,
died 12 April 1821.[88]

Some time later Sophia left Muzaffarpur. There is little in the records about Nathaniel's own return to Calcutta, but, at least initially, it was quicker than the outward journey had been. His return home had been scheduled by the Government for mid-December 1821, so he was in a hurry when he left Kathmandu on 8 November. The mountains adjoining the Kathmandu Valley to the south were quickly crossed and only two days later Wallich reached the Bicchiakor (now Amlekhganj). On 22 November, he was in Patna and must have immediately boarded a boat because only a week later he was to be met in Bhagalpur.[89] However, he was not to reach Calcutta as quickly as he had hoped, because he contracted a severe fever that put him out of action for a month. He was forced to stay in Bhagalpur with the surgeon John Glas to recover at least a little. He sent his baggage ahead,[90] but did not himself return to Calcutta until 9 January 1822, where he immediately resumed management of the Botanic Garden though still weakened by fever.[91]

While his deteriorating health did not allow him to start to prepare the detailed expedition report immediately, he commented on some aspects of the journey in a long letter to the Government only two weeks after his return. Without Edward Gardner's support the expedition would have been far less successful and, recollecting his friend Colebrooke's admonition, he also thanked his supporters in England. Wallich suggested that a large part of his Nepal collection be transferred to the museum of the East India Company in London, but he did keep a considerable amount of the Nepalese material for his own use and study. The resulting work would find expression in his unfinished edition of Roxburgh's *Flora Indica*, as already mentioned in his own *Tentamen Florae Nepalensis* and, later, while in London in his great *Plantae Asiaticae Rariores* (1829-32).[92]

NOTES

1. Sanwal, *Nepal and the East India Company*, preface.
2. Allen, *Prisoner*, p. 4-10.
3. Sanwal, *Nepal and the East India Company*, p. 4.
4. M.F. Watson & H.J. Noltie, 'Career, Collection, Reports and Publications of Dr Francis Buchanan (later Hamilton), 1762-1829. Natural History Studies in Nepal, Burma (Myanmar), Bangladesh and India', *Annals of Science*, vol. 71, 2016, p. 23; Allan, *Prisoner*, p. 42.
5. C.R. Fraser-Jenkins, *The First Botanical Collectors in Nepal: the Fern Collections of Hamilton, Gardner and Wallich, Lost Herbaria, a Lost Botanist, Lost Letters and Lost Books Somewhat Rediscovered*, Dehra Dun: Bishen Singh Mahendrapal Singh, 2006, p. 6.
6. Watson & Noltie, *Career, Collection, Reports*, p. 25.
7. Ibid., pp. 4, 27.
8. F. Buchanan Hamilton, *An Account of the Kingdom of Nepal and of the Territories Annexed to this Dominion by the House of Gorkha*, rep. New Delhi: Rupa, 2007.
9. Fraser-Jenkins, *First Botanical Collectors in Nepal*, p. 36.
10. Allen, *Prisoner*, pp. 39-58.
11. BL IOR, F/4/621/15534, Bengal Public Letter, Wallich to Government, 25 September 1817.
12. Ibid.
13. Ibid., Trotter to Wallich, 26 September 1817.
14. Kind information by Dr Mark Watson, Edinburgh, December 2020.
15. CNH, Wallich letters, Gardner to Wallich, 4 March 1818.

16. SNM, Letters from Wallich, I, 9, Wallich to Hornemann, 1 July 1818.
17. CNH, Wallich letters, Wallich to Colebrooke, 20 April 1819.
18. Fraser-Jenkins, *First Botanical Collectors in Nepal*, pp. 20-4.
19. CNH, Wallich letters, Wallich to Colebrooke, 20 April 1819.
20. Ibid., p. 39-58.
21. Ibid.
22. Ibid.
23. BL IOR, F/4/621/15534, Bengal Public Letter, Wallich to Lushington, 25 December 1818.
24. Ibid.
25. Ibid., Lushington to Wallich, 15 January 1819; ibid., 5 April 1819; ibid., Wallich to Lushington, 25 December 1818.
26. M. Krieger, *Tee. Eine Kulturgeschichte*, Cologne, Weimar & Vienna: Böhlau, 2009, pp. 144f.
27. Ibid., p. 184.
28. Ibid., p. 185.
29. CNH, Wallich letters, Gardner to Wallich, 12 November 1818.
30. Ibid., 26 September 1818.
31. Nair, *Proceedings*, vol. 3.2, pp. 1028f.
32. Dr Mark Watson, pers. comm., 8 September 2014.
33. Dr Devajit Borthakur, Tocklai Research Institute, Jorhat, pers. comm., 20 November 2014.
34. Dr Mark Watson, pers. comm., 8 September 2014.
35. CNH, Wallich letters, Gardner to Wallich, 6 December 1818.
36. N. Wallich, 'New Camellia', *Asiatick Researches*, vol. 13, 1820. David Don published the plant under the name *Camellia keina*, which may have been due to a misreading of the herbarium label. Dr Mark Watson, pers. comm., 8 September 2014.
37. CNH, Wallich letters, Gardner to Wallich, 26 September 1818; ibid., 22 October 1818.
38. Ibid., Gardner to Wallich, 21 November 1818; ibid., 5 November 1818.
39. Ibid., Gardner to Wallich, 12 November 1818.
40. Ibid., 30 November 1818.
41. Nair, *Proceedings*, vol. 3.2, p. 1029.
42. CNH, Wallich letters, Gardner to Wallich, 11 December 1818.
43. SNM, Letters from Wallich, I, 11, Wallich to Hornemann, 1 January 1819.
44. CNH, Wallich letters, Wallich to Colebrooke, 20 April 1819.

45. Allen, *Prisoner*, pp. 50f.
46. CNH, Wallich letters, Wallich to Lushington, 4 April 1820.
47. BL IOR, F/4/655/18040, Board's Collections 1815-22, Lushington to Wallich, 14 April 1820.
48. BL IOR, F/4/655/18040, Wallich to Lushington, 2 July 1821; on Leycester see Nair, *Proceedings*, vol. 3, 2, pp. 1969f.
49. Landsarkivet for Sjælland, QA-035, Engelholm Gods, 1811-52, Wolff family private archive, correspondence 29-8, Wallich to Wolff, 4 October 1820.
50. Ibid., 27 January 1821.
51. Allen, *Prisoner*, pp. 28ff.
52. Flora, 7 February 1823, p. 67.
53. BL IOR, F/4/1139, Board's Collections, Wallich to Moloney, 8 January 1828.
54. Ibid.
55. Ibid.
56. Landsarkivet for Sjælland, QA-035, Engelholm Gods, 1811-52, Wolff family private archive, correspondence 29-8, Wallich to Wolff, 4 October 1820.
57. Ibid., 4 October 1820.
58. Ibid., 'a little occasioned grumbling'.
59. CNH, Wallich letters, Gardner to Wallich, 22 November 1820.
60. Landsarkivet for Sjælland, QA-035, Engelholm Gods, 1811-52, Wolff family private archive, correspondence 29-8, Sophia Wallich to Benjamin Wolff, 19 December 1820.
61. Ibid.
62. Ibid.
63. CNH, Walllich letters, Wallich to Colebrooke, 15 July 1821.
64. Fraser-Jenkins, *First Botanical Collectors*, p. 44.
65. BL IOR, F/4/712/19459, Extract Bengal Public Consultations, 25 January 1822.
66. Ibid.
67. Fraser-Jenkins, *First Botanical Collectors*, p. 45.
68. BL IOR, F/4/712/19459, Extract Bengal Public Consultations, 25 January 1822.
69. Burkill, *Chapters on the History of Botany*, p. ix.
70. Ibid., p. 65.
71. CNH, Wallich letters, Wallich to Colebrooke, 15 July 1821: 'Not only in the Vegetable productions, but also in Insects is this Country partaking in the features of Europe, America & China'.

72. Ibid.; *Flora*, 6,1, 1823, pp. 68f.
73. CNH, Wallich letters, Wallich to Colebrooke, 15 July 1821.
74. For example, Landsarkivet for Sjælland, QA-035, Engelholm Gods, 1811-52, Wolff family private archive, correspondence 29-8, Wallich to Wolff, 4 October 1820: 'my conscience had often smote me of late, for having omitted to fulfill my engagement of writing to you now & then'.
75. CNH, Wallich letters, Wallich to Colebrooke, 15 July 1821; SNM, Letters from Wallich, I, 15, Wallich to Hornemann, 18 July 1821.
76. 'Af et brev fra Dr N. Wallich, Directeur ved den botaniske Have af Calcutta, til Professor J.W. Hornemann', in Tidsskrift for Naturvidenskaberne, 1, 2, 1822, pp. 257-64.
77. Ibid.
78. The manuscript of 'Filicologia Nepalensis' is in the Wallich papers in the Calcutta Botanic Garden. Fraser-Jenkins, *First Botanical Collectors*, pp. 45f.
79. Flora, 6.1, 1823, pp. 65-73.
80. Ibid.
81. N. Wallich, *Tentamen Florae Napalensis illustratae, Consisting of Botanical Descriptions and Lithographic Figures of Select Nipal Plants*, 2 vols., Calcutta & Serampore, 1824-6 (repr. Dehra Dun: Bishen Singh Mahendra Pal Singh, 1984).
82. Landsarkivet for Sjælland, Engelholm Gods, Wolff family private archive, correspondence 1811-52, Sophia Wallich to Wolff, 29 December 1820.
83. Ibid., Wallich to Wolff, 27 January 1821.
84. Ibid., Sophia Wallich to Wolff, 29 December 1820.
85. Ibid.
86. Ibid., 20 March 1821.
87. M. Krieger, *European Cemeteries in South India (Seventeenth to Nineteenth Centuries)*, New Delhi: Manohar, 2013, pp. 41-9.
88. Holmes & Co., *Bengal Obituary*, p. 394.
89. Fraser-Jenkins, *First Botanical Collectors*, p. 44.
90. BL IOR, F/4/712/19459, Extract Bengal Public Consultations, Wallich to Lushington, 25 January 1822.
91. Ibid.
92. Ibid.

CHAPTER 9

The Straits of Malacca

A few months after his return from Nepal, Wallich still complained of recurring fever attacks almost daily.[1] Some treatment or recuperation, therefore, seemed to be necessary, and he may have recalled with pleasure the benefits brought by the weeks of relaxation and botanizing spent on Mauritius a decade earlier. Perhaps, he had learned from Raffles that a trip further east could also be beneficial to health.[2]

Wallich's request for sick leave was quickly approved by the Government, suggesting the seriousness of his illness, but perhaps also excellent contacts with the Calcutta authorities, and he was allowed to sail to 'China' for a total of six months. It quickly became clear that his destination was not China itself, but that he intended to stop halfway there at Singapore.[3] On 10 August 1822, he left Calcutta on the company ship *Sir David Scott*, this time without his family,[4] but accompanied by his head gardener George Porter and two servants.[5]

The first stop was Prince of Wales Island (Penang), about which William Jack had already reported to him in detail. Wallich himself stayed there for a few days while Porter, who was to remain there, immediately got to work.[6] Porter's laborious attempts to set up an experimental garden in the jungle of the island are reported in the detailed letters that he regularly addressed to his boss who travelled onwards. Porter identified a plot of land that was cultivated by prisoners but his initial optimism quickly evaporated and on 22 October, he complained about the great resistance and problems: 'I wish it were in my power to give you a favourable account of the nursery you have been pleased to place under my care, but it really is not; I have met with so many obstacles in my endeavours to bring it into a favoured state'.[7] Porter complained that the prisoners provided were almost constantly sick or absent. Moreover, he could only be present himself early in the morning to supervise the work because of his simultaneous obligation as a teacher at the local school. Nevertheless, Porter's nursery existed for twelve years before being abandoned.[8]

Wallich arrived in Singapore in early September and on 10 October, Raffles also went ashore for his third and final stay there. The pair exchanged news not only over breakfast but on excursions outside the young settlement when they had plenty of time to talk about natural history and the future of Singapore. On one of these walks, they came across an unusual epiphytic plant. Some of its leaves are flask-shaped and filled with soil by ants; into this grow some of the plant's roots, in order to absorb additional nutrients. Later, in London, in his *Plantae Asiaticae Rariores* (1831), Wallich named this

Plate 9.1: Pongamia macrophylla. In 1845, many plant-specimens collected by Wallich were sent to Kiel University.
(Botanical Garden, Kiel University)

plant as *Dischidia rafflesiana* in memory of his esteemed, but by now deceased friend.[9]

The stay in Singapore achieved its purpose and already by the beginning of October, Wallich felt well again.[10] He was greatly impressed by the fertility of the island and by the almost unimaginable abundance of plants and, as he later wrote to Raffles, he considered that a naturalist would need several years simply to get a general overview.[11] Hardly a dozen of the botanical specialities of Singapore were as yet known to science, and probably not a single plant had made it from the island to the botanical gardens of Europe.[12]

Wallich met virgin forests on Singapore island and immediately recognized its potential as a timber plantation. Although there was no teak, he discovered other native trees that were ideal for shipbuilding and thought that others, such as sissoo, mahogany and bamboo, could easily be naturalised there. Full of enthusiasm, he believed that practically any useful plant could be cultivated successfully there, from pepper and ginger to sugarcane, cotton, tea, and coffee. Wallich also claimed, if rather dubiously so, to have discovered Chinese tea plants: 'even tea grows freely and seems to lose nothing in luxuriance of flower and fruit by the change from its natural climate'.[13] The probably spurious claim that dangerous predators were said to be absent made the island particularly attractive to him.

The idea of founding a botanical garden in Singapore, based on the model of Calcutta and comparable with the experimental garden on Penang, quickly crystallized. The matter was apparently settled with a handshake, but then had to be legitimized through official correspondence. On 2 November 1822, in a detailed official letter to Raffles, he extolled Singapore in the highest tones as a particularly suitable location for a botanical garden: 'It would perhaps be impossible to picture to the mind a situation better calculated in every respect to accomplish the ends of such an institution than that, which Singapore represents in reality, placed under circumstances the most favourable for indigenous as well as foreign vegetation, and forming part of the richest archipelago in the world—its soil yielding to none in fertility, its climate not exceeded by any in uniformity, mildness and salubrity'.[14] In the end, the letter was little more than a formality, for Raffles himself had personally scouted out a suitable site on Government Hill for the future botanical garden and recommended it to Wallich for closer inspection.[15]

The garden was immediately established with funds from the East India Company, though Wallich seems to have paid no further attention to its progress after his departure. In the long-run, Singapore might have seemed to be too insignificant and too small for Wallich's wide-ranging projects. Assistant Surgeon William Montgomerie was entrusted with the supervision of the new garden but no correspondence with Wallich has survived if it ever existed. In 1829, the garden was dissolved and so neither of Wallich's horticultural establishments, in Penang or in Singapore, were destined for permanence.[16]

Botany was not Wallich's only concern during his stay in the young city. He became a member of a short-lived commission to investigate the question of whether warehouses for the growing number of European merchants could be built on the southern bank of the Singapore River. The work was quickly completed, and the Committee submitted its report after only a few days.[17] Although the Committee pointed out that the country in question was located at a very low level, was correspondingly humid and subject to occasional inundation, it was not aware of the fact that the country was in the middle of a flood plain. It considered that good, healthy building land could be gained by means of appropriate drainage measures and the construction of a quay wall, in which case the south bank would become even more suitable in the long term than the already populated north side. The river itself could also serve as the main artery of an efficient drainage system, which would improve the healthiness of the entire settlement. Wallich could not have foreseen that with this report one of the foundation stones for the origin of the modern metropolis of Singapore was laid.[18]

The relationship with Raffles may have started on a professional basis and through shared scientific interests, but during their six-weeks together in Singapore, it developed into a friendship.[19] Raffles' later letters to the botanist prove how close this friendship was, which resulted in the asking of small private favours, such as sending baby drinking bottles to the pregnant Lady Raffles. He knew no one else to whom he could make such a request, as he wrote to Nathaniel.[20]

Wallich's stay in Singapore had been a happy one. He may even have had the idea of settling there permanently with his family at some point in the future as in November he asked to be provided with a plot of land as close as possible to the European Quarter. The local authorities granted him a hilltop property, visible from afar, which was initially known as 'Daimebrog Hill' (doubtless a misreading for 'Danebrog') and later as Mount Wallich, but the hill has long since been levelled and built over.[21]

On 23 November, Wallich set off for the return journey to Bengal on the ship *John Adams*. Also on board were John Crawfurd and George Finlayson, returning to India from a British embassy to Siam and Cochin China (Vietnam).[22] Crawfurd, who had led the mission, came from Scotland, and had studied medicine in Edinburgh. From 1803, he served as a physician in India, was stationed in Penang shortly afterwards and in 1811 had taken part with Raffles in the invasion of Java, on the basis of which he published his 'History of the Indian Archipelago'; from 1815 he was a member of the Asiatic Society. He would hold later high administrative positions in Singapore and Pegu and in 1826 was sent as envoy of the embassy to the Court of Ava in Burma on which he would be accompanied by Wallich.[23] Finlayson, another talented young surgeon and naturalist, was already in poor health in Singapore and died the following year.

The ship passed between the islands of the southern Straits of Malacca and on the first day reached a small stretch of water between Barren and Coney Islands only a few kilometres from Singapore, when the wind died down and the anchor was dropped.[24] As always Wallich was guided by restlessness, so he used the opportunity to roam around some of the islands and botanize.[25] Soon the world of islands was left behind and the open route from Malacca leading north-westwards reached. On 12 December, the island of Junk Ceylon was passed and four days later the wind carried the *John Adams* into the Bay of Bengal. On 29 December 1822, Wallich was back in Calcutta,[26] never again to return to Singapore.

NOTES

1. CNH, Wallich to Lushington, 19 July 1822.
2. Noltie, *Raffles' Ark Redrawn*, p. 27.
3. Desmond, *European Discovery*, p. 86.
4. Bastin, *Letters of Sir Stamford Raffles*, p. 6.
5. Desmond, *European Discovery*, p. 86; Noltie, *Raffles' Ark Redrawn*, p. 133; CNH, Wallich letters, Porter to Wallich, 22 October 1822.
6. CNH, Wallich letters, Porter to Wallich, 20 September 1822.
7. Ibid., 22 October 1822.
8. Ibid.
9. Noltie, *Raffles' Ark Redrawn*, p. 43.
10. CNH, Wallich letters, Porter to Wallich, 22 October 1822.
11. Wallich to Raffles, 2 November 1822, in R. Hanitsch (ed.), 'Letters of Nathaniel Wallich Relating to the Botanical Garden in Singapore', *Journal of the Malayan Branch of the Royal Asiatic Society*, vol. 65, 1913, pp. 39-48 (reprinted in *Journal of the Malayan Branch of the Royal Asiatic Society*, vol. 42, 1, 1969).
12. Wallich to Raffles, 2 November 1822, in Hanitsch, 'Letters of Nathaniel Wallich'.
13. Ibid.
14. Ibid.
15. Ibid., 21 November 1822.
16. Desmond, *European Discovery*, p. 86.
17. Bastin, 'Letters of Sir Stamford Raffles', pp. 6, 44 (note 70).
18. 'the plan is fully practicable'. Report Lumsdaine, Wallich, Salmond to Raffles, 23 October 1822, in Hanitsch, 'Letters of Nathaniel Wallich'.

19. Bastin, 'Letters of Sir Stamford Raffles', p. 6.
20. Raffles to Wallich, 20 July 1823, in: Bastin, 'Letters of Sir Stamford Raffles', p. 29.
21. Noltie, *Raffle's Ark Redrawn*, p. 43.
22. J. Crawfurd, *Journal of an Embassy from the Governor-General of India to the Court of Ava in the Year 1827*, London: Henry Colburn, 1829, p. 457.
23. Nair, *Proceedings*, vol. 2, pp. 579f.
24. Crawfurd, *Journal of an Embassy*, p. 457.
25. Ibid., p. 458: 'Dr Wallich described the vegetable production of all these islands as equally rich and novel, and was, in fact, carrying back with him a curious and extensive botanical collection'. Also see Bastin, 'Letters of Sir Stamford Raffles', p. 45, footnote 47.
26. Bastin, 'Letters of Sir Stamford Raffles', p. 6.

CHAPTER 10

The Forests of India

THE PLANTATION COMMITTEE

Wallich had brought a rich collection of living plants and herbarium material back from Singapore.[1] He dutifully sent part of it to East India House in London's Leadenhall Street.[2] However, most of it remained in Shibpur, where the growing collections attracted more and more attention not only among botanists but also others. Among the enthusiastic admirers of the Garden was the Bishop of Calcutta, Reginald Heber, who came one morning with the Governor-General's wife, Lady Amherst. In an avenue of sago palms, the prelate was reminded of the columns and arches of a Gothic church. Everything, he recollected, was a perfect image of paradise.[3]

After a period of travel, more than two years were to pass during which Wallich ruled his ever-growing empire of botany from his desk in Roxburgh House. The period after 1823 was largely dedicated to a subject that in the long-term was to be of immense importance to the imperial state—forestry. Even in pre-colonial times, India had repeatedly been exposed to phases of severe deforestation, despite a few regional reforestation programmes, but in the colonial era the pressure on forests increased substantially. Calcutta and Bombay, in particular, which were growing rapidly, were thirsting for ever greater quantities of wood, not only for the construction of buildings, but also for the construction of civilian and military ships and for firewood.[4]

The search for exploitable forests increasingly became a motive for territorial conquest in the Indian hinterland, and it was only now that Wallich truly became a representative of imperial botany.[5] Particular attention was paid to the natural resources in the north-western regions that had only recently been conquered during the Maratha wars. This was the area between the Ganga and Yamuna rivers, and the adjacent kingdom of Awadh, still formally independent, but under growing British influence as a 'frontier state'.[6]

Since the 1760s, there had been repeated discussions in India about an increasing shortage of timber, which at that time could be remedied in the short term only by felling in new areas such as the India-Nepal border region.[7] The topic finally took on a new dimension during the wars between Britain and France at the end of the eighteenth century, which brought about an increasing demand for men-of-war—at that time made largely of timber. In the 1790s, for example, a shortage of wood in Britain itself had led to plans to purchase timber from India and eventually to the building of British naval ships there.

The debate initially focused on Bombay, with its densely wooded hinterland along the west coast. Here, since the turn of the century, attempts had been made, with moderate success, to bring the teak trade under the Company's control. In 1800, the short-lived Bengal-Bombay Joint Commission of the East India Company was founded to secure the supply of timber and five-years later, for the first time, a policy for securing long-term resources through sustainable forestry in the west of India was established. The plan was to plant trees under the supervision of the Company in cooperation with Indian landowners. From about 1815 onwards, following initial difficulties, a more or less stable supply of wood to Bombay was actually achieved.[8] However, the transportation of large quantities of timber from Bombay to Calcutta for the shipbuilding industry there proved to be problematic.[9]

Since Roxburgh's time, teak had been cultivated in the Calcutta Botanic Garden.[10] By 1797, thousands of teak saplings were growing there and teak seeds were being sent to all parts of Bengal, to Company representatives and private individuals.[11] Early planting attempts outside Calcutta on land owned or leased by the Company, including Beauleah, Sylhet or in the so-called 'Jungle Mahals' in today's Chota Nagpur region, were successful, but in the long term their effect was limited. In experimental plantings at northern Bengal, there were repeated conflicts of interest with landlords and some plantations reverted to jungle.[12]

Wallich inherited a subject that rapidly grew in importance. Already, in preparation for his trip to Nepal, he had studied different types of timber and thought about the opportunities and risks of a plantation economy. In contrast to the timber debates in Bombay of around 1800, and like Roxburgh before him, he believed from the outset that the only way to meet demand in the long term was to plant new trees. In the meantime, until new plantations had matured, it would be necessary to locate and exploit existing stocks.

In 1820, by virtue of his office as Superintendent, Wallich was also appointed director of the Company's experimental plantations in Bengal, which had been founded by Roxburgh.[13] In a long letter, which almost has the character of a memorandum, he clearly spoke in favour of maintaining the earlier attempts. With due care, and despite signs of neglect, a continuation of the projects started under Roxburgh held promise.[14] He believed it was necessary to centralise control through the Botanic Garden, to request annual reports from the local representatives of the Company, and to be able to intervene if necessary. In order to gain a deeper insight into the condition of the existing plantations, he sent his experienced plant collector Francis de Silva to examine them.[15]

Investigations were no longer restricted to teak, which, though an excellent building material, is slow growing. Wallich, therefore, looked for other, faster growing timber species and came across the *sissu*. *Dalbergia sissoo* is a deciduous tree that can reach a height of up to 25 metres and a trunk circumference of two to three metres, with a dense heartwood that is resistant to insect damage. In its natural state in South Asia, the tree grows mainly along rivers at elevations of up to 900 m and is still of great economic importance in India today.[16]

Wallich carefully studied all the documents on *sissu* available in the Botanic Garden and made verbal enquiries on the subject. In his opinion, *sissu* was the fastest growing hardwood in India that could be cultivated with relative ease. For military purposes it was supposed to be unrivalled. If planted in sufficient quantities, it could, for many uses, replace teak.[17]

In his early period of interest in the subject, around 1819, Wallich was aware of the fact that the naturally existing stocks of *sissu* in Bengal and the conquered areas in the north-west were in sharp decline. Both old and young trees were felled indiscriminately; the survival of the forests seemed increasingly precarious and would, before long, fail to yield any supplies. He was, therefore, aware of the need for sustainable forest management but gave priority to the establishment of new plantations rather than the protection and gradual development of existing natural forests.[18] Wallich also saw the importance of a sufficient supply of bamboo to Calcutta, which he regarded as the most suitable building material for poor people. Bamboo traditionally originated from the area around Murshidabad, where it was in rapid decline. In addition, there was a growing shortage of firewood, and, especially with regard to bamboo and firewood, he saw the Company as having a social responsibility towards the Indian population.[19] However, Wallich was absent from Calcutta for much of the next three years and the issue remained unresolved.

After his travels to Nepal and Singapore, Wallich returned to the topic of timber supplies and forestry in 1823. On 29 January, barely a month after his return from the Straits of Malacca, he again drew the problem to the attention of the Government. Repeating the statements he had made three years earlier he predicted that, in the long term, plantations would save the Company enormous financial expenditure as otherwise it would have to resort to the costly exploitation of forests located further and further from Calcutta or else import wood from other countries. His warnings were heeded, and a Plantation Committee was formed. The Committee was to put the management of the existing tree plantations on a new, systematic basis and develop plans for the future.[20] Its foundation indicates that the colonial state, with Wallich as its representative in the field of botany, now also sought to play a much more active role in Bengal and the newly conquered territories with regard to timber.[21]

William Leycester became the Committee's president, and other members included Wallich's friends and confidants William Carey and Thomas Hardwicke.[22] The appointment of Leycester, though he was soon to leave for Europe, was a wise decision, as he had considerable knowledge of Bengal from his positions as registrar, collector, and as judge. He had been President of the Agricultural and Horticultural Society and had also acted for Wallich during his long absence from his Superintendentship at Shibpur.[23] As the Committee's secretary Wallich himself was not only responsible for coordinating internal discussions, but also for the paperwork, from which he never shied away. On the contrary, by personally writing the minutes of the debates he was able to assert a large measure of interpretative sovereignty. Remarkably, the Committee was initially a purely European undertaking, with Indian experts involved only later and then only in subordinate positions.[24]

The Plantation Committee quickly began its work, with two major topics at the centre of the debate: the identification of existing 'old forests', their limited exploitation and conservation, and, on the other hand, the establishment of new plantations. Already at the first meeting it was contended that a large-scale planting programme would be needed to remedy the foreseeable shortage of timber and not, as had been the case since Roxburgh's time, merely limited experimental planting. The first step was to identify suitable and sufficiently large sites, that were either directly under the control of the Company or which could be leased from Indian owners. Locations were also considered for the establishment of tree nurseries. While Roxburgh had initiated experimental plantings only in Bengal, attention was now increasingly focused on the new western provinces between the rivers Yamuna and Ganga, Nepal being included in the discussions.[25]

At its second meeting, the Committee considered the possible organization of new *sissu* plantations and concluded that Government commissioning of private contractors would seem the most promising way forward.[26] It was clear to all that if new planting was to take place it would take 25 to 30 years before the fully grown *sissu* trees could be felled. It was, therefore, an investment in the future, and no short-term returns were to be expected.[27] Great importance was attached to the appropriate training of local staff. From the outset the members of the Plantation Committee were convinced that the success of the plantations depended on the local knowledge of European officials, and it is noteworthy that indigenous knowledge of natural conditions played hardly any role in the discussions.[28]

Wallich used his rich and extensive communication network to gain the most comprehensive information possible on the relevant areas. One source was Captain Alexander Gerard, who had made a name for himself as a surveyor. He was particularly well versed in the foothills of the Himalaya and in 1821 had even penetrated deep into Tibet via the Himalayan passes.[29] Gerard was one of a select number of Europeans, who had excellent contacts with the Nepali authorities and he promised to mediate in the efforts to use the forests of Nepal.[30] He also pointed out to the Committee extensive land suitable for plantations along the lower reaches of the Mahananda River. There the land was not only fertile, but the timber could also easily be transported to Calcutta via the Mahananda and Ganga. Further west, along the Gandak, which flows into the Ganga at Patna, there was also land highly suitable for tree plantations.[31] From Agra also came promising news with the enclosed ground around Akbar's mausoleum at Sikandra deemed especially suitable for the purpose.[33]

With regard to Nepal the plans quickly fell through. Wallich had asked Edward Gardner in Kathmandu whether it might be possible to clear some forests in the eastern border area with India for use by the Company, while other forests could be preserved for later use. With his own experience of Nepal's restrictive policy towards British India, Wallich should have been able to anticipate the answer, and Gardner pointed out, in brief words, that under no circumstances was support by the Nepali authorities to be expected. On the contrary, any such advances would be extremely damaging to Britain-Nepal relations.[33]

After information had arrived in Calcutta from various places in northern India, the Committee urged the government to allocate or lease land quickly so that the rainy season of 1823 could be taken advantage for sowing or planting. This happened, land was immediately leased, and Company land identified in parts of the north-west. However, land ownership in the periphery of British India was not always clear and conflicts were the result. Already in September 1823, it was reported that there were problems due to the resistance of a large landowner in one of the north Indian districts. Apparently, he had claimed ownership of a piece of land that was also claimed by the Company. The Plantation Committee then called for clear legislation on land ownership by the government, but this was delayed.[34] A first overview was now compiled of the extent to which new *sissu* plantations could be established. Based on the East India Company's anticipated annual demand of 8,000 mature tree trunks over the next 24 years, about 16,000 *bigha* (about 4,000 ha) would initially have to be planted.[35]

AWADH

It was soon obvious to Wallich that he could no longer advance the forest project from his desk without inspecting the localities for the plantations himself. Another phase of travel, therefore, began, which came to an end more than two years later. He had been living alone in the large Roxburgh House for some time as Sophia had left India for Britain in October or November 1824 with their daughter Hannah and their son Leonard Calder, who had been born the year before. Her journey took her via Macao, where she stayed for more than a month and visited the grave of their friend George Cruttenden who had died there. At the beginning of April 1825, Sophia reached St. Helena to deliver a consignment of plants to Georg Wilhelm Jänisch, a keen botanist from Hamburg, who invited her to his country house called Teutonic Hall.[36] When Sophia had left India, she was pregnant again and somewhere on the high seas between Macao and England she gave birth to another son, Nathaniel David. At the beginning of June 1825, she reached London with the children, where she stayed only a few days, probably to set off for her sister in Hull.[37]

Wallich was able to devote himself entirely to preparations for the tour of northern India. His interest focused on areas that had only recently been taken into Company administration and the nominally still independent Kingdom of Awadh. In 1826, large areas of Burma (modern-day Myanmar) had also been added by British conquest and attracted attention. The first journey was, therefore, to take Wallich towards the north of the subcontinent, the second to Burma. These expeditions were to focus on the two major objectives of the forest project: the localization of virgin forests with stands of economically exploitable timber, and the identification of areas suitable for new plantations. Appropriate transport routes in the form of rivers also had to be identified in order, in due course, to be able to transport the timber over long distances to Calcutta.

The southern foothills of the Himalaya were of particular interest. The more accessible lower ranges were deemed most likely to be able to provide natural wood resources, while the lowlands were already largely deforested. Against this backdrop Wallich first wanted to inspect the so-called 'western forests' of Awadh and in the British Indian districts of Rohilkand, Kumaon and Haridwar. In the case of still-independent Awadh botanical development was to precede territorial takeover.[38]

Only one month passed between the initial idea and the start of the expedition. The original intention had been to depart at even shorter notice to spare himself the unbearable heat of the North Indian summer. On 15 January 1825, Wallich set off on his journey by land, with an assistant and two groups of porters. Sixteen porters each carried him and his companion in a palanquin (*palki*), the porters being efficiently changed at the relay stations of the East India Company.[39]

Via Bankura, Sherghati, Benares and Allahabad the teams first went to Kanpur from where Wallich travelled northwards to Awadh by bullock cart. Even here, in the formally still sovereign kingdom, the Company took care of equipment and transportation. He was provided with camp equipment, including tents and trekking oxen, as well as an elephant and driver.[40] Along the Ghagara River, he went northwards through Awadh until he reached the Nepal border.[41] Wallich considered the ruler of Awadh to be well-disposed towards the expedition and to support it to the best of his ability.[42] Special attention was paid to the border region with Nepal, between the Ghagara and Rapti rivers.[43] Here, he found agriculture and cattle breeding in a thriving condition with tobacco and notably indigo grown on a large scale.[44] But from a botanical perspective the country also had much to offer. He discovered orchids, some of which he sent to the king, and came across medicinal plants. He also found Roxburgh's *Gentiana cherayta* (now *Swertia chirayita*), a gentian used as a bitter against fevers. On the eastern bank of the Ghagara river he came across areas rich in *shisham* forests. The trees were still small but, provided they were given appropriate protection, promised to reach a usable size after a decade.[45]

Wallich left Awadh in a hurry and crossed the plains via Kanpur heading north-westwards to Saharanpur. This town had fallen into the hands of the British during the Second Maratha War in 1803. In 1816, the East India Company had founded a botanical garden there under the superintendence of George Govan who had recently, in 1823, been replaced by John Forbes Royle.[46] It was here that Wallich became aware of extensive stands of *sissu* at Dehradun.[47] By mid-August 1825 he had returned to Calcutta, where he immediately turned his attention to another field of research: Burma.[48]

BURMA

The East India Company had for a long time turned to Burma in search of timber. From the first half of the eighteenth century onwards, the country's coastal areas, especially Syriam, had gained importance as suppliers of high-quality timber and as shipbuilding sites, but these were no longer able to satisfy the large European demand.[49]

Europeans first encountered an independent monarchy in Burma,[50] but during the rule of King Bagyidaw, the first Anglo-Burmese war developed out of a local border conflict. This ended in 1826 with the defeat of the Burmese and the peace of Yandabo. Unlike the Sagauli peace treaty with Nepal, this agreement not only brought the British considerable territorial gains in Assam, which had largely been dominated by the Burmese, but also brought the Burmese coastal regions of Arakan and Tenasserim under their control. What remained was a Burmese remnant state on the middle and upper reaches of the Irrawaddy River around the city of Ava. The Burmese were obliged to tolerate a British Resident in Ava and to enter into a trade agreement. As early as September 1826, John Crawfurd was sent as envoy to the court of Ava to achieve beneficial trading terms for the British.[51]

Crawfurd was familiar with mainland and insular Southeast Asia through his previous travels and was particularly aware of the rich natural resources, especially the large stocks of teak, in Burma. It was clear to him from the outset that an experienced botanist should accompany his legation to Ava and Wallich, his travelling companion back from Singapore in 1822, was the obvious choice. Crawfurd, who spent some time in Rangoon, asked the Government in Calcutta to commission Wallich with an expedition to study the flora of the conquered territories, but in particular to gain an insight into the value of their teak forests.[52]

The envoy explicitly denoted the forest issue as of 'national interest'. From the outset the teak forests of the recently conquered Burmese territories became a vital element of the imperial power discourse, resembling the *sissu* debate of northern India. Even less than had been the case in India, there was hardly any talk of conservation, rather of identification and subsequent exploitation.[53]

As on his previous trip, matters developed rapidly. Barely a month after Crawfurd had made his request Wallich was issued with the order to leave. The wording was wide in scope and referred to the botanical examination of all the forests in the conquered territory of Pegu and on the coasts of Tenasserim that were accessible to him. Wallich was requested to start preparations immediately.[54]

The travel order may have aroused ambivalent feelings in him: on the one hand the botanical secrets of a yet unexplored area were attractive; on the other hand his beloved wife Sophia had left Calcutta for Europe the year before and, after almost two decades abroad, he now himself hoped for furlough and a reunion with his family.[55] However, as a servant of the East India Company, officially still in the rank of Assistant Surgeon, he could hardly question the order.

It was particularly important for Wallich to be accompanied by experienced assistants. So he put together a substantial travel party all chosen on the basis of experience, skill and efficiency. Wallich relied on his team, many of whom had already proven themselves in Nepal; and the party consisted of five Indian draughtsmen, William Gomez, and his European apprentice Bernard Fury. Among the artists were the highly skilled Gorachand and Vishnuprasad.[56]

At the beginning of August 1826, Wallich once again began a journey into the unknown. Always interested in technology, it must have been particularly exciting to him that the *Enterprize*, which had been moored off Calcutta for some time, was a steamship.[57] The beginning of the expedition was under an unlucky star. In Rangoon it rained incessantly, the city was 'abominably dirty and ugly'; the accommodation was shabby and almost all the travelling companions were ill. Wallich was particularly dismayed by the unexpected death, from dysentery, of his experienced chief draughtsman Gorachand. Gorachand left behind a widow and son for whom Wallich later arranged a government pension.[58] He himself felt well, which he attributed to good medication, a strict diet, and the use of tobacco, especially in the form of the 'Cigar'. He wrote to Colebrooke that in this part of the world tobacco was a necessary luxury, as practised by many people.[59]

Immediately after arriving in Rangoon, Wallich gathered any information on teak that he could, especially from the areas directly under Company control.[60] Time was pressing, but he nevertheless found a little leisure in Rangoon to botanize. He collected and pressed about 200 plants and came across a hitherto unknown waterlily, of which he hurriedly made a rough drawing and a brief description, which he sent to Colebrooke with the request to send it on to the botanists William Hooker or John Lindley. Following their feedback, Colebrooke was to print the revised draft in London, which he duly did in the 'Transactions of the Linnean Society', under Wallich's authorship and using the name that he had coined for the plant, *Barclaya longifolia*.[61]

In Rangoon, Wallich also met Crawfurd, and a detailed travel programme emerged. Contrary to the original plan, he was first to go north to Ava to investigate the mountainous region there (which was not controlled by the British) and then to return to Rangoon. Wallich would then inspect the teak forests in the south.[62] On 1 September, they set off north together, accompanied by their retinues.[63] For two months, they travelled up the Irrawaddy River by steamer, and Wallich eagerly explored the unknown flora, taking a special interest in aquatic plants and, with Crawfurd, in geology. Crawfurd himself was quickly convinced that he had requested the right man from Calcutta, as he was later to record in his travel journal.[64]

On 24 September, a highlight of the journey was reached— the historical, ruined city of Pagan with its numerous Buddhist shrines, the centre of a once great empire. After dinner the group had the pleasure of wandering through the ruins for more than two hours and climbing one of the highest buildings, from which there was a magnificent view across the ruins towards the hinterland. Some of the sanctuaries they found restored and still in use, while others appeared completely neglected.[65]

Finally, Segaing was reached, situated on the Irrawaddy opposite the capital Ava. Even before he was able to set off into the mountains, Wallich encountered mistrust from the authorities of the only recently defeated Burmese. For a whole month, he was practically interned with his small party, his radius reduced to the limit of a few rice fields, as he wrote to Benjamin Wolff.[66] He found little to admire in the way that members of the local elites treated each other. He once witnessed a public punishment carried out on a seventy-year-old confidant of the king. Following denouncement to the royal court by a competitor the unfortunate man had to lie on his back, entirely exposed to the blazing sun for about six hours. With irony he penned down to Benjamin Wolff the rhetorical question relating to the British Prime Minister: 'Now can you imagine anything equal to this in brutality? Lord Liverpool spread & dried!?'[67] The distrust of the Burmese authorities made it hard enough even to send letters to India and unthinkable to send one to Europe, so he asked Wolff in Calcutta to inform Sophia about his present situation.[68]

It was not until 22 November that he was able to leave Segaing, without Crawfurd, for his short expedition to the hills east of Ava. The same day he crossed the Irrawaddy and the route continued through villages, rice and cotton fields. Even though the roads were good to start with, progress was slow due to the lack of a sufficient number of porters; heavy rainfall also impeded progress. An elderly lady, who identifed herself as a member of the royal family, passed by on an elephant in a long procession. Again and again Wallich saw ancient sanctuaries that reminded him of Pagan and on the evening of the first day the hills of the mountainous country announced themselves far away on the eastern horizon.[69]

The roads became even worse and the land more rugged. Wallich stayed overnight in public inns. A caravan loaded with dried fish passed by into the land of the Shan. As the terrain became steeper, travel by ox-cart was impossible and the hired porters often asked for a break on their way through the lonely bamboo forests. Finally, it became rocky and by a serpentine path, with Wallich riding a pony, the party went up into the mountains. In a lonely hamlet rice and millet were cultivated on barren fields and some oaks and teak trees were spotted. This unexpected coexistence of teak and supposedly European oak aroused sentimental feelings: 'So that here probably, for the first time, by a European at least, was seen growing naturally, side by side, the two greatest glories of the forests of Europe and Asia'.[70]

In the mountains there were no more inns, so they spent one night in the house of a village headman, together with a man dubbed by Wallich a 'cicerone', a local guide who was addicted to alcohol.[71] The air was clear, the night cold, and the botanist was glad to be able to hide under a warm blanket to sleep. Despite the elevation the gardens now appeared more varied. Ginger, papaya, jackfruit and guavas were cultivated and, in the fields, grew sesame, corn and tobacco. In the wilderness, Wallich discovered an unknown species of strawberry and another large oak species. Larger teak forests were not, however, encountered.[72]

Only five days after the departure from Segaing the party started its way back. Considering the long journey from Rangoon the expedition is likely to have been seen as disappointing, at least in terms of identifying teak forests, but Wallich was satisfied with the botanical yield. He wrote that he had brought with him an exquisite collection of living and dried plants: five boxes alone (which were at least all made of teak) full of herbarium material, four others with living plants, seven baskets of roots, and various packages of seeds, which he sent by ship to Calcutta.[73]

On 8 February 1827, Wallich stayed in Amherst Town, a British naval base at the mouth of the Salween on the Bay of Bengal.[74] From there, he made three short journeys to the south: the first in February 1827 along the coast of Tenasserim, the second in March on the river Salween, and the third in May on the river Attram.

Wallich had heard from an Indian about extensive teak forests along the coasts of Tenasserim, and a gunboat was put at his disposal for a trip to investigate this area. With good wind and clear weather, he headed along the coast southwards, passing dense virgin forests, among which *Casuarina* trees stood out prominently.[75] In the evening, the boat was anchored beside small promontories or river mouths, but the large number of roving tigers prevented spontaneous evening excursions into the interior of the country. Where possible, however, small rivers were ascended by boat until stopped by rocks or oyster beds. Plants such as mangroves, rattans, and hibiscus dominated the vegetation, and traces of campfires and fishing tackle indicated the presence of people nearby. But here, as in Ava, the hoped-for teak forests failed to appear, so Wallich and his companions turned back after a few days.[76] At least he returned with the knowledge that the wood of the Casuarina was not suitable for shipbuilding and he reported that, although hard, it rotted quickly and had a strong tendency to crack.[77]

Between 10 and 18 March, he made the second trip, up the Salween River. Here, he did find teak forests and though the trees were small, they offered prospects for future use. Finally, in May, he sailed up the Attram River. His observations there seemed to be promising as regards future use by the Government of India. As he reported to Archibald Campbell, Political Agent of the conquered coastal areas: 'I hesitate not offering it as my humble opinion that the forests in question will prove a source of very excellent supplies. They contain at this moment several thousand trees of a size and quality capable of yielding every description of material in use by our army'.[78] By the end of May, Wallich was back on board the *Enterprize* on the way to Calcutta. He left behind a part of his entourage, who were to continue with the collecting and drawing of plants.[79] In addition to plants and seeds he took with him notes for a two-volume manuscript, a plant catalogue, which is now held by the Linnean Society of London.[80]

Despite all his efforts, Wallich's attempts to establish or extend plantations proved to be only a drop in the ocean. Individual plantations did indeed develop, but the demand for wood in colonial India continued to grow relentlessly, and large-scale deforestation continued to increase in many regions. A more systematic inventory of the remaining forests and efforts to institutionalise protection began only around the middle of the nineteenth century.[81]

NOTES

1. CNH, Wallich letters, Wallich to Lushington, 7 January 1823.
2. BL IOR, F/4/1139, Committee of Correspondence, 11 November 1839.
3. Desmond, *European Discovery*, p. 85.
4. Grove, *Green Imperialism*, pp. 386f.
5. Ibid., p. 389.
6. On the third Maratha War, see S. Förster, *Die mächtigen Diener der East India Company. Ursachen und Hintergründe der britischen Expansionspolitik*, Stuttgart: Franz Steiner, 1992, pp. 352-76.
7. Grove, *Green Imperialism*, p. 388.
8. Man, *Flottenbau und Forstbetrieb in Indien*, pp. 28-106.
9. Grove, *Green Imperialism*, pp. 410f.
10. Harrison, 'Calcutta Botanic Garden', p. 237.
11. Robinson, *William Roxburgh*, p. 130.
12. Grove, *Green Imperialism*, pp. 405ff.; Mann, *Flottenbau und Forstbetrieb in Indien*, pp. 126-9; K. Sivaramakrishnan, *Modern Forests: Statemaking and Environmental Change in Colonial Eastern India*, Stamford: Stamford University Press, 1999, pp. 107f.
13. Mann, *Flottenbau und Forstbetrieb in Indien*, p. 130.
14. BL IOR, F/4/655/15, Board's Collections, Wallich to Lushington, 24 May 1820, 'that the climate of that district [= Sylhet] is especially calculated for the cultivation of the Teak tree'.
15. Ibid.
16. BL IOR, P/11/2, First Report of the Plantation Committee, 25 March 1823.
17. BL IOR, F/4/655/15, Board's Collections, Wallich to Lushington, 24 May 1820.
18. Ibid.

19. Grove, *Green Imperialism*, p. 411.
20. Ibid., p. 407.
21. Ibid., p. 384; Arnold, 'Plant Capitalism and Company Science', p. 914.
22. BL IOR, P/11/2, First Report of the Plantation Committee, 25 March 1823.
23. Nair, *Proceedings*, vol. 3.2, pp. 1969f.
24. Richard Grove's assertion of a much stronger indigenous Indian element in the forest debate at this time must be questioned. Cf. Grove, *Green Imperialism*, p. 382.
25. BL IOR, P/11/2, First Report of the Plantation Committee, 25 March 1823.
26. BL IOR, 8/11/6, Second Report of the Plantation Committee, 26 June 1823.
27. BL IOR, P/11/6, Second Report of the Plantation Committee, 26 June 1823, Wallich to Secretary to the Board of Commissioners in the Ceded and Conquered Provinces, 14 May 1823.
28. BL IOR, P/11/2, First Report of the Plantation Committee, 25 March 1823.
29. Nair, *Proceedings*, vol. 2.2, p. 1951.
30. BL IOR, P/11/6, Second Report of the Plantation Committee, 26 June 1823, Gerard to Plantation Committee, 4 April 1823.
31. BL IOR, P/11/10, Fourth Report of the Plantation Committee, 18 September 1823; BL IOR, P/11/46, Tenth Report of the Plantation Committee, 5 December 1825.
32. BL IOR, P/11/6, Second Report of the Plantation Committee, 26 June 1823.
33. BL IOR, P/11/17, Seventh Report of the Plantation Committee, 5 January 1824.
34. BL IOR, P/11/10, Fourth Report of the Plantation Committee, 18 September 1823.
35. BL IOR, P/11/17, Seventh Report of the Plantation Committee, 5 January 1824.
36. CNH, Wallich letters, Jenisch to Sophia Wallich, 8 April 1825.
37. Ibid., Alexander Jack to Wallich, 17 May 1825; CA, A 515, 74, Wallich to Mary Maclear, 19 November 1846; CNH, Wallich letters, Sophia Wallich to Marjoribanks, 3 June 1825.
38. Bastin, 'Letters of Sir Stamford Raffles', p. 3.
39. CNH, Wallich letters, Shakespear to Deputy Post Master Bancoorah, 4 January 1825.

40. Ibid., Wallich to Swinton, 25 April 1826.
41. BL IOR, P/124/14, Bengal Proceedings, Wallich to Ricketts, 15 March 1825.
42. Ibid.; H. Kulke & D. Rothermund, *Geschichte Indiens. Von der Induskultur bis heute*, 2nd ed., Munich: Beck, 1998, p. 316.
43. BL IOR, P/124/14, Bengal Proceedings, Wallich to Ricketts, 15 March 1825.
44. Ibid.
45. Ibid.
46. CNH, Wallich letters, Govan to Hare, 18 April 1816.
47. BL IOR, P/11/46, Tenth Report of the Plantation Committee, 5 December 1825.
48. CNH, Wallich letters, Jack to Wallich, 2 June 1825.
49. Mann, *Flottenbau und Forstbetrieb in Indien*, p. 4.
50. M. Aung-Thwin & M. Aung-Thwin, *A History of Myanmar since Ancient Times: Traditions and Transformations*, London: Reaction Books, 2012, pp. 167f.
51. E. Gait, *A History of Assam*, Dibrugarh, Guwahati, Tezpur & Jorhat: Bani Mandir, 2010, pp. 405-45; Aung-Thwin & Aung-Thwin, *History of Myanmar*, pp. 178-81.
52. CNH, Wallich letters, Crawfurd to Government, 28 March 1826.
53. Ibid.
54. Ibid.
55. CNH, Wallich letters, Sophia Wallich to Marjoribanks, 3 June 1825.
56. Ibid., Wallich to Swinton, 25 April 1826; BL IOR, F/4/1068, Board's Collections, Wallich to Government, 25 June 1827.
57. CNH, Wallich letters, Wallich to Greenlaw, 8 June 1826.
58. Ibid. Lushington, 21 September 1826.
59. Royal Library Copenhagen, Håndskriftsamlingen, Wallich to Colebrooke, 31 August 1826.
60. Ibid.
61. Ibid.
62. Ibid.
63. Ibid.
64. Crawfurd, *Journal of an Embassy*, pp. 50, 52f., 62.
65. Ibid.
66. Landsarkivet for Sjælland, QA-035, Engelholm Gods, 1811-52, Wolff family private archive, correspondence 29-8, Wallich to Wolff, 8 February 1827.
67. Ibid.

68. Landsarkivet for Sjælland, QA-035, Engelholm Gods, 1811-52, Wolff family private archive, correspondence 29-8, Wallich to Wolff, 8 February 1827.

69. Nathaniel Wallich, *Brief Excursion to the Hills to the East of Ava in November 1826*, in: SOAS Bulletin of Burma Research, vol. 3,2, 2005, pp. 476f.

70. Ibid., p. 478.

71. Ibid., p. 479.

72. Ibid.

73. Landsarkivet for Sjælland, QA-035, Engelholm Gods, 1811-52, Wolff family private archive, correspondence 29-8, Wallich to Wolff, 8 February 1827.

74. Ibid.

75. CNH, Wallich letters, Wallich, An Account of Several Excursions, February 1827.

76. Ibid.

77. Ibid.

78. CNH, Wallich letters, Wallich to Campbell, 25 April 1827.

79. Harrison, 'Calcutta Botanic Garden', p. 239.

80. N. Wallich, Catalogus plantarum quas in itinere Burmanico a mense Augusti 1826 ad finem Maii 1827 observavit, 2 vols., manuscript.

81. Grove, *Green Imperialism*, pp. 441-62.

CHAPTER 11

London

FURLOUGH

Wallich had now spent just over two decades in India, interrupted only by expeditions to neighbouring countries. His parents and friends were waiting for him in Denmark, but, although he had been in close contact with Britain by correspondence for more than a decade, he had never visited the country himself. In the meantime, a huge treasure of herbarium material had accumulated in the Calcutta Botanic Garden, much of it representing species unknown outside India. Due to lack of time, it had not been possible to arrange all the dried plants and even less to identify or describe many individual specimens. In addition, the printing of high-quality illustrated books in India had proved to be technically difficult to carry out. Wallich also suffered repeated attacks of fever, which might be remedied by a stay in the cooler climate of Europe. He had not seen his wife Sophia and the children for almost three years. Many good reasons, therefore, came together to travel to Europe on home leave.

Soon after his stay in Singapore, Wallich had considered such a furlough and, on her departure for London in 1824, he had asked Sophia to apply for one to the Court of Directors.[1] However, these plans had been thwarted for the time being by the expeditions to Awadh and Burma. He turned to the government in November 1827 with a medical certificate confirming the need for rest. In a detailed accompanying letter, he described the state of his health as almost life-threatening: 'my own feelings now plainly tell me that unless the measures, which have been recommended can be adopted I shall not long survive the repeated attacks of a fever, which I have lately experienced'.[2] He complained that the pain was not only noticeable physically, but also affected the mind. The enormous workload, borne more or less entirely by himself, added to the strain, but scientific motives also played a role. In recent years, he had practically no time to publish his discoveries, and he now intended to do so. He also hoped to take the Garden's large herbarium collection to Europe to distribute it from London on behalf of the Company.[3] Given the size of the collection, it was clear that a great deal of work awaited him, so he also requested that two assistants should accompany him, William Gomez, who had proven himself in Nepal and Burma, and James George Watson, who had just completed his training at the Botanic Garden.[4] When the Company's administrators in Calcutta were informed about Wallich's poor state of health they recognized the seriousness of the situation and reacted quickly. Only ten days later, he was granted leave and allowed to take the herbarium with him at the Company's expense. During his absence Charles Metcalfe, a member of the government, was to take over the superintendence of the Botanic Garden.[5]

However, departure was not straightforward, as it turned out that no East India Company man with enough room to take the large collection of plants was due to sail to Europe in the foreseeable future, so Wallich had to travel on the private ship *Orient*.[6] Taken on board were 56 large boxes of dried plants and seeds, 13 of living plants, 12 of roots, 12 baskets of epiphytic plants, wood samples including six whole tree trunks, more than a thousand drawings by Indian artists and various living animals.[7] The latter included two Tibetan mastiffs. Hodgson had sent the dogs to Wallich from Kathmandu with a request to take them to London.[8] In haste, just before the departure of the *Orient* on 10 March, Wallich wrote a short note to Benjamin Wolff. He apologized for not having contacted him earlier and reminded Wolff that he himself probably realised what it meant to leave the country for Europe after so many years.[9] On the long voyage he used a short stopover on St. Helena to botanise and probably also to visit Georg Wilhelm Jänisch in his Teutonic Hall.[10] In mid-July 1828, he reached London.

On 20 July, he transferred the two Tibetan mastiffs to the Zoological Society of London—a mistake, as it soon turned out for the intended recipient of the dogs was none other than King George IV himself. The King immediately forwarded them to the Zoological Gardens in Regent's Park, where they died soon afterwards.[11]

We do not know anything about how Wallich adapted himself to his new environment, but some significant differences from Calcutta must immediately have struck him. Until then, he had been used to the autocratic rule of the East India Company, which in many ways exerted a profound influence on everyday life. In the city of the Company's headquarters, things were very different. Here countless privileges, often stemming from past centuries, determined the maintenance of public order. Matters such as sewerage, road maintenance, the poor and public safety were the responsibility of parishes, and other somewhat archaic bodies. The London, he got to know, was a city of great social contrasts, it was the world of Charles Dickens who, as a ten-year-old, had moved with his parents to the rapidly growing metropolis.[12]

First and foremost, the entire city constituted an enormous construction site. Wallich may not only have admired the new, magnificent rows of houses along Regent Street, but he also witnessed the incipient revolution in transport that began with horse-drawn trains and would later continue with railways, trams and the London Underground to be.[13] Full of admiration, he looked at the steam locomotives that pulled hitherto unimaginable loads across the country. Years later he metaphorically toasted the railway: 'long life to it with plenty of improvements!'[14]

Wallich had no permanent place to stay in his first few weeks in London. He lodged at 6 Princess Street, Hanover Square for some time and was then to be found at the Tavistock Hotel in Bloomsbury.[15] Finally, in a letter to the astronomer John

Herschel in early September, he wrote that he had rented a house at Turnham Green, just outside the city.[16] This was in line with the trend of the time, when the better-off middle classes were moving to the fashionable western suburbs, though this necessitated considerable travel to the city centre.[17] Almost at the same time, on 28 August 1828, his parents celebrated their Golden Wedding in Copenhagen. Perhaps, Wulf Lazarus and Hannah thought of their son, but for him the herbarium and his botanical work seemed more important.[18]

Before Wallich moved into an apartment at 8 Turnham Green Terrace, he had to reconnect with his family, whom he had not seen for more than three and a half years.[19] At Mary Smith's house near Hull, not only was his sister Sophia herself waiting, but also their elder son George Charles, who had come from Copenhagen some time earlier, and the three younger children Hannah, Leon Calder and Nathaniel David. Once reunited in London, the boundaries between work and family life became blurred, and often the little ones would come together when their father was talking about botany. Years later, George Bentham still remembered with joy the lively, happy boys who introduced themselves to him as 'Leonard Scott Wallich, Esq.' and the chubby 'David Nathaniel Scott Wallich, Esq.'[20]

Wallich devoted a large portion of time to his family and after the loss of two newborns in India, was all the more concerned when illnesses circulated in the family.[21] He had to worry above all about Sophia who was not only ill at the beginning of 1829, but also pregnant again.[22] It proved increasingly difficult for him to leave his family alone, and Turnham Green was not the ideal address from which to travel to his pressing work in the centre of London.[23] Wallich, therefore, soon started to look around for accommodation closer to the premises of the East India Company, the British Museum and the Linnean Society. From May, his new address was in Bloomsbury at 49 Great Coram Street, Brunswick Square,[24] approximately where the Brunswick Shopping Centre is located today.

On 9 August, Sophia gave birth to a daughter. But the relief was to be short-lived, for the infant died the following January and a small funeral service was held at St. Pancras Church.[25] In October 1830, another daughter, Mary Sophia, was born,[26] so once again the botanist's family had five children.

In Calcutta, the length of the furlough had not been decided. To gain sufficient time necessary for his major projects—the distribution of the herbarium and the publication of a major botanical work—he applied to the Court of Directors for a leave totalling eighteen months, calculated from the date of his arrival in London. The Board of Directors agreed but stipulated that he should not be absent from the Botanic Garden for more than two and a half years in total.[27]

AT THE CENTRE OF NATURAL SCIENCE

At this time, London was one of the undisputed centres of natural science in the world. With their telescopes, astronomers penetrated to the most distant regions of our galaxy and beyond; the microscope was used to study the smallest objects that had ever been seen, which allowed major contributions to plant physiology; mathematics also made enormous progress. Much of this work was undertaken by unsalaried savants, as supposedly altruistic and purely academic research, but some of it also directly served the power interests of the steadily growing British Empire. While the available sources report little about family matters, they provide much information about Wallich's academic contacts while on leave in London. While some existing 'pen friendships' were strengthened by personal meetings, other new connections found their beginnings here. Much of the communication must have developed informally and orally, and not all the acquaintances were such frequent writers as William Jackson Hooker, then based in Glasgow.[28]

One of the first contacts was John Lindley, who lived with his family near Turnham Green and whose house became a focal point for Wallich's integration into London social life from the outset. Still plagued by money worries Lindley was an assistant secretary at the Horticultural Society and at the same time looked after the garden of the 6th Duke of Devonshire at nearby Chiswick House. In 1829, he was appointed to the chair of botany at University College London. Lindley was of interest to Wallich not only for his own research but for his links with Robert Brown and Hooker. On the other hand, Wallich was useful to Lindley for his knowledge of Indian and Nepalese orchids.

It was in Lindley's house that Wallich met George Bentham, a nephew of the philosopher and lawyer Jeremy Bentham. Though not yet thirty, Bentham had already travelled extensively, with visits to St. Petersburg and a period of residence near Montpellier from where he had explored the flora of the Pyrenees. When he met Wallich, Bentham was studying law in London, but he was a naturalist at heart. In connection with the current debate on the natural system, he had become interested in botanical classification systems, and in 1827 published his 'Outline of a New System of Logic'. A close relationship of trust developed between the pair, which was to last until Wallich's death.

Lindley may also have provided the personal introduction to Robert Brown. Since the first indirect contact between the two in 1815, Brown had refined his thoughts on the natural system and the distinguishing characteristics of plants through his increasing use of the microscope. His achievements in this field would be one of the reasons for Humboldt's designation of Brown as 'botanicorum princeps'.[29] In 1827, Brown had discovered the movements of the smallest, microscopically visible particles in liquids and gases, which was later named 'Brownian motion' after him.[30]

Although only a few letters between them have survived evidence suggests that contact between Wallich and Brown must have been close. In November 1828, for example, Brown accepted a Sunday invitation to the Wallichs at Turnham Green.[31] The memorable meeting with a demonstration of the molecular movement through microscope lenses ('some molecules before dinner') had to take place without Herschel, who had also been invited but had had to stay at home with his indisposed wife.[32] Wallich himself did not acquire a microscope until later and then used it only rather superficially. Brown himself was among the signatories of Wallich's nomination by the Royal Society, who was then duly elected. Furthermore, he joined meetings of the Linnean Society to be elected on to Council in 1829.[33]

Wallich's friend Sir Edward Ryan, a judge in Calcutta, had already arranged from India an introduction to John Frederick William Herschel.[34] Herschel was at that time one of the most famous natural scientists in Britain. As an astronomer, he had followed in the footsteps of his father Wilhelm Herschel and had made a name for himself with his investigations into stellar nebulae and double stars. At the same time, his research on light had a considerable influence on the production of ever more high-quality optical lenses.[35] Immediately after his arrival in London, Wallich wrote to Herschel, who lived in Slough, and their first meeting took place in early December 1828.[36] Among other scientists whom Wallich met this year was Charles Babbage, an outstanding mathematician and one of the forefathers of the computer.[37]

With scholars living outside London Wallich was able to correspond. Whereas letters took four or more months to reach Britain from India the post took only days or at most a few weeks within the country and the frequency of correspondence could, therefore, increase. In this way, a long-distance and long-standing friendship was consolidated with William Jackson Hooker in Scotland, with whom he had been in correspondence since 1818. Hooker, like Wallich, had shown himself to be a talented natural scientist from youth. At the age of twenty, he had discovered a species of moss (*Buxbaumia aphylla*) new to Britain, in recognition of which he was accepted into the Linnean Society a year later. There he met Joseph Banks and his assistant Robert Brown. In 1809, Banks arranged for Hooker to sail to Iceland, but the collection he made there was unfortunately lost in a fire on board. Banks now encouraged the young man to make a trip to Asia and though this project never came about, he nevertheless began to study the flora of the continent. Hooker was appointed Professor of Botany at the University of Glasgow in 1820, where he spent twenty years during which he lectured, wrote and edited and drew plants prolifically, and for which he was knighted in 1836. In 1827, he accepted and then turned down the chair at University College London, and in 1841 achieved his major ambition with his appointment as Director of the Royal Botanic Gardens of Kew.[38] Countless letters dealing with botanical matters, but also many personal ones, travelled between London and Glasgow and Wallich frequently sought Hooker's opinion as to whether a plant he had described was new or had already been published.[39]

From London, Wallich's botanical correspondence extended not only towards Scotland, but also to the European continent. While German botanists had previously played virtually no role in Wallich's network, they now became important as directed to specialists in particular plant families. One of these was the Hamburg botanist Johann Georg Christian Lehmann to whom Wallich had an introduction from his cousin Ludvig Levin Jacobson. Lehmann had studied medicine in Copenhagen and had been Professor of Physics and Natural History at the Hamburg Academic Gymnasium since 1818. In 1820, with the gardener Johann Heinrich Ohlendorff, he founded Hamburg's botanical garden and became its first director.[40] Lehmann hoped to welcome Wallich to the ninth meeting of German natural scientists and surgeons in Hamburg in September 1830, but Wallich could not spare the time. The botanical section of the congress did, however, issue an official note of recognition of Wallich's scientific achievements.[41]

More lasting was the connection with Carl Friedrich Philipp von Martius in Munich. Martius had spent four years in Brazil on behalf of the Bavarian Academy of Sciences, after which he was appointed professor at Munich University and director of the botanical garden there. He gained an international

Plate 11.1: Daniel Macnee, Nathaniel Wallich during
his furlough in London, chalk drawing, *c*.1830.
(Royal Botanic Gardens Kew)

reputation through his great works on the Brazilian flora and
on the palm family.[42] Martius had tried to contact Wallich as
early as 1825, but on 24 November 1829 Wallich wrote a
letter of apology, explaining that he had found this first
communication only two years later, following his return to
Calcutta from Burma, at which point he had felt too ill even
to think of replying.[43]

Another major correspondent in Germany was Christian
Gottfried Daniel Nees von Esenbeck. Nees was a brilliant
systematic botanist, with broad taxonomic interests, initially
in Cryptograms, but who would develop a particular interest
in Indian members of the families Acanthaceae, Gramineae
and Cyperaceae. Until 1830, he was director of the Bonn
Botanical Garden, from where he moved in the same capacity
to Breslau.[44] He was always keen to recognize the botanical
knowledge developed in Britain and made a name for himself as a translator of Robert Brown's works into German.[45]

However, Nees also had a wide European network including Stephan Ladislaus Endlicher in Vienna, the father and son Augustin Pyramus and Alphonse de Candolle in Geneva and Adrien de Jussieu in Paris—with all of whom Wallich would enter into correspondence.

Although Brown, the Candolles and Endlicher were leading exponents of the natural system,[46] Wallich's correspondence with them, somewhat surprisingly, contains no evidence of a professional exchange on this subject. The countless letters from and to Wallich chiefly contain information on the practice of botany—the collection and dispatch of plants, plant descriptions and determinations, though information on the networks of the correspondents, and even personal matters, does also emerge. Theoretical thoughts are almost never found, which reinforces the impression that Wallich was first and foremost a practitioner and networker, who, due to his long stay in India, had little involvement, or even interest, in the debates then being discussed in Europe.

THE DISTRIBUTION OF THE HERBARIUM

The strengthening of his European communication network, starting in 1828, primarily served the two major projects in which Wallich sought to engage from his London base: the distribution of the East India Company herbarium and an illustrated publication of a selection of South and South East Asian plants. He probably took heed of the fate that had befallen Buchanan's Bengal collection, forgotten by the scientific world, and languishing in the rooms of East India House, and wanted to avoid this for his own much larger herbarium.[47]

Immediately after his arrival the boxes had been transferred from the *Orient* to the East India Company's baggage house in Little St. Helens. The wheels of bureaucracy ground slowly and the order for their release dragged on.[48] In addition to his efforts to obtain customs clearance, Wallich also had to look for suitable premises in which to curate his plant collection (involving identification, cataloguing and arranging into sets of duplicates) and prepare it for distribution. He asked the Court of Directors to allow him to seek a suitable apartment and to furnish it with large open shelves on all the walls.[49] Shortly after this he rented the first and second floors of 61 Frith Street in Soho, which he fitted out with the desired furniture.[50] For the next three years the Frith Street rooms, Wallich's 'botanical workshop', became a centre of botanical activity of pan-European reputation.

The herbarium that Wallich brought from India contained multiple duplicates of most of the collections. There was never any doubt that a complete set should remain in the possession of the Company; at least initially, it should be kept in East India House. But even before leaving Calcutta Wallich had formulated the plan to make use of experts, wherever they might be, by sending them a set of duplicates of the families in which they were specialist, and which they could retain.[51] However, the proposal to transfer precious treasures from the Company's possessions abroad was a political issue, to which the Company agreed only after some hesitation.[52]

It soon proved to be impossible to manage the distribution of thousands of herbarium specimens by himself, and Wallich found an eager assistant in George Bentham. Bentham agreed to visit Frith Street regularly, and for a longer period during the summer holidays, 'to assist him in the general sorting and distribution'.[53] Bentham, thus, became Wallich's closest collaborator and over a long period they worked together almost daily, arranging, labelling and dispatching specimens.[54] In Frith Street, Wallich was a warm-hearted and generous host, who did not hesitate to offer his visitors an 'oyster luncheon' in between the piles of thousands of dried plants. It was only when he realized that his hospitality was also attracting second-rate, self-proclaimed botanists, such as one from Northumbria referred to ironically as 'borealis', that Wallich stopped the oyster snacks.[55] Bentham himself named and curated the family Labiatae, which involved the description of many new species, and in November 1829 completed a summary of the tribes and genera of the family.[56] Much of this was based on Wallich's specimens and it was published in *Edwards' Botanical Register*, a periodical edited by Lindley.

Before the actual dispatch of the herbarium material started, a 'Numerical List' of all the plant specimens was compiled, commonly known as the 'Wallich Catalogue'.[57] This was not intended as an authoritative floristic publication and, although it included large numbers of new plant names, these were not accompanied by descriptions. The intention, rather, was to produce several copies using the inexpensive and still young process of lithography, and to send the relevant pages to the recipients of individual plant batches. Recipients would be able to cut out sections with the name of the respective plant, location and year and use them as labels on the appropriate herbarium sheets. In this way, Wallich saved himself the production of several hundred thousand labels, because he only had to number the herbarium sheets and record the same number in the catalogue. The first plants and catalogue sheets left Frith Street in 1828 and the last shipment was sent in the summer of 1832 by which time Wallich and Bentham had reached page 253 of the catalogue and species number 7683.[58]

For the sorting, naming and processing of the specimens, Wallich enlisted the help of a number of leading botanists besides Bentham, each of whom well known in his own field. These included Lindley and Brown, George Arnott Walker Arnott, John Prescott, Robert Kaye Greville, Adrian Hardy Haworth, Robert Graham, Alphonse de Candolle, Jules Paul Benjamin Delessert, Adrien de Jussieu, Achille Richard, Lehmann, Martius, Nees von Esenbeck, Karl Sigismund Kunth, Stephan Ladislaus Endlicher, Joseph August Schultes, Johannes August Christian Roeper, Karl Friedrich Meisner and Nicolas Charles Seringe. Some of these forwarded their material by post, others made their way to London in person.

For example, in the summer of 1829 Hooker visited the Wallichs from Scotland, probably being among the first to receive specimens.[59] The following year Lehmann came from Hamburg and worked for a few days in Frith Street.[60] In 1830, the Swiss law student Alphonse de Candolle spent several months in London, having made a shorter visit two years earlier. Alphonse was the son of the famous Geneva botanist Augustin Pyramus de Candolle and on his way to becoming a leading authority on plant geography.[61] Wallich and Bentham had an intensive exchange with de Candolle and together they visited the botanical garden of Kew.[62] Only a week after de Candolle's arrival, the professor of botany at Berlin, Karl Sigismund Kunth, arrived from Germany. Bentham acted as host and introduced de Candolle and Kunth to the Linnean Society and took them to meet the elderly patron of science, Aylmer Bourke Lambert.[63]

With the help of such prominent support the astonishing number of 641 packages and 83 pieces of palm trees left Frith Street, accompanied by printed sheets of the catalogue. The Scottish botanist Robert Graham, who had helped with the legumes, received the greatest number of packages (48), followed by Brown (35), Alphonse de Candolle (34), Hooker (32), the British Museum (29), Delessert (27) and Kunth (25). Nees von Esenbeck (20) and Martius (19) were also generously treated, while Bentham himself received 16 packages. The four surviving shipping lists give a total of 64 recipients, including Lehmann and Wallich's old teacher Jens Wilken Hornemann.[64]

Some of the parcels and palm segments were bulky goods, which had to be handled with special care and required careful transport. Treuttel & Würtz, a trading company and bookshop founded in Strasbourg in 1770, which had a London branch in Soho Square, had great expertise in this field. The firm was under the direction of the German Adolph Richter and specialised in importing books from France, but also the dispatch of shipping orders.[65] While in London, Wallich had very close links with Treuttel & Würtz; the firm acted not only as a forwarding agent for the herbarium material, but as the publisher of his great botanical work. From February 1829, Wallich used its services, for example, to send herbarium specimens to Hooker in Glasgow, as well as to recipients in

Germany.[66] The bookseller and agent for dried plants John Hunneman, who also lived in Frith Street, also played a central role in Wallich's distribution network,[67] as did companies on the continent, such as the brethren Ruedorffer in Munich who were also entrusted with consignments.[68]

For all these activities, the goodwill of the Court of Directors was essential, because Wallich always regarded the herbarium as the exclusive property of the Company.[69] The Company was to ensure that the plant shipments were effective—not only as objects of research, but also as a means to enhance the Company's reputation abroad as a patron of science. Accordingly, Wallich did not hesitate to instruct recipients to write appreciative letters of thanks.[70] Over time, many acknowledgements, as well as precious book gifts, were received by the Court of Directors in Leadenhall Street from both home and abroad.[71]

The value of the system of plant dispatch had proved itself so that Wallich, at the end of 1829, tried to expand the distribution to include other earlier herbaria already in the possession of the Company. He requested that the collections of Roxburgh, Buchanan, Robert Wight, Patrick Russell, Benjamin Heyne, and the plants that he himself had sent to London in earlier years, be sent to him for distribution as duplicates.[72]

After some time, it became apparent that Wallich would not be able to complete the distribution of the herbarium without further extending his stay in London. In a detailed letter to the Company on 3 April 1830 he asked for an extension to his furlough. Once again he highlighted the great achievements of his Botanic Garden, referred to the countless acknowledgements that had already reached the Court of Directors and pointed out that, due to time constraints, he had hardly ever left London and had not even visited his native country Denmark.[73] Ten days later, the Management Committee ordered the extension of his stay for a further year.[74] Even with this, Bentham and Wallich did not manage to complete the distribution of the enormous herbarium collection and shortly before his return to India, Wallich sent the remaining specimens to Bentham's country house, Pontrilas House, near Hereford.[75]

The fact that Wallich took almost all the Botanic Garden's herbarium material with him from Calcutta to London can from today's perspective seem problematic, as it did to some of his Indian contemporaries. In doing so, he deprived subsequent generations of researchers in India of the opportunity to work with Indian specimens in their own country and in the long term it greatly diminished the Garden in its role as a research institution. Even though the distribution of specimens did make the Garden at Shibpur known in Europe in the short term, this measure led to a loss of reputation in the long run.[76] While Wallich originally intended to take back a set of specimens with him to Calcutta, this did not happen, and it was later Superintendents who had to attempt to obtain duplicates from various sources—Thomas Anderson requested duplicates from the Linnean Society in 1863, and others were transferred from Geneva in 1958-9.[77] One advantage was that the 'top set', the only complete set of specimens, has been well looked after in Britain, initially by the Linnean Society to which the East India Company presented it in 1832, and after its transfer to Kew in 1912. The temperate climate of London, and relative scarcity of insects that feed on dried plant material, has favoured the preservation of the specimens as compared with the humid tropical climate of Bengal, and the herbarium was made available in the early 1970s by means of microfiche, and more recently digitally.

PLANTAE ASIATICAE RARIORES

Until Wallich's time, global correspondence networks were one of the most important means by which to communicate new scientific knowledge. Botanical journals were beginning to establish themselves but very few books on the flora of India existed, illustrated or not. Botanists had to rely on works of the seventeenth century including the *Hortus Malabaricus*,

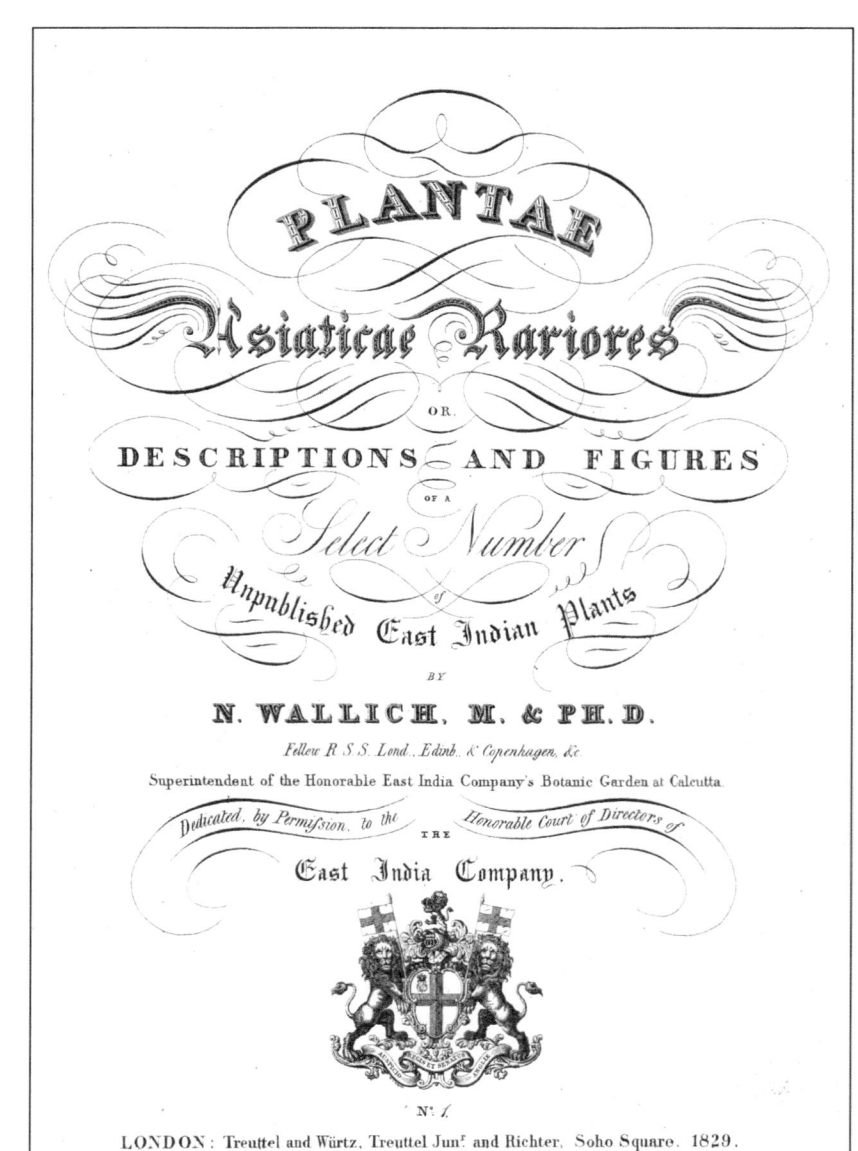

PLANTAE

Asiaticae Rariores

OR.

DESCRIPTIONS AND FIGURES

OF A

Select Number

of

Unpublished East Indian Plants

BY

N. WALLICH, M. & PH.D.

Fellow R.S.S. Lond., Edinb. & Copenhagen, &c.

Superintendent of the Honorable East India Company's Botanic Garden at Calcutta.

Dedicated, by Permission, to the THE *Honorable Court of Directors of*

East India Company.

N.º 1.

LONDON: Treuttel and Würtz, Treuttel Jun.ʳ and Richter, Soho Square. 1829.

Engelmann. Graf. Londed & Co lithog.

Plate 11.2: Plantae Asiaticae Rariores. Title page of Nathaniel Wallich's magnum opus.

the much more recent, but relatively slight work based on König's specimens by Anders Johan Retzius, or else find references to Indian species in publications of worldwide scope such as those of Linnaeus.[78] Roxburgh's posthumously published 'Flora Indica' represented a major step forward, but still only covered a fraction of the plants to be found in South Asia. At the same time, the visual representation of botanical knowledge by means of reproductions of drawings was becoming increasingly important.[79] Wallich recognized that there was a real deficiency, especially with regard to the rapidly increasing number of plants newly discovered in Asia.

In November 1828, he, therefore, planned an illustrated work to be called *Plantae Rariores Indica Orientalis*, which, to gain their financial support, he intended to dedicate to the Court of Directors.[80] This sort of publication was extremely expensive to produce, and one way to gain funds was to ask the Company to subscribe for several copies. In fact, they agreed to the remarkable number of 50 copies. However, at this early stage it was also necessary to acquire many other subscribers to cover the enormous cost of publication. For this he used all the communication channels available to him and identified not only professional naturalists as potential interested parties, but wealthy landowners and aristocrats with interests in botany and horticulture. The method proved to be successful, as can be seen from the lengthy list of subscribers printed in the first volume.[81]

In December an advertisement was published for the work under the slightly altered title of *Plantae Asiaticae Rariores*. It represented the fruits of Wallich's long experience in India, which abundantly justified the production of such a lavish publication.[82] Further advertisements were to follow, such as one in the *Magazine of Natural History*.[83] To increase the reach of his publicity, he also advertised on the continent, with his efforts reaching as far as Denmark and Norway. On 16 February 1829, readers of the newspaper *Norske Rigstidende* in Norwegian Christiania learned (rather misleadingly) that the botanist Wallich, Knight of the Danebrog order, was currently in London and intended to publish a splendid work under the title *Flora Birmanniensis* in three folio volumes of 100 illustrations each. The whole thing was to appear in a total of twelve instalments and, to cover the costs, the publisher had agreed to publish when 100 copies had been pre-ordered by subscribers.[84]

Treuttel & Würtz was commissioned as publisher, but, in contrast to Wallich's satisfactory experience with this firm over the shipping of plants, cooperation over the publication of the book was to prove problematic. Wallich had a direct dealing with the managing director, Adolph Richter, and soon felt annoyed by what he considered to be Richter's arrogant manner, which he felt obliged to point out at the beginning of their business relationship.[85] Despite the initial difficulties, a contract was concluded on 10 April 1829 for the publication of three volumes, each of four parts.[86] Wallich began with the preparation and arrangements with the printers of the plates, Engelmann, Graf, Coindet & Co, and especially the Maltese artist Massimo Gauci, who transferred the Indian artists' drawings to the lithographic stones.[87] Of these, 81 were by Gorachand and 114 by Vishnuprasad.

Problems with Richter did not, however, stop and a few months later Wallich complained about what he considered the slow progress with the plates and urged haste: 'My time is too precious to me to admit any further delays'.[88] Time was running out; Wallich began to get nervous and expected a written reply within two days at the latest.[89]

Next to his own text, Wallich asked other botanists to send taxonomic accounts of the plants that had been sent to them, though many were to disappoint him. In the end, the only other contributors to the *Plantae Asiaticae Rariores* were Nees (the families *Lauraceae* and *Acanthaceae*), Bentham (*Labiatae*), Martius (*Eriocaulaceae* and *Xyridaceae*) and Meisner (*Polygonaceae*). However, Wallich's use of Linnaean classification was not always accepted by the fellow-botanists without demur and Nees, for example, rearranged the plants and revised some of the designations given by Wallich.[90] Nevertheless, Wallich

Plate 11.3: Dischidia rafflesiana, lithography from
Plantae Asiaticae Rariores, vol. 2, London 1831.

received delivery of the first part of the first volume of his
magnum opus, containing 25 plates, in October 1829 and
immediately, and with justifiable pride, sent a copy to the Court
of Directors, full of gratitude.[91] The twelfth and last part
appeared in August 1832 shortly before his return to India.[92]
The work was enormous, both in its large folio scale and the
richness of its content, with detailed Latin plant descriptions
and, as in his unpublished *Filicologia Nepalensis*, short notes in
English on the localities of the plants depicted. Of these, there
are 295 plates of plant portraits, and a double-page map of
India inscribed with the itineraries of himself and of other
botanists.

COPENHAGEN AT LAST

During his stay in London greetings from Denmark were received from time to time. A letter from Cornelius Gottlieb Roll, city physician of Hadersleben, may have brought back memories of their student days at the Surgical Academy. From the newspaper Roll had learned about Wallich's stay in England and about the project '*Flora Birmanniensis*'.[93] Roll invited him to his home in the Duchy of Schleswig—an invitation that Wallich was unable to accept due to lack of time.[94] In the end there was only a single short visit to his birthplace Copenhagen.[95] He had not seen his relations for a quarter of a century, and it seems astonishing that he had not made the short journey across the North Sea earlier. But botany weighed more heavily, and the purpose for even this visit was not solely for the reunion with his parents, siblings and former companions.

In the early morning of 18 August 1832, the steamship *Sir Edward Banks* left London for Hamburg with Wallich and Bentham on board. Bentham was planning to travel on from Copenhagen to Vienna and reported in detail about the journey in his memoirs. In Hamburg the pair spent a day with Lehmann and at night rented carriage to drive to Lübeck. Bentham complained about the poor condition of the road, which once must have been well maintained, but was now in a deplorable state.[96] The following morning there was time for a walk through the quiet old town, which in Bentham's eyes had also seen better days. The gabled houses were more antiquated than those in Hamburg, the cathedral was simple and lacking in elegance, but St. Mary's Church, the masterpiece of Hanseatic ecclesiastical brick architecture, did meet with his approval.[97]

From Travemünde, they sailed to Copenhagen on the Danish ship *Frederik den Sjette*, but before the relations could be greeted, health checks and customs first had to be passed. In Denmark, there was great fear of an outbreak of cholera, which was already circulating in Hamburg. While Bentham went to the comfortable, but in his eyes somewhat dirty Hotel d'Angleterre, Nathaniel found himself immediately surrounded by his old Danish friends. It is not known exactly when and where he first saw his parents and siblings again, but we may assume that he embraced his closest relations in the afternoon after his arrival, while Bentham struggled with Danish newspapers and shop advertisements in the city centre.[98]

Bentham recorded that all Wallich's close relations were well-established and that during the long period of absence there had been no deaths; on the contrary, the large family had grown. Among them were Nathaniel's nephews Theodor Edvard and Carl Cantor, sons of his sister Nanine, who will be met again some years later in Calcutta. The parents were also in good shape, the mother, now old and small, was delighted with the progress of her now famous son, who lovingly addressed her in Danish as 'min gammel moder'.[99] The wealthy Bentham correctly assessed Wallich's family environment: his relations were not rich, they belonged to the middle class of society, but were even more distinguished by their warm-heartedness. There is no doubt that the family was proud of the eminent botanist; Nathaniel had left Copenhagen 25 years ago young and poor and had returned home as an internationally renowned celebrity.[100]

While Wallich made some official appointments the following day, Bentham visited the herbarium of the Copenhagen Botanical Garden where he found, among other plant collections, the ones Wallich had sent home from the East Indies over the years. He was shocked by the neglect and confusion of the elderly Jens Wilken Hornemann's study and herbarium.[101] At the same time, Wallich paid a visit to the Royal Palace, where he met King Frederik VI and Crown Prince Christian Frederik, later to become King Christian VIII. The Crown Prince in particular showed great interest in natural history research, especially in the further development of the royal palaeontological collection, which was under the direction of the zoologist Henrich Henrichsen Beck. Beck had been commissioned by the Crown Prince to give Wallich a list of desiderata for the collection that he was asked to obtain either through his London contacts or directly from the East Indies.[102] At the end of the day, the Jacobsons invited Wallich and Bentham to a party with tea, music on the pianoforte and a sumptuous dinner.[103]

The great Danish scholar Rasmus Rask, on his visit to India, had been unable to meet Wallich who was travelling in Nepal at the time. Rask, nevertheless, acknowledged the botanist's scientific achievements and later tried to attract his interest, for example by dedicating his 1828 book on the Hebrew calendar to him.[104] Fate again intervened and during Wallich's short visit to Copenhagen, Rask, now seriously ill and close to death, felt neglected. Rask tried to meet him at Wallich's sister Nanine's home, but did not find him there. In the afternoon of the same day, he finally saw Wallich at his parents' house, but, surrounded by a large circle of relations and family members, Rask returned home without having spoken to him, but at least with a book for the university library. He had no choice but to send Wallich a written thank you note the following day, in which he could hardly conceal his disappointment.[105]

The day of 25 August was a splendid and sunny one and Wallich, Bentham, and Ludvig Levin Jacobson set off to visit the botanical garden and Hornemann. In the afternoon, the three met the famous natural scientist and president of the Royal Academy of Sciences, Hans Christian Ørsted.[106] In the evening the society gathered for dinner at the house of his brother, the theatre painter Arnold Wallich.[107] The days passed quickly, the next day sister Nanine gave a farewell party, and the following day the ship left for Travemünde. After an absence of more than two decades Nathaniel had taken no more than five days to visit his parents and siblings in his home country, and at the same time to complete a significant academic program. As a farewell gift, he received a porcelain cup bearing a portrait of his great Copenhagen teacher Martin Vahl.[108]

From Lübeck, they took a different route back to Hamburg, which Bentham considered the worst in the whole of Europe. Around eleven in the evening, while trying to avoid a bump, the carriage hit a stone with one wheel, while another sank into the sand, causing the vehicle to overturn. Wallich was sound asleep at the time and did not wake up until Bentham and their traveling companions descended upon him. A short time later the man who had survived the rigours of travels in Nepal and Burma stood on his feet again and murmured in German 'Ach mein Gott!'[109]

On 15 October, Nathaniel left London, accompanied by Robert Wight, to travel by stagecoach to the port of Deal in Kent, from where he took the *Exmouth* back to India. The children were left with relations in England for further education. Sophia, again pregnant, also stayed on for a while in the home of her ancestors, where in 1833 she gave birth to another daughter Ann; she then followed her husband back to Calcutta. Full of tension and disappointment that he had not completed all the work he had contemplated, Wallich now had to follow the orders of the Company. He wrote to Hooker: 'My distress is beyond all utterance—it is almost beyond endurance, and my nerves are deserting me'.[110] In retrospect, this gloomy assessment is scarcely justified, since Wallich had not only succeeded in distributing the larger part of one of the greatest herbaria ever assembled (which provided research materials for numerous European botanists for generations to come), but had also completed and published one of the most magnificent of all colour-plate botanical books, his *Plantae Asiaticae Rariories*.

NOTES

1. CNH, Wallich letters, Sophia Wallich to Marjoribanks, 3 June 1825.
2. CNH Wallich letters, Wallich to Moloney, 5 November 1827.
3. Ibid.
4. G. Bentham, *Autobiography 1800-34*, ed. by M. Filipauk, Toronto, Buffalo & London: University of Toronto Press, 1997, p. 495, footnote 2.
5. BL IOR, F/4/1139, Board's Collection, Wallich to Moloney, 8 January 1828.

6. Ibid., Moloney to Wallich, 10 January 1828; Farrington, Catalogue, p. 492.

7. CNH, Wallich letters, Wallich to Siddons, 25 February 1828.

8. D. Lowther, A. Sylph & M. Watson, 'Hodgson's Tibetan Mastiffs', twice presented to the Zoological Society of London. *Archives of Natural History*, vol 46, 2019, pp. 220-9.

9. Landsarkivet for Sjælland, QA-035, Engelholm Gods, 1811-52, Wolff family private archive, correspondence 29-8, Wallich to Wolff, March 1828.

10. Wallich, Numerical List of Dried Specimens, nos. 64, 362, 1116, 1160, 2078, 7609, 7659.

11. Lowther, Sylph & Watson, 'Hodgson's Tibetan Mastiffs'.

12. F. Sheppard, *London 1808-70. The Infernal Wen*, Berkeley-Los Angeles: Universiy of California Press, 1971, pp. 2f. 19-45.

13. Ibid., p. 84.

14. CA, A 515, Maclear Mann Papers, 74, Wallich to Mary Maclear, 30 October 1847.

15. Royal Society, Herschel Letters, HS 18.28 Wallich to Herschel, 4 September 1828; ibid., HS 18.29, Wallich to Herschel, 9 September 1828.

16. Ibid., HS 18.29, Wallich to Herschel, 9 September 1828.

17. Sheppard, *London 1808-70*, p. 109.

18. Diary Rasmus Rask, P.S. Ramanujan, pers. comm, 29 November 2016, Rask noted 'Wallichs Guldbryllup' for 28 August 1828.

19. Royal Society, Herschel Letters, HS 18.29, Wallich to Herschel, 9 September 1828.

20. CNH, Wallich letters, Bentham to Wallich, 10 February 1847.

21. RBG Kew, Director's Correspondence, Wallich to Hooker, 52/55, 3 February 1829.

22. Ibid., 52/56, 16 February 1829.

23. Ibid., 52/57, 19 February 1829; ibid., 27 February 1829.

24. Ibid., 52/59, 7 May 1829.

25. Ibid., 52/66, 12 January 1830; ibid., 13 February 1830.

26. Ibid., 52/104, 29 July 1831.

27. BL IOR,F/4/1139, Board's Collection, Wallich to Court of Directors, 29 July 1829; ibid., Minutes of Court, 6 August 1828.

28. Arnold, *The Tropics and the Travelling Gaze*, pp. 154ff.

29. Mägdefrau, *Geschichte der Botanik*, p. 81.

30. RBG Kew, Director's Correspondence, Wallich to Hooker, 52/53, 2 April 1820.

31. Royal Society, Herschel Letters, HS 18.33, Wallich to Herschel, 20 November 1828: 'Mr Robt. Brown has promised to spend the day with me, and if you could honor me also—especy if you could make it convenient to come a little early, we should have some microscopia—insbesondere some Molecules before dinner'.

32. Ibid., Herschel Letters, 18.34, Wallich to Herschel, 22 November 1828.

33. Kind notice by Mark Watson, Edinburgh.

34. Nair, *Proceedings*, vol. 3.2, p. 1995.

35. A. M. Clerke, 'Herschel, Johann Frederick William', *Dictionary of National Biography*, vol. 26, New York, 1891, pp. 263-8.

36. Royal Society, Herschel Letters, HS 18.28, Wallich to Herschel, 4 September 1828; ibid. 18.30, Wallich to Herschel, 8 December 1828.

37. Ibid.

38. R. Desmond, *Kew. The History of the Royal Botanic Gardens*, London: The Harvill Press, 1998, pp. 152ff.

39. RBG Kew, Director's Correspondence, Wallich to Hooker, 52/56, 16 February 1829.

40. E. Wunschmann, 'Lehmann, Johann Georg Christian', *Allgemeine Deutsche Biographie*, vol. 18, Munich: Duncker & Humblot, 1883, p. 144.

41. CNH, Wallich letters, Lehmann to Wallich, 30 September 1830; see also: J.H. Bartels & J.C.G. Fricke, Amtlicher Bericht über die Versammlung Deutscher Naturforscher und Ärzte in Hamburg im September 1830, Hamburg, 1831.

42. J. Helbig (ed.), *Brasilianische Reise 1817-20. Carl Friedrich Philipp von Martius zum 200. Geburtstag*, Munich: Hirmer, 1994.

43. BSB, Martiusiana, II A 2, Wallich to Martius, 24 November 1829.

44. On Nees von Esenbeck's scientific work see B. Hoppe, 'Das naturwissenschaftliche Werk von C.G.D. Nees von Esenbeck als Beitrag zur Entwicklung der Botanik, insbesondere der Systematik', D. Feistauer, U. Monecke, I. Müller & S. Röther (eds.), *Christian Gottfried Nees von Esenbeck. Die Bedeutung der Botanik als Naturwissenschaft in der ersten Hälfte des 19. Jahrhunderts. Methoden und Entwicklungswege*, Stuttgart: Wissenschaftliche Verlagsgesellschaft, 2006, pp. 21-54.

45. Mägdefrau, *Geschichte der Botanik*, p. 81.

46. Ibid., pp. 78-89.

47. BL IOR, F/4/1139, Board's Collections, 15 November 1827.
48. Ibid., 29 October 1828.
49. Ibid.
50. Bentham, *Autobiography*, p. 325; CNH, Wallich letters, extract Committee of Correspondence, 22 September 1831.
51. BL IOR, F/4/961, Board's Collections, Wallich to Moloney, 5 November 1827.
52. BL IOR, F/4/1139, Board's Collections, 15 April 1829.
53. Bentham, *Autobiograhy*, p. 325.
54. RBG Kew, Director's Correspondence, Wallich to Hooker, 52/57a, 21 August 1829.
55. Bentham, *Autobiography*, p. 326.
56. Ibid., p 362
57. A Numerical List of Dried Specimens of Plants in the East India Company's Museum, Collected under the Superintendence of Dr Wallich of the Company's Botanic Garden at Calcutta. See the digital version of the Royal Botanic Garden Edinburgh: http://wallich.rbge.info/
58. CNH, Bentham to Wallich, 16 February 1847.
59. RBG Kew, Director's Correspondence, Wallich to Hooker, 52/57a, 21 August 1829.
60. Bentham, *Autobiography*, p. 333.
61. Mägdefrau, *Geschichte der Botanik*, pp. 126f.
62. Bentham, *Autobiography*, p. 332.
63. Ibid.
64. Cf. correspondence with Mark Watson.
65. Homepage British Museum, Treuttel & Wurtz, http://www.british-museum.org/research/search_the_collection_database/term_details.aspx?bioId=74336, (retreived 23 February 2016).
66. RBG Kew, Director's Correspondence, Wallich to Hooker, 52-5, 3 February 1829; CNH, Wallich letters, Richter to Wallich, 3 June 1829.
67. See for example CNH, Wallich letters, Hunnemann to Wallich, 26 June 1829; ibid., 30 April 1831.
68. This concerned, for example, a consignment in the opposite direction, from Munich to London—see CNH, Wallich letters, Martius to Wallich, 13 December 1831.
69. For another interpretation see A. P. Thomas, *Calcutta Botanic Garden. Knowledge Formation and the Expectations of Botany in a Colonial Context, 1833-1914*, Diss. Phil, London, 2016, p. 105.

70. For example, RBG Kew, Director's Correspondence, Wallich to Hooker, 52/57a, 21 August 1829.

71. For example, BL IOR, F/4/1139, Board's Collections, 21 October, 18 & 19 November, 10 December 1829; ibid., 10 & 17 February & 10 March 1830.

72. BL IOR, F/4/1139, Board's Collections, 5 May 1830; H. J. Noltie, *The Botany of Robert Wight*, Ruggell, Liechtenstein: A.R.G. Gantner, 2005, pp. 8-12.

73. BL IOR, F/4/1139, Board's Collections, Wallich to Auber, 3 April 1830: 'Since my arrival in England I have scarcely been beyond the Suburbs of London, and have not even been able to revisit my Native Country after an absence of 23 years'.

74. BL IOR, F/4/1139, Board's Collections, 13 April 1830.

75. CNH, Bentham to Wallich, 16 February 1847.

76. Harrison, 'Calcutta Botanic Garden', p. 241.

77. Mark Watson, pers. comm., August 2020; Fraser-Jenkins, *First Botanical Collectors*, p. 49

78. Harrison, 'Calcutta Botanic Garden', pp. 242f.

79. Secord, 'Botany on a Plate. Pleasure and the Power of Pictures in Promoting Early Nineteenth-Century Scientific Knowledge', *Isis. An International Review Devoted to the History of Science and its Cultural Influences*, 93/2002, pp. 28-57.

80. BL IOR, F/4/1139, Board's Collections, 26 November 1828.

81. N. Wallich, *Plantae Asiaticae Rariores*, vol. 1, London: Treuttel & Würtz, 1829, pp. 13ff.

82. BL, 2.23.C.11 (47), Proposals for Publishing by Subscription, *Plantae Asiaticae Rariores; or, Descriptions and Figures of a Select Number of Unpublished East India Plants*, London, 1828.

83. *The Magazine of Natural History*, vol. 2, 1829, p. 61.

84. *Det Norske Rigstidende*, 16 February 1829.

85. RBG Kew, Director's Correspondence, Wallich to Hooker, 52 February, 1829.

86. CNH, Wallich letters, Wallich to Treuttel & Würtz, 10 April 1829.

87. Ibid., Richter to Wallich, 25 March 1829.

88. Ibid., Wallich to Richter, 13 August 1829.

89. Ibid., Wallich to Richter, 25 March 1829; ibid., 15 August 1829.

90. H.W. Lack, 'Nees von Esenbeck und die Biodiversität von Gefäßpflanzen', D. Feistauer, U. Monecke, I. Müller & B. Röther (Hgg.), *Christian Gottfried Nees von Esenbeck. Die Bedeutung der Botanik als Naturwissenschaft in der ersten Hälfte des 19. Jahrhunderts*.

Methoden und Entwicklungswege, Stuttgart: Wissenschaftliche Verlagsgesellschaft, 2006, pp. 159, 161; Wallich, *Plantae Asiaticae Rariores*, vol. 3, pp. 70-117: 'Acanthaceae Indiae Orientalis'.

91. BL IOR, F/4/1139, Board's Collections, 21 October 1829.
92. RBG Kew, Director's Correspondence, Wallich to Hooker, 53/151, 17 September 1832.
93. CNH, Wallich letters, Roll to Wallich, 19 April 1829.
94. Ibid.
95. BSB, Martiusiana, II A 2, Wallich to Martius, 19 July 1831.
96. Bentham, *Autobiography*, p. 388.
97. Ibid., p. 388.
98. Ibid., p. 389.
99. Ibid., p. 390.
100. Bentham, *Autobiography*, p. 390: 'His relations are not rich nor high in rank, but warm in their feelings, and elated at seeing him again after a 25 years' absence'.
101. Ibid., pp. 390f.
102. CNH, Wallich letters, List of Desiderata of the Royal Natural History Museum, 25 August 1832.
103. Bentham, *Autobiography*, p. 391.
104. R. Rask, *Den Ældste Hebraiske Tidsregning indtil Moses, efter kilderne auf ny bearbejdet og forsynet mit einer Kårt over Paradis*, Copenhagen: J. Hostrup Schultz, 1828.
105. Diary Rasmus Rask, 24 August 1828; P.S. Ramanujan, pers. comm., 29 November 2016; CNH, Wallich letters, Rask to Wallich, 25 August 1832.
106. Bentham, *Autobiography*, pp. 389f.
107. Ibid., p. 391.
108. CNH, Wallich letters, Boye to Wallich, 27 August 1832.
109. Bentham, *Autobiography*, p. 393.
110. RBG Kew, Director's Correspondence, Wallich to W.J. Hooker, 53/152, 15 October 1832.

CHAPTER 12

Tea

ASSAM AND THE EAST INDIA COMPANY

Wallich took back with him from London interest in a topic that was to become one of the major natural history and imperial debates in India from the mid-1830s, that of tea. His stay in Europe had coincided with the negotiations for an extension of the East India Company's charter in the British parliament. In the new privilege, which was finally granted in 1833, politicians had ruled that the Company should, henceforth, cease its economic activities and limit itself to administration and political rule. In this context, the exploitation of natural resources had largely been shifted to become the preserve of Indian and European private investors. A first phase of British-Indian entrepreneurship began, and among the new stars in the firmament of economic life in Calcutta was Wallich's companion from the Agricultural and Horticultural Society, Dwarkanath Tagore, and his firm Carr, Tagore & Company.[1]

In addition to a strong boost for indigo cultivation and the silk industry, the question of the cultivation of Chinese tea in India—until now grown commercially only in eastern Asia, was again raised. It was known in London and Calcutta that the Dutch had been successfully growing Chinese tea plantations on Java for several years.[2] While still in London, Wallich was asked for his opinion on the subject by the Board of Control, the parliamentary body responsible for overseeing the activities of the East India Company. Wallich, who had taken little interest in tea since the exchange with Edward Gardner about *Camellia kissi* a decade and a half earlier, was on the spot and quickly presented the Board with a statement on the prospects of tea cultivation in India based on the Chinese plant.[3]

In view of his previous disinterest a certain political opportunism might, perhaps, be read into his statement in the report that the time was now ripe.[4] The best chances of success would be to identify areas in India with the greatest similarity in terms of vegetation to China's tea-growing regions: 'If it should appear that there is an identity or a considerable similarity in their vegetable productions, it is probable that any plant taken from one will thrive in the other'.[5] This idea, taking into consideration principles of plant geography that he had already displayed in Nepal, was henceforth, to support his efforts to establish tea cultivation in India. Banks' and Macartney's idea of transferring Chinese tea plants to India experienced a rebirth.

Apparently unnoticed by Wallich at the time, a small, but in the long-term an all-important step towards tea production in India had already been taken. Its actors were stationed in Assam in the north-east, which had only entered the sphere of influence of British India in the mid-1820s. It was European merchants and Company servants who independently made a remarkable discovery; in the jungles of Assam they identified a plant whose leaves had the same characteristics as those of Chinese tea, except that they were considerably larger. These people soon asked themselves if the plant might be a wild relative of the Chinese plant. This impression was confirmed by the fact that some indigenous peoples in the surrounding mountainous regions of eastern Assam prepared the leaves as an infusion in the same way as the Chinese and Europeans did with 'real' tea.[6]

Three individuals are to be credited with making this plant a little better known—David Scott, Robert Bruce, and Andrew Charleton. The judge, David Scott, founder of the hill station of Cherrapunji and one of the first Company representatives in Assam, is said to have discovered plants of the supposed wild tea at the village Gubroo Purbat near Jorhat in 1826 and sent it to various Europeans, but apparently not to Wallich himself.[7] The explorations of Robert Bruce proved to be more significant. Before the outbreak of the first Anglo-Burmese War, he had settled as an independent merchant in the small village of Sadiya in the far east of Assam, worked for various princes, and finally married a local woman. His brother Charles commanded a British gunboat on the Brahmaputra.[8] Robert was one of the Europeans who knew the border region between Assam, Burma, and China best and was possibly the first to discover specimens of what would later be described as *Camellia sinensis (var. assamica)* and to share this knowledge with British administrative officials. Wallich had no direct contact with Bruce, which again supports the impression that tea had been of little interest to him for many years.[9] Independently of Bruce, Lieutenant Andrew Charleton of the Assam Light Infantry also discovered the mysterious plant at Sadiya. He reported to the Agricultural and Horticultural Society in Calcutta that the locals brewed its dried leaves with hot water and that the resulting beverage had the same taste as Chinese tea.[10]

In fact, Assam represents a botanical treasure chest. Topographically, the region is in a protected position, surrounded by mountains on three sides—the Khasia and Jaintia hills to the south, the hills of Nagaland to the southeast and to the north the great wall of the Himalayas. Lying between them is the wide and majestic valley of the Brahmaputra, one of the mightiest rivers on earth, which joins the lower reaches of the Ganga and finally flows into the Bay of Bengal. Until the beginning of the nineteenth century, the Brahmaputra Valley was ruled by the independent kings of the Ahom Dynasty. For a long time, they had succeeded in keeping the country free of invaders, or in rapidly driving out those who did succeed. But eventually their rule fell to Burmese power in 1816. The Burmese took control of the country for several years.[11] After the first Anglo-Burmese War and the Peace of Yandabo of 1826, Assam finally fell into the hands of the British. While the East India Company brought the western part of the country under its direct control, it transferred power in the eastern Upper Assam to the last Ahom King, Purandar Singh, as a tributary lord.[12] The surrounding mountainous countries, however, escaped from colonial rule for a considerable time.[13]

The British takeover brought Assam further into crisis, as

tax collection put heavy pressure on the peasant population. The main problem, however, was that Assam produced hardly any goods for the Indian or European markets so that no money came into the country, while British administration and troops proved costly.[14] Against this backdrop, the new charter of the East India Company brought about a fundamental change. While large-scale entrepreneurship in India had previously been prohibited to private European companies, enormous investment opportunities now presented themselves. Even though the private purchase of land remained prohibited, Europeans were now able to lease it at favourable rates. This was especially true for what were denoted 'waste-lands', including the extensive savannah and jungle areas in Assam and the surrounding mountains. These, despite what European imperialists might have wished to believe, were by no means 'uninhabited'.

It was Francis Jenkins, the British governor of Assam, who made the public aware of the opportunities now available. Captain Jenkins had been 'Commissioner and Agent to Governor-General in Assam and north-east parts of Rangpur' since early 1834 and thus the highest-ranking representative of the colonial power on the spot, residing in Cherrapunji on the southern slope of the Khasia hills. He envisaged the future development of an export-oriented agricultural production of the region entirely in the hands of Europeans: the only thing missing was a suitable crop. A year after the renewal of the Company's charter, evidence was growing that there might indeed be a wild relative of Chinese tea growing in eastern Assam. It was Jenkins who first formulated the idea of sending a botanical expedition there in order to confirm the identity of the plant as tea.[15]

THE TEA COMMITTEE

Governor-General Bentinck pushed for an answer to the tea question as early as the beginning of 1834, and initiated the establishment of a Tea Committee, thus, bringing the debate within an institutional framework. Membership of the Committee was rapidly decided, and it was composed of eleven members, two of whom were Indian. Among the Indian members was Radhakanta Deb, whose grandfather had been secretary to Robert Clive. Although conservative, and an opponent of liberal reforms in India, he was a great thinker.[16] It seems surprising that Wallich himself was not initially asked to chair the Committee and the post, instead, went to George James Gordon, a merchant of the trading house Mackintosh & Co. in Calcutta. It was only when Gordon left for China that the management was temporarily transferred to Wallich.[17]

The leading question put before the Committee was not so much botanical as economic in nature; it was to find out to what extent tea could be planted and commercially used in India.[18] The aim was to develop a concept for the introduction and cultivation of Chinese tea in the territory of the East India Company and to find out the best way to obtain seeds, seedlings and technical expertise from China.[19] At this point there was no mention of using the supposedly native Assam tea.

The Committee and the Government were well aware of the difficulties involved in transferring plants and knowledge from China to India, because it was forbidden by the Chinese government. The first consideration was, therefore, how to make indirect contact with the closed country. To this end, it was considered that a suitable person should be sent to Penang and Singapore to make contact with Chinese intermediaries, who would in turn seek to obtain healthy Chinese tea plants.[20] Such a person was quickly identified—George James Gordon, the chairman of the Tea Committee himself.[21] Wallich, despite his experience in Penang and Singapore, but approaching his fiftieth birthday, was never suggested for the role.

At the same time, the Committee suggested to the government that plantations (the 'experiment') be established in India. In the spirit of the new Charter, these were rapidly to be transferred into private ownership after an initial experimental phase.[22] In order to be informed as precisely as possible about the best possible locations for future plantations, it was decided

Plate 12.1: T. Morris, Radhakanta Deb, oil painting.
(Victoria Memorial Hall, Kolkata)

to contact various gentlemen in the country parallel with Gordon's trip.[23] For already at the initial meeting it was contended that there must be areas in India suitable for experimental planting, but that the details of such localities were still too little known. Three regions, however, were immediately highlighted: the foothills of the Himalaya, the recently occupied Assam, and 'the Neilgherries' (the Nilgiri Mountains in the south). From the outset, the Committee made efforts to identify suitable locations in the Kumaon region where Hugh Falconer, Superintendent of the Saharanpur Botanical Garden, was to play a decisive role.[24] Robert Bruce was also commissioned to prepare future tea gardens in eastern Assam.[25]

The importance given to the subject is shown by the fact that Gordon left Calcutta by ship for the east as early as June 1834.[26] It was expected that he would return not only with tea plants, but also with up to fifty experts in their cultivation and processing. While Falconer and Bruce simultaneously showed great zeal, difficulties soon became apparent. Only one month after his departure, Gordon discovered that it would not be as easy as hoped to attract tea specialists to India. The prospect of a sea-voyage in itself proved to be a stumbling block for would-be Chinese experts from far inland.[27]

It was the indefatigable Jenkins, having moved from Cherrapunji to Guwahati, who for the time turned the Tea Committee's gaze in a different direction. If it was not possible to transport Chinese tea and experts to India by sea, then it might be possible overland. It was not far from the Chinese province of Yunnan over the mountain passes into the Burmese Ava and from there on to Assam. Lieutenant Charleton stated that the journey through the mountains from the Chinese border to Sadiya would take only thirty days.[28]

At the same time, Gordon contacted Karl Gützlaff, a Lutheran missionary knowledgeable about southern China. On 23 January 1835, after long decades, Chinese tea seeds once again reached the Calcutta Botanic Garden where, to Wallich's delight, they proved to be fresh and good. The Committee immediately ordered the seeds to be forwarded to the prospective tea-growing regions for the establishment of experimental gardens—to Kumaon, the Nilgiris, and Assam.[29]

At this time, the focus was still exclusively on Chinese tea plants. Wallich, perhaps reminded of the exchange with Gardner about the *Camellia kissi* in Nepal, would long believe that the samples collected in Assam represented a completely different species of *Camellia* from the Chinese one. However, his assessment may also have been influenced by the fact that the few specimens that reached him from eastern Assam were usually in a very poor state of preservation after a journey of several months, so that a definitive botanical identification was not possible. Wallich was careful, but apparently took no steps to try to get better specimens.[30]

However, on 8 November 1834, Charleton sent better leaves and seeds from Sadiya in a box to Jenkins in Guwahati who forwarded them to Calcutta.[31] Based on these, and at the end of the year, Wallich was finally able to make a positive identification, the significance of which would only later become apparent. Wallich wrote: 'It was ascertained that the Tea plant was a native of Hindostan, on its remotest North-Eastern frontier of Assam, growing wild and used as tea, although in a peculiar manner by the Singpo's and other barbarous tribes inhabiting those parts, stretching to the southwards and eastwards through a vast extant of (partly Burmese) territories until these spontaneous or natural tea forests reached the Chinese frontier province of Yunnan, where the shrub is most extensively cultivated and the leaf prepared in the Chinese fashion'.[32] Wallich finally made it clear that the tea plant is naturally native to India. Further tea samples, which were now packed in corked bottles and, thus, better preserved, followed and supported Wallich's assessment.[33] Gradually, the fact that two varieties of the tea plant exist became clear—the fine China tea (*Camellia sinensis* var. *sinensis*), which is adapted to higher altitude, and the more robust Assam tea (*Camellia sinensis* var. *assamica*), which is native to the warm and humid foothills of the Brahmaputra valley. Innumerable hybrids of these two varieties today produce a wide spectrum of tea cultivars.[34]

Once the tea plant was clearly identified as native to India, Wallich immediately understood the enormous potential of this discovery. The significance was not greatly of a botanical nature, but it served the economic and imperial interests of the Company. That tea grew in India as well as in China allowed the possibility that, long ago, it might have spread naturally from India to China, which would give the British all the more reason to have a right to the tea plant.[35]

Between January and March 1835, a remarkable change in the views of the Tea Committee took place, to which Wallich, with his change of opinion, made a major contribution. If there was wild tea in Assam, would it even be necessary to try to extract more tea plants out of China under difficult circumstances? It should actually be sufficient to build up an independent tea production using the existing Chinese seeds already sent by Gordon as well as Assam tea seeds that were available in any quantity. While until then all hopes had been pinned solely on Chinese tea, both varieties were now to be tried at the same time. The Tea Committee, therefore, recommended to the Government that Gordon be recalled from China.[36]

In September 1835, Gordon was back again. However, contrary to initial hopes, it had become apparent in the meantime that it would not be possible to bring Chinese experts to India overland, so it was decided to send him to China a second time. The Government approved this second about-turn of the Committee and again provided funds.[37] Gordon's second excursion proved partly successful, and in May of the following year, Wallich reported that three or four Chinese experts had reached Calcutta from Canton and were already on their way to Assam.[38]

IN THE JUNGLES OF ASSAM

In addition to the efforts to obtain expertise from China, the Tea Committee also tried to gain as much knowledge as possible about the home of the wild tea plant in eastern Assam. Immediately after it was established at the end of 1834 that tea was native to India, it was decided to send an investigative expedition to Assam.[39] Since Gordon was still away, Wallich himself was to undertake this mission. According to his own statement, he initially had no interest in participating himself, citing as a reason the poor state of his health. As modesty was not one of Wallich's characteristics, it is likely that he was unwilling to face a demanding expedition because he really was feeling old, ill and exhausted.[40] Finally he agreed to join and his companions, two Assistant Surgeons, were quickly nominated: William Griffith as botanist and John McClelland as geologist.[41]

McClelland and Griffith had known each other since their student days in London and Wallich, through Lindley, had met Griffith as a medical student at University College London. Griffith had contributed some outstanding drawings of microscopic details to *Plantae Asiaticae Rariores* from which Wallich entertained high hopes of the brilliant young man. In the postscript to the third volume he wrote of Griffith, about to set out for India, that 'future exertions . . . will shed much additional light on the botany of that country'.[42] Even after Griffith had accepted a position as an Assistant Surgeon in Madras Wallich made every effort to further the career of the young natural scientist. The later, truly deadly enmity between the pair, was not yet foreseeable. John McClelland was also a Company physician, whose interests were in zoology and geology,[43] and was chosen as the tea question was by no means a purely botanical topic—soil was also important, for which geological knowledge was required.

The aim of the expedition was to identify the areas in which the wild tea plant grew and to find out whether, and if so, where in Assam growing conditions were comparable to those in southern China. Wallich made it clear that it was not possible or even necessary to know all the details about the regions in question and that local climatic data could also be useful.[44] In this is an awareness of Humboldt's views on plant geography, but Wallich did not develop the idea any further.

On 29 August 1835, the small group left Calcutta.[45] The time was wisely chosen; there was still heavy rainfall in Assam, but the dry season would follow from November to January, when the fieldwork was to take place. Wallich was to be on the road for a total of nine months and while little information is available from his own hand, we do have the travel journal of his companion Griffith, printed posthumously in 1847.[46]

The route was up the Hooghly northwards to Pabna. Steadily upstream the group continued their journey, through a seemingly endless jungle of reeds and channels of the Ganga, to Sirajganj.[47] It must have been a feast for the eyes when, on 14 September, the Khasia hills became visible on the northern horizon, rising above the monotony of the river system. The three of them stayed only briefly in Sylhet, where since Roxburgh's days a nursery of the East India Company had been located.[48] The air became progressively cooler until they reached a serpentine path that led directly to the plateau of Cherrapunji. On the steep slopes of the Ghat were remarkable limestone rocks with caves, where a great variety of ferns and mosses flourished abundantly in the humid environment. As Griffith wrote of the mosses: 'I gathered four species of four genera without moving a foot'.[49]

On 10 October 1835, Cherrapunji was reached.[50] This was one of the recently established 'hill stations', where Europeans were able to recover their health in the cool mountain air. Cherrapunji had one disadvantage: in the hot season (i.e. during the months between April and September, when Europeans repaired there from the hot and humid climate of the Bengal lowlands), it rains ceaselessly and extremely heavily. To the east of the settlement was a deep valley clothed on its western side in a dense jungle of small trees, and on its opposite side, facing the bungalow where the three were accommodated, was a series of deep ravines presenting 'a most picturesque and varied surface'.[51]

Wallich found Camellias, which suggested a plant-geographical closeness with southwest China,[52] and Griffith also came to the conclusion that, from the vegetation around

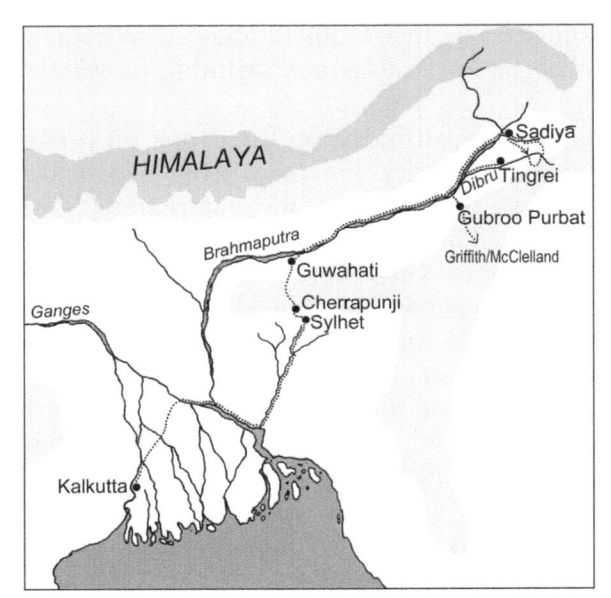

Plate 12.2: The expedion to Assam, 1835-1836.

Cherrapunji, 'an affinity is indicated with the botany of China'.[53] Wallich proudly reported to the Tea Committee: 'Our botanical and geological collections are already immense'.[54] At the same time, McClelland analyzed soil samples that he had received from China via Gordon and compared them with the local findings.[55]

From Cherrapunji, the group crossed the Khasia hills, where many previously unknown plants were collected and soil samples taken.[56] At the hamlet of Surureem they saw large trees of what is now called *Exbucklandia populnea* and, for the first time on the trip, *Rhododendron arboreum*. Between here and the village of Moflong the group split—while Wallich and McClelland took the main route, Griffith chose a side route from which he was able to see for the first time the spectacular panorama of the Himalayas to the north of the wide Assam valley.[57] That Griffith's route was for botanical reasons, rather than an indication of later problems is suggested by his discovery of two new species, a climbing gentian (*Crawfurdia campanulacea*), and a submerged aquatic plant of fast flowing streams that Wallich intended to name after his young colleague as 'Podostemon griffithii' (now *Hydrobryum griffithii*).

With increasing altitude, the flora took on progressively European characteristics. For three days, rain held them in the small village of Moflong before the reunited group went downhill again. The coniferous trees gradually disappeared and made way for oaks and other deciduous trees. The weather cleared up and the panorama of the Himalayas was spectacular, as Griffith wrote: 'Altogether this view is the finest which, in my limited experience, I have ever seen'.[58] With a shiver, the three may have passed the tombs of Lieutenants Burlton and Beddingfield near the bungalow at Nongklaw, where the soldiers had been killed by locals six years earlier.[59]

On the way down into the Assam valley Wallich, to his delight, came across an abundance of one of his favourite ferns, *Polypodium wallichianum*, which a self-righteous and already carping Griffith blamed as the cause of a delay: 'I may accuse

[it] with justice of being an additional reason for our benight-ment'. On 23 November, the British garrison at Guwahati on the Brahmaputra was reached, where Captain Jenkins awaited the small party.[60] It is not possible to determine exactly, when the party reached Sadiya in the east of the Brahmaputra Valley, where they were received by Robert Bruce and from where they made a shorter expedition to their ultimate goal, the land of the Singpho tribe. Wallich, Griffith and McClelland first headed south and came across wild tea plants for the first time on 16 January 1836 in the middle of the jungle near the village of Kujoo. Griffith recorded in his diary: 'This day we gave up to the examination of the tea in its native place. It occurs in a deep jungle to the south of the village, and at a distance of about three miles from it. Our route thither lay through first a rather extensive grass jungle, then through a deep jungle'.[61] From Kujoo they continued further south to the small river Manmoo, where more specimens of wild tea were found. The way back led the group a little further east on the Lohit to Sanpura, twelve miles above Sadiya, from where they returned to Bruce on 29 January and remained at Sadiya for seven days before returning to the west.[62]

Already at the beginning of November 1835, a shipment of Chinese tea seedlings from the Botanic Garden, sprouted from the seeds sent by Gordon, had been sent to Assam on eight boats. Seven boats finally reached their destination at the mouth of the river Dibru into the Brahmaputra, where Wallich, Griffith, and McClelland received the shipment, but many of the plants were in an unfortunate state.[63] Of 20,000 seedlings sent out, only 8,000 reached their destination in a good condition, and Wallich found that those that had been trans-ported in pots were in much better shape than those in crates. He suggested that the plants should be sent not to Sadiya, as originally planned, as transport there by water was dangerous due to the rapids in the upper reaches of the Brahmaputra. Instead, he decided on Saikowa, a place further to the west.[64]

On 16 February the group set off from the mouth of the Dibru for another trip inland. The march lasted three days, accompanied by incessant rain, before they reached the village of Rangagura. The heavy rainfall made the journey difficult, as Wallich plaintively reported: 'This is awfully distressing, considering the rough mode of travelling which we are obliged to adopt, and the horrid jungles we have to pass through'. Even these adverse circumstances did not slow him down in his thirst for results, as he continued: 'But *jacta est alea*, the object of my mission must be accomplished this season, unless the obstacles should become absolutely insurmountable. My only fear is that the seasons have changed manners, and that the rains have been anticipating their usual period by a couple of months or so, and that this, in fact, is the beginning of them. Such is Assam!'[65] But the rain eventually eased off and now and again the sun appeared between the clouds. A few miles before Rangagura the group met a jungle with tea plants: 'The spot appears to be very small, but although it is very probable that there are others in the same direction'.[66] Wallich was of the opinion that the land could undoubtedly be bought by the Company at a low price.[67]

From Rangagura they went to Tingrai, where they again saw wild tea plants: 'The tea looks remarkably healthy and vigorous, consisting of plants of all ages, between quite young seedlings and tall shrubs of 12, 16 to 20 feet in height, with stems mostly under an inch in diameter, and in no instance reaching beyond two inches; almost all the full-grown plants had abundance of seed-buds, a few had still some flowers on them'.[68]

While Wallich was travelling with his companions a letter arrived from a British major in Jorhat. It was reported that the tea plant was still to be met where it had been discovered many years earlier, about 18 to 20 miles south of that town in Gubroo Purbat. It was here that tea was sighted for the last time on 8 March.[69] In total five localities for the wild Assam tea were identified during the course of the journey.

In Gubroo Purbat on 9 March, the group finally split up. While Griffith and McClelland set off for further field research in the direction of Nagaland and across the Burmese border to Ava, Wallich started his return journey to Calcutta. By the time the three parted a deep rift had opened up between Wallich and Griffith. The younger man later complained bitterly about Walllich, that he had hindered his search for plants, destroyed material already collected, and claimed some as his own discoveries. McClelland took Griffith's side in the dispute and later described Wallich as worn-out and solely intent on returning as quickly as possible out of concern for his health.[70]

After the trip, Wallich forbade his young competitor to publish his own results, some of which contradicted his own, but Griffith, nevertheless, did so two years later in a small, polemical paper in which he fiercely attacked and tried to play down the performance of his former patron.[71] Griffith's bitterness may also have been due to the fact that Wallich himself failed to publish anything about the Assam expedition and only gave a brief summary of it in a letter to Radhakanta Deb. In this, he stated that the journey had resulted in the certainty that the tea plant was at home not just in the far east of the Brahmaputra valley, but much further west than had previously been believed—namely in areas that were firmly in the grip of the Ahoms as tributary princes of the East India Company. Behind this was a clear message to policy makers: 'Instead of being obliged to establish new plantations, which would have been indispensable, if the shrub had only been ascertained to grow among the Singpoo, we have natural forests readily prepared for our experiments among our own, far more civilized friends and allies'. He clearly believed that 'a good saleable and potable tea will be produced ere long from our Assam forests'.[72] Wallich suggested that the natural tea jungle be put under European management, and to cultivate tea there with the help of Chinese experts.[73] Even more, he recognized the great opportunity this would present for India and, in prophetic words, wrote: 'Patience and perseverance will enable us to compete with China in respect to the superior sorts of that great and invaluable comfort of life'.[74] Almost metaphorically, he saw tea as a necessity as well as a means of well-being and implicitly presented himself as its mediator.

Wallich, however, left the carrying out of further cultivation trials to others. It was above all thanks to Jenkins and Bruce, and their deep knowledge of the regional languages and customs, that European knowledge of the existence and use of the Assam tea plant had developed. The first planting trials in the Assam valley had quickly made it clear that Chinese tea would not grow there due to unsuitable environmental conditions, and thereafter the British concentrated mainly on the Assam variety. Already in October 1836, Bruce received six Chinese, who were well-versed in tea processing and who produced a first batch of usable Assam tea.[75]

In 1838, the first lots of it appeared on the British market and a year later it was first offered at a London tea auction. Contrary to initial fears, the strong, dark infusion met with a positive response in Britain; in the same year an Assam Company was founded as a focus for European private sector involvement in the far north-east of the subcontinent. The foundation stone was thus laid for large-scale tea production, but at a considerable social and ecological cost. In 1864, ten years after Wallich's death, there were already 12,000 ha, the plants grown being mainly hybrids derived from the Chinese and Assamese varieties.[76]

NOTES

1. Kulke & Rothermund, *Geschichte Indiens*, p. 310.
2. Krieger, *Tee*, p. 236.
3. N. Wallich, 'Observations on the Cultivation of the Tea Plant, for commercial purposes, in the mountainous parts of Hindustan; drawn up at the desire of the Right Honourable C. Grant, President of the Board of Control for Indian Affairs', *Parliamentary Papers*, vol. 39, 1839, document 63.
4. Ibid., p. 15.
5. Ibid., p. 14.
6. Krieger, *Tee*, pp. 186f.
7. White to Wallich, 24 December 1835, in R. Gordon (ed.), *Copy of Papers from India relating to the Measures adopted for Introducing the*

Cultivation of the Tea Plant within the British Possessions in India, [London], 1839, p. 52.

8. A. Macfarlane & I. Macfarlane, *Green Gold. The Empire of Tea: the Remarkable History of One of the Most Important Plants Known to Mankind*, London: Ebury Press, 2004, pp. 124, 130.

9. Jenkins to Wallich, 6 January 1835, in Gordon, *Copy of Papers from India*, p. 37.

10. Quoted from Macfarlane & Macfarlane, *Green Gold*, p. 130.

11. Geit, *History of Assam*, pp. 290-8.

12. Macfarlane & Macfarlane, *Green Gold*, p. 120.

13. Ibid., pp. 126f.

14. A. Guha, *Medieval and Early Colonial Assam*, Calcutta & New Delhi: K.P. Bagchi & Co., 1991, pp. 145-8.

15. Jenkins to Secretary Tea Committee, 7 May 1834, in Gordon, *Copy of Papers from India*, pp. 33f.

16. Nair, *Proceedings*, vol. 4,2, pp. 1923f.

17. Extract India Revenue Consultations, 12 May 1834, in Gordon, *Copy of Papers from India*, p. 18.

18. CNH, Wallich letters, Wallich to Radhakanta Deb, 20 May 1836.

19. BL IOR, F/4/1586/64547, Board's Collections, Macsween, 1 February 1834.

20. Gordon, *Copy of Papers from India*, p. 17.

21. BL IOR, F/4/1586/64547, Board's Collections, Macsween, 1 February 1834.

22. Gordon, *Copy of Papers from India*, p. 17.

23. Ibid. pp. 16f., 21.

24. Wallich to Traill, 28 June 28, in Gordon, *Copy of Papers from India*, p. 29.

25. Macnaghten to Wallich, 11 February 1835, ibid., p. 40.

26. Tea Committee to C. Macsween, 23 July 1834, ibid., p. 27.

27. Gordon to Wallich, 24 July 1834, ibid., p. 30: 'The difficulty is enhanced in our case by our requiring men that have been born and brought up at a distance from the sea, and to whom the idea of a long voyage to a barbarous land is likely to be very terrific, independently of natural aversion to long separation from friends and family'.

28. Charleton to Jenkins, 30 March 1835, Gordon, ibid., p. 45.

29. Wallich to Macnaghten, 24 January 1835, ibid., p. 42.

30. Krieger, *Tee*, pp. 187ff.

31. Charleton to Jenkins, 8 November 1834, in Gordon, *Copy of Papers from India*, p. 35.

32. CNH, Wallich letters, Wallich to Radhakanta Deb, 20 May 1836.
33. For example, Wallich to Macnaghten, 11 August 1835, in Gordon, *Copy of Papers from India*, p. 47.
34. Krieger, *Tee*, pp. 26ff.
35. CNH, Wallich letters, Wallich to Radhakanta Deb, 20 May 1836.
36. Tea Committee to Macnaghten, 12 March 1835, in Gordon, *Copy of Papers from India*, p. 39: 'The discovery of the growth of the tea in Upper Assam, and the reports which we have received of the facility of multiplying it to any extent by seeds, renders all supplies from China unnecessary, inasmuch as there is every reason to suppose, that seeds even of the best sorts of tea, will produce only inferior sorts of plants when removed from their native soil'.
37. Ibid., 18 September 1835, in Gordon, *Copy of Papers from India*, p. 47.
38. CNH, Wallich letters, Wallich to Radhakanta Deb, 20 May 1836.
39. Ibid.
40. Ibid.
41. Tea Committee to Mactnaghten, in Gordon, *Copy of Papers from India*, p. 38.
42. Wallich, *Plantae Asiaticae Rariores*, vol. 3, postscript.
43. Nair, *Proceedings*, vol. 4.1, p. 174.
44. Gordon, *Copy of Papers from India*, p. 13: 'But since it does not often happen that accurate or sufficient information can be obtained upon those points in remote parts of the world, we must have recourse to the general laws that have been found to prevail in the distribution of heat and the other conditions of the atmosphere, with regard to latitude and other well-known circumstances, and a judgement has to be formed from a calculation of probabilities, instead of from a comparison of exact data'.
45. W. Griffith, *Report on the Tea Plant of Upper Assam*, Calcutta: N.N., [c. 1838], p. 2.
46. W. Griffith, *Journals of Travels in Assam, Burma, Bootan, Afghanistan, and the Neighbouring Countries*, ed. John McClelland, Calcutta: Bishop's College Press, 1847.
47. Ibid., pp. 1f.
48. Gordon, *Copy of Papers from India*, p. 52.
49. Griffith, *Journals*, p. 6.
50. Wallich to Tea Committee, no date, in Gordon, *Copy of Papers from India*, p. 48.
51. Ibid., p. 4.

52. Wallich to Tea Committee, no date, ibid., p. 49.
53. Griffith, *Journals*, p. 7.
54. Wallich to Tea Committee, no date, in Gordon, *Copy of Papers from India*, p. 49.
55. McClelland, *Examination of Soils in which the Tea Plant is Cultivated in China*, in ibid., pp. 49-52.
56. Griffith, *Report on the Tea Plant*, p. 2.
57. Griffith, *Journals*, p. 8.
58. Ibid., p. 9.
59. Ibid.
60. Ibid., p. 11.
61. Ibid., p. 14.
62. Griffith, *Report on the Tea Plant*, p. 2.
63. Wallich to Grant, 12 February 1836, in Gordon, *Copy of Papers from India*, pp. 53f. 'I regret to say, that a great number of the seedlings have died on their way there far, owing partly to the protracted durations and difficulties of the journey . . . and the numerous rats which infest the boats.'
64. Ibid.
65. Wallich to Grant, 19 February 1836, in Gordon, *Copy of Papers from India*, p. 58.
66. Ibid.
67. Ibid.
68. Wallich to Grant, 26 February 1836, ibid., pp. 59f.
69. Gordon, *Copy of Papers Received from India*, pp. 66f.
70. Arnold, *Plant Capitalism and Company Science*, pp. 925f.
71. Griffith, *Report on the Tea Plant*, p. 3 'At the expiration of this period the deputation had been in Assam bearly four months, of which about two were passed on a most uninteresting river the Burrampootur. And in addition to this disadvantage it returned in every instance, but one, by the `same route.'
72. CNH, Wallich letters, Wallich to Radhakanta Deb, 20 May 1836.
73. Ibid.
74. Ibid.
75. Macfarlane & Macfarlane, *Green Gold*, pp. 135-9.
76. Krieger, *Tee*, pp. 190f.

CHAPTER 13

The Medical College

TEACHING STUDENTS

Despite some interesting botanical finds, the expedition to Assam had shown that Wallich's star was on the wane. He was no longer unchallenged for his expertise in the field of Indian botany. A younger generation, brought up in the natural system, had grown up and increasingly questioned the authority of someone wedded to the Linnaean tradition. In the middle of the jungles of Assam, Wallich had celebrated his fiftieth birthday, which in colonial India of the time made him an old man. Instead of going on the offensive as he would once have done, he chose the path of quiet retreat.

After returning from Assam, however, his daily work routine resumed. The first priority continued to be the care of the plants, the herbarium material newly collected since his return from London, and the maintenance of his communication network. In the garden steps were taken to provide each plant with the most favourable living conditions. For plants sensitive to moisture raised beds were created, the so-called 'high nursery', which were better drained than the others.[1] The Governor-General himself, Lord Auckland, took an interest in the development of the garden and in 1836 sent a magnificent specimen of a palm tree to be planted there.[2] The damage caused outside by storms, floods or drought, was mirrored inside by the havoc wrought by ants. The cabinets containing the precious dried plant specimens could only be protected from the voracious insects by having their feet placed in bowls of water. One employee was busy solely to refill the quickly evaporating water.[3]

The dispatch of seeds, plants and herbarium material to institutions and individuals continued unabated, as the herbarium started to accumulate more. Approximately 2,00,000 individual plants left the garden between 1836 and 1840 to destinations all over the world.[4] A special role was played by John Forbes Royle, the former director of the Saharanpur botanical garden, who had returned to England and at East India House was responsible for the reception of plants and seeds from India.[5]

However, the garden was not only a site of research, but was also a popular place of recreation for the inhabitants of Calcutta and their guests.[6] This also applied to Wallich himself, who, to his personal delight, was given a small building there known as a 'summer house'.[7] Perhaps, he used this in his limited free time to read the books and magazines that regularly reached him from near and far.[8] One of the most popular attractions was the mighty banyan tree, with its numerous aerial roots, which was probably already more than fifty years old,[9] and is still one of the great sights of the garden.

Plate 13.1: Charles D'Oyly, Banyan tree, *c*.1830.
(Victoria Memorial Hall, Kolkata)

In addition to fulfilling his duties in the Garden, Wallich was keen to pass on his knowledge to a younger generation. He had always been concerned with the advancement of promising young botanists including William Jack and William Griffith. From 1837, he lectured at the Medical College of Calcutta. Since the late eighteenth century medical care for Europeans had mainly been provided by European doctors but the idea arose to train Indian personnel in Western medicine to serve in subordinate roles and for the benefit of the local population. In 1822, the 'Native Medical Institution' was established in Calcutta, where Indian doctors were taught. Courses in traditional Indian medicine were likewise offered at the Sanskrit College. After criticism of the training in 'native' medicine was voiced, it was decided to establish a college for the training of Indians in Western medicine and the previous courses of study were dissolved. On 28 January 1835, the Medical College opened its doors and barely a month later began its work with 49 Indian students. The training was to last four to six years to be completed with an examination for qualification as a 'Native Doctor'.[10]

Wallich, who had worked closely with Indian staff for many years, was open-minded towards the project. Remembering his own practical studies in Copenhagen with Holbøll, he considered it as important to provide professional training for young doctors in the field of botany and took it upon himself to do so. He already had some experience as during the 1820s Indian students of the 'Native Medical Institution' had occasionally visited the garden.[11] His perseverance paid-off and on 1 February 1837 Wallich was appointed professor of botany at the Medical College.[12] From then on, he gave regular lectures, on Tuesdays and Thursdays, on general and medical botany, for which he did not prepare notes. The lectures were informal, based on his wealth of experience and illustrated with real plants, presumably both dried and living. He also offered practical exercises in the garden including exercises in microscopy.[13]

The courses meant a considerable expenditure of time for

Wallich since the college was in the north of Calcutta, a long distance away from the Garden. The most comfortable way to reach it was by boat on the Hooghly, though after this a mile and a half still had to be covered on foot or by carriage. This was not, however, always practical as the outward journey could only be taken on an incoming tide with which the lecture schedule often failed to conform. Most of the time, there was no choice but to cross the river by ferry from the Ghat at his house to Garden Reach and from there to travel the seven miles on the east bank through Calcutta by carriage.[14]

The high-point of the botanical session at the College was the annual award of botanical prizes by the Governor-General. For this purpose, Wallich brought live plants from his garden to the College for a practical identification exercise. Wallich enjoyed it when the examination sometimes turned into a professional discussion between students and teachers, allowing the spotting of talented students. In 1842, for instance, the best three were Suttkai Dutt, Oondatje and Prasanna Kumar. Dutt received a large microscope as the first prize, while Oondatje, in second place, was given a pocket microscope.[15] There was also talent among the students of European origin, which Wallich encouraged whenever possible. One such student was Charles Simons, who developed a passion for botany and later worked as a pharmacist in Guwahati, where he studied the flora of Assam with Jenkins.[16]

A heavy workload was unlikely to leave Wallich's commitment to the Medical College unaffected and in 1839-40 his work for the Tea Committee kept him away from teaching for more than a year.[17] He had hoped to have his life made easier by an increase in the allowance for his travels to the College, but was brusquely dismissed with the remark that teaching was one of his official duties and, moreover, he was reminded that he did not pay to live in Roxburgh House.[18] Times had changed and Wallich was no longer as fast or efficient in carrying out official duties as he had once been. Increasing age was doubtless one reason, but the result was dissatisfaction on the part of the Government, which noted

NATH¹ WALLICH.M.D.F.R.S.
Professor of Botany.
Medical College Calcutta.

Plate 13.2: Nathaniel Wallich as a teacher
at the Medical College, Calcutta.
(British Library, London)

with growing displeasure that Wallich no longer replied to the official letters addressed to him, or only after a delay of up to two months.[19] He also found it increasingly hard to cope with his enormous private and scientific correspondence and his apologies to correspondents, who had to wait ever longer for an answer, became more frequent.

Contact with his Danish compatriots in nearby Serampore gradually diminished and latterly he exchanged ideas and letters only with Johannes Rehling and Joachim Otto Voigt. Rehling was a veteran in the Danish East Indies. Originally from Odsherred on the island of Zealand, he had been appointed bailiff of Tranquebar in 1804 and remained there during the British occupation and started a family. Over time, he rose to become member of the government of Tranquebar, returned to Denmark for a while, then became head of the Serampore colony in 1834. Four years later, he returned to Tranquebar as Governor and died there in 1841.[20] Wallich occasionally visited Rehling in Serampore or invited him to the Botanic Garden,[21] and Rehling supplied him with Danish and German literature. But Wallich's increasing workload left its mark on his contact with his fellow countryman and Rehling, himself bearing the signs of age, did not hesitate to remind him to write to him more often and to reply more quickly.[22]

While Rehling had little interest in botany, this did not apply to Joachim Otto Voigt from the Duchy of Schleswig. Voigt had studied at the Surgical Academy in Copenhagen about fifteen years after Wallich and in March 1827 took up the post of Royal Danish Surgeon of Serampore. There, in 1830, he married Rachel Shepherd Marshman, one of the daughters of the prominent missionary. The fact that Voigt was about to deputise for Wallich as Superintendent of the Garden at Shibpur for several months in 1842 indicates a relationship of trust and mutual respect.[23]

FAMILY MAN

Sophia had returned to India, where in 1835 the last of the couple's children was born, a daughter Fanny. But at the end of the 1830s, we find Sophia back in England, close to her sister Mary Smith near Hull. The weaker her husband's professional position in Calcutta became, the more he became involved from a distance in the planning of the lives of his children, who were also in England. For them, he could imagine nothing but a life in India, either in the service of the East India Company for the boys, or as a caring wife of a Company servant in the case of his daughters.

Wallich's sense of family duty extended to the children of his sister Nanine, who was married to the merchant Levin Isaac Cantor. Wallich's nephew, Theodor Edvard Cantor, was six years older than his own son George Charles, and was, therefore, the first to be taken under his wing. Cantor studied at the Surgical Academy in Copenhagen and then at Halle where he received his doctorate with a thesis entitled *De absessu lymphatico.*[24] His uncle had met Cantor briefly in the summer of 1832 but did not turn his attention to him until after his return to India. Wallich finally invited the young man to Calcutta, probably with a hint as to how he could impress the elite of Calcutta, since he brought with him prehistoric artefacts from Denmark as a gift for the Asiatic Museum – a method of establishing contacts that by now was probably rather outmoded in view of the growing professionalisation and institutionalisation of academic life.[25]

In India, Theodor Edvard developed his existing interest in zoology under Wallich's supervision and specialized in snakes,[26] but he was also interested in fossils including some bones that he found in a sedimentary layer at Diamond Harbour.[27] He compiled a catalogue of the collection of snakes and fish in the Asiatic Museum, which he presented to the Asiatic Society and was accepted as a member.[28] Next to Hodgson and McClelland, Theodor Edvard Cantor was one of the most significant contributors of zoological material to the Museum.[29]

Wallich tried to secure an appointment for his nephew in the service of the East India Company, and on 19 July 1836 wrote a cleverly worded letter to Governor-General Lord Auckland. He praised Cantor's zeal and his deep knowledge of natural history and said that he was strongly built and with a healthy physical constitution. He suggested that Cantor could accompany a natural history expedition to Darjeeling in the foothills of the Himalayas in the service of the Company or undertake studies in some other place that required investigation.[30]

Though this approach failed, Theodor Edvard was given temporary employment with the Marine Survey, and he also worked at the General Hospital in Calcutta. To get ahead it would be necessary to present himself personally at East India House,[31] and in February 1839, Cantor was in London to apply for admission to the Company's medical service. Through the mediation of his uncle, he was able to provide an impressive list of testimonials from Wallich's old companions Herschel, Brown, Lindley, and Royle. He passed the examinations and was appointed Assistant Surgeon on 12 September 1838. Cantor returned to India as a surgeon-naturalist and in 1840-1 undertook a research trip to China on behalf of the Company on which he published some of the results. In 1853, he was promoted to Surgeon and six years later to Surgeon Major.[32]

Relationship between Nathaniel and his second nephew, Carl Cantor, is unclear. He also probably reached Calcutta at the end of the 1830s, launched his own business and founded the house of Charles Cantor & Co at 3 Fairlie Place in Calcutta; he also acted as an agent for the shipment of plants between Calcutta and Great Britain,[33] but later went bankrupt and returned to Europe.[34]

It was now time to turn to his own two oldest children. His eldest son, George Charles, born in 1815, had spent a short time in Denmark after leaving India in 1820; after that he went to Britain to his mother's relations. He attended the Grammar School in Reading, went on to study at King's College, Aberdeen, and then pursued medicine in Edinburgh where he graduated with an MD in 1836. Finally, he followed in his father's footsteps and applied for admission to the Company as an Assistant Surgeon in 1838. The application came from Wallich himself, who would have liked to see his son in Bengal near him. George first had to undergo a medical examination with the senior physician of Hull General Infirmary, which he passed with flying colours, after which he was officially nominated as a candidate.[35] Sophia pursued the matter vigorously from Hull, and the appointment as Assistant Surgeon was soon confirmed in London.[36] George Charles, then, went to India, but his orders took him not to his father in Calcutta, but to a posting in distant Punjab.

The couple's eldest daughter Hannah was particularly close to her father during his last years in India. Already as a small child, she had accompanied her parents as far as the Nepal border but had then travelled to England with Sophia in 1824. It is no longer possible to determine when Hannah returned to India but on 17 April 1841, at the age of twenty, she married Captain William Biddulph in Calcutta, and in January of the following year Nathaniel and Sophia became grandparents for the first time.[37]

Nathaniel had last seen his parents in 1832 during his brief visit to the Danish capital. Seven years later, his mother died, and his father gave up the household and moved into a rented apartment. His life savings had been spent, and in the last years of his life he had to be supported by his children until his death in 1843.[38]

THE BLUE MOUNTAINS

Few new opportunities to contribute to botanical knowledge or practice opened up for Wallich after his return from Assam, and then only vicariously—the most important again related to mountainous regions of South Asia. Wallich himself had climbed the mountains surrounding the Kathmandu valley as well as those of Ava, and the Khasia Hills in Assam. The latter continued to attract his interest and an occasion for further explanation came from Britain. In 1836 the 6th Duke of Devonshire, a keen botanist and horticulturist, sent one of his gardeners, John Gibson, to hunt for plants in northern India. The Duke had large greenhouses both in London at Chiswick House, and an even more spectacular one at Chatsworth (the model for his gardener Joseph Paxton's famous Crystal Palace), for which he wanted exotic plants.[39] With Wallich's support Gibson travelled to the Khasia Hills from where he regularly sent living plants to Calcutta, which Wallich took care of and forwarded to Europe. He was greatly impressed with Gibson's collection 'which would in all probability exceed in value anything of the sort ever seen or received [in Britain]'.[40]

At the beginning of July 1836, Gibson was in Cherrapunji, where precious orchids were to be collected. Wallich took the opportunity to send a group of his own plant collectors to assist Gibson, but also to enrich the Calcutta collection, camouflaged as the best way to ensure the success of the plant hunt for the Duke.[41] After their return, he applied for funds for another collecting trip to the hills,[42] but, contrary to previous occasions, the Government flatly rejected his request on the grounds that his plant collection system had supposedly not proved to be effective. In view of Wallich's rich experience since Singh and de Silva collection tours, this accusation seems grossly unfair, but is clear evidence of Wallich's gradually weakening position of influence with the government.[43]

Nevertheless, he was also to be involved with one final excursion into applied botany, if only from his desk. This related to the Nilgiri Hills in the south, to which he gave importance for the introduction of new crops. The Nilgiris had been acquired by the British in 1799 because of the Third Mysore War, but were still largely unknown at the beginning of the nineteenth century. British rule was at first largely nominal and hardly any European had ever seen the wide plateau high up in the hills, where drinking water in bottles froze at night. Francis Buchanan had reached the edge of the hills on his Mysore Survey in 1800, but it would be almost two decades before Europeans made further progress. In 1818, the Company employees John Wish and Nathaniel Kindersley reached the plateau, allegedly in search of a gang of tobacco smugglers. The botanical development of the Nilgiris began with enthusiastic reports about the pleasant, cool climate, and the almost European vegetation. The following year, John Sullivan, Collector of Coimbatore and the highest-ranking British official in the region, climbed the hills in person for the first time. He reported clear, cool streams in the gentle slopes and that malaria, omnipresent in the plains, was unknown there. He encountered a luxuriant flora and told of roses, marigolds, wheat, barley, peas, opium and garlic cultivated by the local tribal populations.[44] In the same year, Sullivan set off again, this time in the company of the French botanist Jean-Baptiste Leschenault de la Tour. Leschenault had been sent by the French government to study the natural history of India; he soon succumbed to the diseases of the lowlands, but the mountain climate would suit him well.[45]

More and more frequently the prospect of establishing a 'hill station' in the Nilgiris was discussed, and in 1822, Sullivan had the first permanent house built in Ootacamund, 'Stone House', which became the nucleus of imperial, European possession of the Nilgiris. The founder of European Oota-camund hoped that in the long run European settlers, if at the expense of the tribal people, could live from agriculture alone, which is why knowledge from the Calcutta Botanic Garden about the acclimatization of plants became important to him. Simultaneously, Sullivan's project of creating a sanatorium in the cool Nilgiris for Europeans plagued by the heat and diseases of the plains soon took on more concrete form.[46]

Wallich took notice of the quick development of the Nilgiris and used the inquiries of British officials from the region to expand his contacts there. His first contact was not Sullivan, who was then on home leave, but the British soldier Lieutenant William Munro, later to become a General. Born in Glou-cestershire, Munro was stationed in the southern Indian city of Bangalore in 1834 where, soon after his arrival, the keen naturalist began to botanize and to write a manuscript, *Hortus bangalorensis*.[47]

Munro had written to Wallich seeking advice and was sent seeds to try out in Bangalore. To restore his health, Munro travelled to the Nilgiris, with an Indian draughtsman, in the first half of 1836. Like his predecessors, he was overwhelmed by the abundant flora, including large numbers of crypto-grams and wrote to Calcutta: 'The Neilgherries offer a superb field for a botanist'.[48] He considered many of the plants growing there to be unknown and planned to make a her-barium with duplicates.[49] Wallich also received information from Munro about the occurrence of timber in the Nilgiris and asked him to send seeds and herbarium material, which resulted in a significant transfer of plants.[50]

The contact with John Sullivan came slightly later. Already informed by Munro about the vegetation in the Nilgiris, Wallich approached him in 1839 with a request for plants: 'In case you should be able to indulge me with some such of the production of your delightful Hills you would confer a very great favour upon me indeed by granting me your powerful aid in this respect'.[51] Sullivan obliged and sent Wallich specimens and seeds on several occasions, some of which were passed on to other correspondents, others cultivated at Shibpur.[52]

Wallich also shared Sullivan's vision of naturalising European crops in the Nilgiris to implement European-style agriculture there. So partly by sea, and partly overland by banghy,[53] he sent Sullivan Indian grains and seeds that he had received from Royle at East India House, such as red currants and European strawberries, and, from Chile, the oil-rich seeds of *madia sativa*, which he also arranged to be sent for trial in the Nilgiris. Of potential economic importance were the trees that might provide useful timber, so Wallich also forwarded seeds of Himalayan trees such as oaks and the cedar (*Cedrus deodara*) from the mountains between western Nepal and Afghanistan.[54] Wallich was still acting as a global intermediary of plants and botanical knowledge, an art he had mastered since the beginning of his career.

Tea was again a topic and already during the course of the debates of the Tea Committee seedlings of Chinese tea had arrived in the Nilgiris in 1835 from Gordon's delivery from China. These had been taken to an experimental garden in the village of Keti, but had not been properly planted and were quickly neglected. Two years later, the Swiss botanist George Samuel Perottet found the plants almost dead but managed to revive them by exposing their roots. On returning to the hills the following year he found them laden with flowers and fruit.

In October 1839, eighteen boxes of living Assam tea plants were waiting to be shipped from Calcutta to Madras for Sullivan in Ootacamund. At the same time Wallich also promised to send tea seeds from Assam as soon as he had received some.[55] In contrast to the Chinese tea plants, which are accustomed to higher altitudes, the Assam tea from the lowlands of the Brahmaputra were unsuited to the climate of the Nilgiris,[56] which at this stage were not yet considered for a large-scale European plantation economy; the first commercial tea plantation in the Nilgiris did not appear until 1856.[57]

Through his interest in the Nilgiris, Wallich came into contact in the 1830s with a rather new kind of botanist: the commercial plant collector, who made a business out of his knowledge and love of flora and earned his living by the sale of herbarium specimens. Around the same time there was a growing demand for 'exotic' plants from the temperate mountain climates of India that might thrive in the climate of west and central Europe—for example rhododendrons.[58] Such plants or their seeds were largely collected by professional plant hunters and the major destination was Britain. One who ended up as such a collector was Bernhard Schmid from Jena in Germany. He had originally worked in south India as a missionary for the Church Missionary Society (CMS) and pursued botanical interests in the Nilgiris, which he discussed in correspondence with Wallich,[59] but in 1838 he returned to Europe, broken by the loss of three sons and because he found no support for a mission in the Nilgiris. Eight years later Schmid returned to the hills, on his own initiative, with his wife and six children, and supplemented his CMS pension by selling herbarium plants in Europe. He planned to run his own nursery for 'exotic' plants over which he had first contacted Sir William Hooker, who referred him to Wallich. But by now, with only a year left in India, Wallich had no longer any interest in how such a project could benefit the Calcutta Garden.[60]

One of Wallich's most frequent correspondents was the Scottish Company surgeon Robert Wight, the most productive botanist of his time in southern India. Of him, 231 letters are recorded in the index to Wallich's correspondence, but of these only three remain. Wight was the last of the Company's official Madras Naturalists and when this post was scrapped in 1826, he sent his collections from this period to East India House. In 1831, Wight returned on furlough to Britain, and one of the first people he sought out was Wallich, over shared interests in the distribution of their respective enormous herbaria. Wallich amalgamated the early Wight collections sent to India House with the East India Herbarium distribution, but Wight distributed his subsequent collections on his own, like Wallich's, accompanied by a lithographic catalogue. After they had both returned to India, their correspondence continued, and one of the most important subjects in the 1840s was over the publication by Wight of 419 of the Roxburgh Icones, which were sent to Madras in the form of pencil copies possibly made by Wallich's artist Lachman Singh. Wight unintendedly, and regrettably, became involved in the Wallich–Griffith falling out, which continued after Griffith's death in 1845. The issue concerned the posthumous fate of Griffith's specimens and publication of his papers, and an accusation made by Wight, due to a misunderstanding, about Wallich's removal and distribution of the Calcutta herbarium. Although Wight apologised to the always hyper-sensitive Wallich, their friendship never fully recovered, even after they had both retired to Britain.[61]

NOTES

1. BSB, Martiusiana, II A 2, Wallich to Martius, 14 February 1848.
2. Ibid.
3. Candolle & Radcliffe-Smith, 'Nathaniel Wallich', p. 330.
4. Ibid.
5. CNH, Wallich letters, Wallich to Royle, 17 February 1841.
6. Bille, *Steen Billes Bericht*, p. 129.
7. RBG Kew, Director's Correspondence, J.D. Hooker to W.J. Hooker, 7 April 1850.
8. For example, CNH, Wallich letters, Wallich to Sullivan, 17 October 1839.
9. Bille, *Steen Billes Bericht*, p. 130.
10. J. Bhattacharya, 'From Hospitals to Hospital Medicine. Epistemological Transformation of Medical Knowledge in India', G. Stollberg, C. Vanj & E. Kraas (eds.), *Außereuropäische und europäische Hospital- und Krankenhausgeschichte*, Berlin: Lit-Verlag, 2013, pp. 62-9.
11. CNH, Wallich letters, Wallich to Adam, 8 October 1825.
12. Ibid., Wallich to Secretary to Government of Bengal, 30 September 1840.

13. Ibid.
14. Ibid., Wallich to Bushby, 14 May 1842.
15. CNH, Wallich letters, Wallich to Council of Medical College, 1 April 1842.
16. RBG Kew, Director's Correspondence, 54/275, Jenkins to Hooker, 21 July 1850.
17. CNH, Wallich letters, Wallich to Secretary to Government of Bengal, 30 September 1840.
18. Ibid., Bushby to Wallich, 18 May 1842.
19. Ibid., Wallich letters, Wallich to Secretary to Government of Bengal, 30 September 1840.
20. Larsen, Dansk Ostindiske Personalier og Data, entry 'Rehling, Johannes'.
21. CNH, Wallich letters, Rehling to Wallich, 31 January 1830.
22. Ibid., (c. 1837).
23. Ibid., Voigt to Wallich, ca. January/February 1838.
24. J. Collin, article 'Cantor, Theodor Edvard', in *Dansk Biografisk Lexikon*, vol. 3, ed. by C.F. Bricka, Copenhagen: Gyldendal, 1889, p. 352.
25. Nair, *Proceedings*, vol. 4.1, p. 212.
26. Ibid., vol. 4,1, p. 77.
27. Ibid., p. 243.
28. Ibid., vol. 4,1, p. 269; ibid., vol. 4,2, p. 1914.
29. Ibid., vol. 4,1, p. 249.
30. CNH, Wallich letters, Wallich to Lord Auckland, 19 July 1836.
31. BL IOR, L/MIL/9/386, Assistant Surgeons' Papers, Groves to Clarke, 2 April 1839.
32. Nair, *Proceedings*, vol. 4.2, p. 1914.
33. RBG Kew, Director's Correspondence, 54/275, Jenkins to W. J. Hooker, 21 July 1850; ibid., 4 December 1850.
34. F. Mount, *The Tears of the Rajas: Mutiny, Money and Marriage in India 1805–1905*, London: Simon & Schuster, 2015, p. 351.
35. BL IOR, L/MIL/31385, May 1838.
36. BL IOR, L/MIL/9/385, Assistant Surgeons' Papers, N.N. to Clark, 18 May 1838.
37. *The Asiatic Journal and Monthly Register for British and Foreign India, China, and Australasia, May-August 1841*, London, 1841, p. 132.
38. FT-1840, C9482.
39. E. Bradlow, 'Nathaniel Wallich: A Man for all Seasons', *Quarterly Bulletin of the South African Library*, vol 52,3, 1998, pp. 98f.
40. CNH, Wallich letters, Memorandum respecting the Duke of Devonshire's Gardener to Lord Auckland, May 1836.

41. CNH, Wallich letters, Wallich to Government, 27 June 1836.
42. BL IOR, P/13/24, Bengal Public Consultations, Wallich to Government, 4 August 1837.
43. Ibid., Government to Wallich, 9 August 1837.
44. Ibid., p. 108.
45. Ibid., pp. 108f.
46. Ibid., pp. 110f., 116.
47. J. Archer, *General William Munro, C.B., 39th Regiment – Soldier and Plantsman*, Homepage The Keep Military Museum. Home of the Regiments of Devon and Dorset, http://www.keepmilitarymuseum.org/info/general+william+ munro+c+b++39th+regiment+-+soldier +and+plantsman, (retrieved 5 September 2016).
48. CNH, Wallich letters, Munro to Wallich, 24 July 1836.
49. Ibid.
50. Ibid.
51. Ibid., Wallich to Sullivan, 17 October 1839.
52. Ibid.
53. The Banghy is a shoulder yoke carried by persons, to which loads of the same weight were attached on both sides.
54. CNH, Wallich letters, Wallich to Sullivan, 21 September 1840.
55. Ibid., 17 October 1839.
56. Ibid., Sullivan to Wallich, 21 September 1840.
57. A. Raman, 'Georges Guerrard-Samuel Perrottet. A Forgotten Swiss French Plant Collector, Experimental Botanist and Biologist in India', *Current Science*, vol. 107,9, 2014, p. 1609.
58. CNH, Wallich letters, Wallich to Hodgson, 24 January 1841.
59. CNH, Wallich letters, Schmid to Wallich, 16 October 1835; ibid., 28 October 1836; ibid., 23 February 1838.
60. CNH, Wallich letters, Schmid to Wallich, 25 August 1845: 'and shall make collections of dried Hill plants for sale in England'.
61. For more on Schmid see Noltie, *Robert Wight*, pp. 111f.

CHAPTER 14

At the Cape of Good Hope

PLANT HUNTERS FROM GERMANY

The years following his return from Assam were largely ones of decline, which threatened to overshadow Wallich's earlier considerable achievements. Major field explorations were a thing of the past and only from a distance could he even passively observe current debates on the natural history exploration of new regions. Old companions like Robert Brown and Hooker had long since outstripped him and younger, ambitious natural scientists such as William Griffith and Joseph Dalton Hooker were establishing their own considerable reputations. The mere collection and description of new species had gone out of fashion and classification was more concerned with synthesis, which frequently involved the reduction of species to synonym. Botany was no longer restricted to systematics and with the work of Augustin-Pyrame and Alphonse Pyrame de Candolle, Ludolf Christian Treviranus and Franz Julius Ferdinand Meyen, the sub-discipline of plant physiology had also grown out of its infancy;[1] plant geography (and even the inklings of ecology) had developed from the basis established by Humboldt, and the microscopy was becoming increasingly important. In retrospect Wallich's last great journey, which was to South Africa, turns out to have been more of a retreat into the private sphere than the discovery of a new field of work. On the other hand, the botanical treasures of the southern tip of the African continent, with some of the richest flora in the world, were still only partly explored, and even in Wallich's place of retreat one or two new things could perhaps be discovered.

For almost two centuries South Africa, with its Mediterranean climate, had held great fascination for European botanists. One of the major reasons for the establishment of Cape Town, situated at the junction between the Atlantic and Indian Oceans, was horticultural. In 1652 the Dutch United East India Company established its first settlement there, though modest in scale. Next to the fortress, which was initially built of clay and wood, was the 'Company Garden'—an extensive area in which to grow vegetables and other crops to provision passing Company ships. In this was also the beginnings of South African viticulture.[2]

Conflicts with the semi-nomadic tribes of the Khoi have occurred again and again since then, and only gradually did Dutch freemen establish private farms outside the Company grounds in the early days, especially beyond the prominent Table Mountain along the course of the small Liesbeek River. By the end of the eighteenth century, Cape Town and its environs fell to the British, but it was not until the middle of the subsequent century that the loose settlement began to develop into a real city—one that was heavily shaped by slavery.[3]

From the very beginning, Europeans admired the enormous variety of plants and animals in the region, and during the eighteenth century the area became of increasing interest to botanists. Francis Masson, for example, was first sent to the Cape for two years in 1772 to collect for Sir Joseph Banks, through which many varieties of *Erica*, *Mesembryanthemum*, *Oxalis* and *Pelargonium* were introduced to Britain.[4] On Masson's second visit of 1786-95, he accompanied the Linnaean pupil Carl Peter Thunberg.[5] The Company garden no longer served the sole purpose of growing vegetables, and became more like the Calcutta garden, a base for botanical research.[6]

The growing city performed another important role to that of provisioning of ships. Before the establishment of the hill stations in South and Southeast Asia, the Cape was the most easily accessible place with a favourable climate for the recuperation of Europeans living in India suffering from exhaustion and disease. These visited the cape in ever increasing numbers and the country houses along the Liesbeek River became particularly sought-after addresses.

In 1798, William Roxburgh went to the Cape for the sake of his health, but during an eighteen-month stay, he travelled long distances by cart and on horseback, actively collecting plants.[7] Above all, however, Roxburgh recognised the enormous importance that the Cape could play as an acclimatisation station for the transfer of plants between Asia and Europe and suggested the establishment of a botanical garden independent of the old Company Garden. Even if this plan did not immediately work out, he took back to India a large number of herbarium specimens and sent many to Britain. Some of these, including 200 species of *Erica* and 100 of the family *Proteaceae*, were still with him in Calcutta in 1812, but in the course of time they increasingly fell victim to insect damage.[8] It is likely that Wallich became acquainted with these specimens in his early visits to Roxburgh from Serampore.

In the 1820s, South Africa increasingly became a domain of German amateur and professional collectors, but they were to gain importance in Wallich's network only after his return from Assam. His first contact at the Cape was Carl Ferdinand Heinrich Baron von Ludwig, a nobleman from southwest Germany who had applied for a vacant position as a pharmacist in Cape Town. After completing a pharmaceutical apprenticeship, he set off for the settlement in 1805 and in 1816 married the wealthy widow Alida Maria Altenstaedt, who gained a name in her own right as a successful entrepreneur in the production of snuff and beer. His wife's income not only enabled the Baron to live a life of leisure, but the freedom to pursue his passion for research on natural history. This included extensive collecting tours, and in 1826, he sent a large number of herbarium specimens to the Royal Natural History Museum in Stuttgart. Two years after a visit to his home country, he acquired a piece of land on Kloof Road near Cape Town, where he founded a private botanical garden that became known as Ludwigsburg Garden.[9] Here, he planted large numbers of plants, not only native South African ones, but also ones from Europe, America, and Australia.[10] Among other celebrities, as the baron proudly reported to Wallich, these included Wallich's friend from London days, John Herschel, who visited the garden during his astronomical studies at the Cape in 1834.[11]

In 1833, Ludwig had sent Wallich, among other things, a yam from the South African dry regions, which apparently fulfilled its purpose of establishing an exchange. The following year Wallich returned the favour with a letter and 'a box of the rarest and best seeds of India'. Ludwig sowed some of these in pots in his botanical garden and others he sent on to the Eastern Cape region.[12] At the same time, Ludwig arranged an introduction to the botanist Karl Wilhelm Ludwig Pappe, who came from Hamburg, but with whom Wallich appears to have had little contact.

Wallich's connections in South Africa also included Karl Ludwig Philipp Zeyher, who came from the German town Dillenburg and had learned the gardening trade in the Schwetzingen park. Zeyher profited from the gradual commercialization of collecting, by which he was enabled to make a living. He had set off from Germany for the East in 1822 with the collector Franz Sieber, but instead of travelling to Mauritius with Sieber as originally planned, Zeyher got stuck at the Cape. There he entered into a business partnership with Christian Friedrich Ecklon, a plant collector from the Duchy of Schleswig.[13] In 1837, Zeyher wrote to Wallich requesting plants from India for the acclimatisation garden he planned. He asked for specific plants, above all rare or hitherto little-known species, which were apparently easy to sell in Europe,[14] but communication between the scientist Wallich and the commercial plant collector Zeyher seems not to have developed greatly.

Ecklon had gone to Cape Town in 1823 having, like Baron Ludwig, initially trained as a pharmacist. Already during his first stay in South Africa, he botanized and published on the plants of the lily family of the Cape region. Five years later he returned to Germany with a large collection of plants, which he distributed to scholars at home, including Lehmann in

Hamburg. While in Europe, Hornemann arranged a scholarship for him to enable a further stay at the Cape. From 1829, Zeyher and Ecklon initially collaborated, and while Ecklon worked in the Eastern Cape region, Zeyher travelled north towards the Orange River but became disappointed with Ecklon and the two parted ways again.[15]

In 1833 Ecklon returned to live in Hamburg with another large collection and published the Flora of South Africa under joint authorship with Zeyher. Botanical and zoological samples were sent to Copenhagen and Kiel and in 1838 he received an honorary doctorate from Kiel. In the same year, he set off on a third voyage to the Cape, from where he did not return except for a short visit to Europe in 1844.[16]

CAPE TOWN

Wallich's links with South Africa were thin until the early 1840s, and the initiative to develop them came more from German collectors at the Cape than from himself. More surprising, therefore, is the deep interest in the region that came about in 1842, but it was probably more a reflection of his deplorable mental and physical state than from scientific considerations. At the end of 1841, Wallich had suffered from cholera, which followed a certain degree of official fatigue and resignation that had developed over the previous years. As almost a decade had passed since his last stay there, he briefly considered a furlough in Europe, but once again his tried and tested method gained the upper hand—the idea of combining sick leave with botanizing in an area still unknown to him. As he wrote to Hooker: 'I need not tell you, my highly valued friend, that I will by no means remain idle in this glorious part of the world'.[17]

Wallich obtained several medical certificates in early January 1842, which confirmed the urgent need for sick leave. For several months, however, he could not bring himself to make the decision to leave Calcutta. The hesitation was, perhaps, since his position with the Government had weakened, and he obviously had difficulty in finding someone of whom he approved to deputise for him at the Garden. Such an appointment would be of some significance as it was far from certain that the botanist, already approaching sixty, would return to live at Roxburgh House or instead move from the Cape to European retirement. Wallich's main consideration was, at all costs, to prevent the appointment of William Griffith, who had meanwhile consolidated his reputation as a talented and promising botanist. For the time being, he succeeded in appointing his compatriot from Serampore, Joachim Otto Voigt, as his deputy.[18]

Towards the middle of the year, however, his poor health could hardly be ignored and allowed of no further delay, so Wallich finally submitted the certificates to the Government, with a request for a quick approval of the intended voyage.[19] Voigt took over the garden on Wallich's departure and immediately started to compile a catalogue, which was later published posthumously under the title *Hortus Suburbanus Calcuttensis; A Catalogue of the Plants which have been Cultivated in the Hon. East India Company's Botanical Garden, Calcutta, and in the Serampore Botanical Garden.* However, Voigt's health was also weakened and, only a short time after Wallich's departure, he himself went to England where he died soon after.[20] When Voigt left India Wallich was already in South Africa, from where he could no longer prevent his enemy Griffith from finally being entrusted by the Government with the management of the Garden.[21]

Wallich reached the Cape of Good Hope in August 1842, and stayed there for more than a year and a half. During the voyage, he had regained strength and the plan for a longer botanical expedition with tent and bullock cart through the Cape Colony began to mature.[22] The weather on his arrival was changeable: cool, rainy days were followed by plentiful sunshine.[23] In any case, it was a welcome change from the sultriness of Bengal. He first took up an accommodation in St. George's Street in the town centre, but later moved out into the green suburbs.[24] So, some time later, we find him in Liesbeek Cottage beside the picturesque Liesbeek River, an area frequented by visitors from India seeking rest and re-creation, but at the same time not far from Cape Town.[25] Here, he was surrounded by gardens and an abundance of nature: 'Good God what a flora', as he wrote to Hooker.

Already in the first few weeks the botanist was a much sought-after conversation partner. Among the guests at Liesbeek Cottage were Thomas and Arabella Roupell, also on leave from India, with whom he made a friendship that would last for many years. Roupell was a servant of the East India Company in Madras, while his wife Arabella cultivated her passion for drawing and painting plants. When Wallich retired to London a few years later he took a selection of her drawings with him, which he showed to Arabella's brother-in-law George Leith Roupell, who was later to become Wallich's own physician. Wallich then showed them to Sir William Hooker and together they made a selection of eight of the drawings for publication. Paul Gauci (son of Massimo who had made the plates for *Plantae Asiaticae Rariores*) made the lithographs, which were published as a book in 1850 under the title *Cape Flowers by a Lady* with text by William Henry Harvey and a dedication to Wallich.[26]

Wallich did not find it difficult to establish good relations with the European members of the community and in this way made contact not only with local plant collectors and professional scientists, but also with members of the political elite, as he had done decades before in Calcutta. From then on he was a regular guest at Government House, hosted by the Governor Sir George Napier and his wife, and he came to know senior military officials and John Fairbairn, one of the leading colonists and editor of the *South African Commercial Advertiser*. He visited the garden of Ludwigsburg and ex-changed plants with Baron Ludwig.[27] The botanical harvest of his efforts was considerable, and he sent numerous dis-patches of material back to Calcutta.[28]

Wallich also developed an interest in the flora of the Cape Colony in the hinterland of the city. A Mr Versfeld from Stellen-bosch enthusiastically assured him of his support in botanising and wanted to undertake his own collecting expedition of several days to collect plants for Wallich. Mrs Versfeld, as he wrote, was also keen to botanise for the famous Danish botanist and Versfeld even hired staff to help with the preparation of herbarium specimens—'two young ladies to dry your plants'. Other young ladies were also busy collecting plants for him under the guidance of a German missionary, but the outcome of these endeavours is unknown.[29] Wallich also corresponded with the famous missionary and subsequent discoverer of the Victoria Falls, David Livingstone. When Livingstone was in Kuruman in the north of the country, Wallich asked him to send him samples of regional crops that might be suitable for cultivation in India. Livingstone obliged and a package duly arrived in Calcutta after Wallich's return there.[30]

Soon after his arrival Wallich met Ecklon, who, at the time, was mired in deep poverty. As in his first years in Calcutta, he responded to the distress of a fellow countryman, even if not completely unselfishly, because through Ludwig's mediation Ecklon entered Wallich's service as a collector. Wallich arranged simple accommodation and clothing for him and ensured that he was provided with regular meals and wine. But he also offered Ecklon paid employment and gave him plant specimens to dry and press for a fee.[31]

From December 1842, Wallich's closest friendship was with Thomas and Mary Maclear. Thomas Maclear was born in Ireland, had studied medicine in London and married Mary (*née* Pearse) from Bedford. The marriage produced a total of eleven children. Astronomy developed into Maclear's great passion; he acquired mathematical knowledge and began his own telescopic observations. He became a close friend of John Herschel and it is, therefore, possible that Wallich had already met Maclear during his stay in London, or at least heard of him. In Biggleswade, England, Maclear established his own observatory, equipped with instruments, some of which had been made available to him by the Royal Astronomical Society. A special research focus was developed on the occultations of the sun and the moon, on which he published extensively.

The result was that Maclear was offered the position of royal astronomer in Cape Town. His contacts with Herschel were to prove not the only stroke of luck for his work, he was also fortunate in his assistants in Cape Town. The first of these was Charles Piazzi Smyth and William Mann the second, who later became his son-in-law. With the best instruments of the day, the three of them devoted themselves to the southern night sky at the Cape, but also to comets and the planets Mars, Uranus, and Neptune. The highly talented Smyth was also one of the pioneers of photography and in the 1840s experimented in South Africa with the then new technique of calotype.[32]

An important topic under discussion at the time was whether the Earth was a perfect sphere, which at that time was calculated accurately by constructing meridians extending hundreds of kilometres in a north-south direction. One of Maclear's largest projects was the meticulous remeasurement of the meridian running through the Cape Colony, which had already been surveyed 80 years earlier by Nicolas-Louis de Lacaille. To this end, Maclear and his staff repeatedly went on extended trips to the hinterland, during which he also regularly made meteorological observations. At the same time he was committed to the exploration of the interior of Africa. Maclear became a member of the 'Cape of Good Hope Association for Exploring Central Africa', which sent its own expeditions to the north, but also supported David Livingstone.[33]

From his first days in the Colony, Wallich regularly visited the Maclears at the Royal Observatory.[34] They also became friends in private, and Wallich found the sort of home he had for so long missed with Mrs Maclear and her numerous children. Now and again, they attended church together and on 21 December 1842 Mary Maclear noted in her diary Wallich's first overnight visit to the Royal Observatory. On Christmas Day, Wallich took the children on an excursion by cart, and he was also a guest on New Year's Eve.

THE CEDERBERG MOUNTAINS

To answer the question of whether the globe was flattened at the South Pole as it was by now known to be at the north, an expedition was planned in 1842 to extend Lacaille's Meridian further north,[35] and Wallich was invited to join.[36] Thomas Maclear planned first to head towards the mouth of the Oliphant River in the northwest, where extreme daytime temperatures prevailed during the southern summer months, and then to move further inland. Versfeld, Wallich's acquaintance from Stellenbosch, warned that the plants there would be withered at that time of year and predicted: 'In the plains you will be roasted and eaten up by the flies.'[37] Wallich was not to be put off, because he was attracted by the Cederberg Mountains, about 200 kilometres from Cape Town, where he presumed there would be an abundance of largely unknown plants.[38]

Originally, the journey was supposed to last about a month, but in the end, it lasted for six. While Maclear travelled by ship along the west coast with the equipment, Wallich and Mann went overland.[39] On 2 January 1843, they set off with horses, bullock carts and plenty of provisions, to be largely independent of supplies from farms. They were accompanied by three Malays and one Khoi and spent the night in tents.[40]

The further north they moved the hotter and drier it became. In the morning between 5.30 and 6.30 the train oxen were harnessed, during the midday heat there was a break, and in the cooler afternoon and evening hours they continued for some time unless a scarcity of water dictated other breaks. Wallich used the interruptions to botanise, and Mann assisted in drying the plants. In the darkness the starry sky was observed.[41] As Mann later recorded, he was impressed by the pleasant nature and rich experience of the man who had spent almost his entire adult life in India.[42]

From Mamre, they went to Hopefield, which was reached on 7 January. The following day they crossed the River Berg and three days later reached Elands Berg (now Bobbejaansberg), the first of the intended survey points. Maclear had reached the place a few days earlier but had great difficulty in getting his equipment ashore on the barren coast.[43] Here the group stayed for a while before reaching the foot of Lambert's Hoek about 50 kilometres east. While Maclear and Wallich stayed in a tent at the base, Mann and his servants had the arduous task of getting all the surveying equipment up to the summit. On the horizon, the band of the Cederbergs finally revealed themselves.[44]

After the initial measurements, Maclear considered it necessary to identify the highest peaks of the Cederbergs to advance the triangulation further to the north. The land became barren and the sandy paths eventually forced the bullock carts to give up; instead, the equipment was now transported up the mountains on wooden sledges. Soon, these too could go no further and the six so-called 'Hottentots' from Clanwilliam, who were supposed to assist with transport, refused to move on. While Mann stayed with the stranded equipment, Maclear explored the area and Wallich, crossing the mountains to the west, headed for the German mission station at Wupperthal. His task was to ask for help for the further ascent of the mountains.[45] Perhaps, his German language skills may have been the decisive factor in entrusting Wallich with this mission.

On 18 March, Wallich returned to Mann and Maclear. In the meantime, the two astronomers had identified the 2026 metre summit of Sneeuwkop in the middle of the Cederbergs as a suitable survey point. Only two days later, reinforcements from Wupperthal arrived, consisting of 26 Khois led by the missionary Christian Schröder. The group was accompanied by four bullock carts loaded with, among other things, dried fruits, meat, cakes, rusks and poultry items. Wallich's negotiating skills had proved their worth once again.[46]

While Maclear conducted his observations, Wallich was in charge of the base camp and three 'Wupperthal Hottentots' employed there.[47] The rich experience from his expeditions through Nepal, northern India, Burma and Assam paid off— 'I have grown grey in that sort of work', as Wallich explained to Maclear.

The party suffered from the low night-time temperatures and violent storms that swept over the mountains at night and in the early morning and which also affected the base camp.

Wallich arranged for something to raise their spirits and sent the 'Brandy-Man' to Rondehat to stock up on alcohol.[48] On another occasion, while congratulating the two astronomers up the mountain on their successful measurements, he sent them coffee with sugar and honey, hard-boiled eggs, potatoes with 'carbonatjes' and sandwiches.[49] On 12 June 1843, Mann and Wallich got back to the Royal Observatory, leaving Maclear in the north to take further measurements.[50]

During his journey to the north, Wallich had missed a visit to Cape Town: in April 1843 the British research ships *Erebus* and *Terror* reached the harbour below Table Mountain. The expedition, under the command of James Ross had come directly from the Antarctic, where never had humans reached a point so far south on the globe. On board was the botanist Joseph Dalton Hooker, son of Wallich's old friend Sir William, who had botanized on the sub-Antartic islands.[51] In mid-April, Baron Ludwig reported to Wallich that 'young Mr Hooker also called on me yesterday, he is in H.H.S. Erebus, & returning to England, he will leave Town tomorrow for Simons Bay where the Exp. Ship lay. He is very sorry he could not see you and wrote a small note which I have the pleasure to enclose herewith'.[52] The letter by the younger Hooker still survives among the Wallich letters at Calcutta.[53]

While Thomas Maclear was at Kamiesberg in the north, Wallich maintained close personal contact with Mary and the children at the Royal Observatory. He regularly visited his friends, whom he had come to appreciate as a substitute family. Mary Maclear, who, as she occasionally noted in her diary, did not always get along well with the children when coping on her own ('very uncomfortable with the children'), was also pleased with the visits, which distracted her from the frequent discomfort and worry about the little ones attending school.[54] The days were cool and Mrs Maclear had a fire lit in the fireplace of her small room.[55] Only a fall while riding the pony while botanizing in Hout Bay kept Wallich from his regular visits for a period.[56]

The last of Wallich's excursions was his participation in an official trip of several weeks led by the judge William Menzies to the Eastern Cape region.[57] The itinerary was via Swellendam and George and to continue across the Outeniqua Mountains, Cradock Pass, Graff Reinet, Somerset East, Uitenhage, Grahamstown, Beaufort West to Worcester. The journey was too rapid for extensive botanizing, but at least Wallich was again in good health.[58] At Uitenhage, Wallich met Joachim Brehm, a pharmacist and botanist from Germany, who had employed Zeyher as a plant collector for some time and now accompanied Wallich to Grahamstown. Wallich's stay in Africa had been a happy time,[59] and he was sorry to bid it farewell.[60] On 30 April 1844, he left the Cape to return once more to India.

NOTES

1. Mägdefrau, *Geschichte der Botanik*, p. 115.
2. M. C. Karsten, *The Old Company's Garden at the Cape and its Superintendents*, Cape Town: Maskew Miller, 1951, pp. 1-43.
3. F. Welsh, *A History of South Africa*, London: Harper Collins, 2000, pp. 88-105.
4. Robinson, *William Roxburgh*, p. 209.
5. Karsten, *The Old Company's Garden*, pp. 142-5.
6. Ibid., pp. 1-43.
7. Robinson, *William Roxburgh*, p. 57.
8. Ibid., pp. 209f.
9. M. Gunn & L.E. Codd, *Botanical Exploration of Southern Africa*. An Illustrated History of Early Botanical Literature on the Cape Flora. Biographical Accounts of the Leading Plant Collectors and their Activities in Southern Africa from the Days of the East India Company until Modern Times, Cape Town: Balkema, 1981, p. 233.
10. CNH, Wallich letters, Ludwig to Wallich, 15 September 1834.
11. Ibid.
12. Ibid.
13. J.P. Frahm & J. Eggers, Lexikon Deutschsprachiger Bryologen, Norderstedt: BoD, 2001, pp. 576f.
14. CNH, Wallich letters, Zeyher to Wallich, 2 June 1837.
15. E. Warming, article 'Ecklon, Christian Friedrich', *Dansk Biografisk Leksikon*, vol. 4, ed. C.F. Bricka, Copenhagen: Gyldendal, 1890, pp. 417f.

16. Ibid.; Gunn & Codd, *Botanical Exploration of South Africa*, p. 147.
17. CNH, Wallich letters, Wallich to Medical Board, 5 March 1842; Bradlow, *Nathaniel Wallich*, p. 100; ibid., Wallich to W.J. Hooker, 6 November 1842.
18. Arnold, *The Tropics and the Traveling Gaze*, p. 174.
19. CNH, Wallich letters, Wallich to Bushby, 27 June 1842.
20. Bille, *Steen Billes Bericht*, p. 127; Larsen, Dansk Ostindiske Personalier og Data, entry 'Voigt, Joachim Otto Voigt'.
21. Thomas, *Calcutta Botanic Garden*, p. 126.
22. CA, A 515, Maclear Mann Papers, 14, Wallich to Thomas Maclear, 4 November 1842.
23. Ibid., 78, Mrs Maclear's Diaries, 10, 12-14, 17, 25-8 August 1842.
24. Ibid., 14, Wallich to Thomas Maclear, 4 November 1842.
25. *Simmond's Colonial Magazine and Foreign Miscellany*, London, September-December 1845, p. 178; CNH, Wallich letters, Wallich to W.J. Hooker, 6 November 1842.
26. However, the year of publication on the volume is 1849. A. Bird, Arabella Roupell. *Pioneer Artist of Cape Flowers*, Johannesburg: The South African Natural History Publication Commission, 1975.
27. Bradlow, *Nathaniel Wallich*, p. 100.
28. Ibid., p. 98.
29. CNH, Wallich letters, Versfeld to Wallich, 20 November 1842.
30. Bradlow, *Wallich*, p. 100.
31. CNH, Wallich letters, Wallich to Ludwig, 19 November 1842.
32. I. S. Glass, *The Royal Observatory at the Cape of Good Hope*, Cape Town: Mons Mesa, 2015, p. 14.
33. C. Plug, Article 'Maclear, Sir Thomas', in Biographical Database of Southern African Science, http://www.s2a3.org.za/bio/Biograph_final.php?serial=1791, (retrieved 7 February 2017).
34. CA, 515, Maclear Mann Papers, 74, Wallich to Arabella Roupell, no date (February 1844).
35. William Mann to Sarah Mann, 21 June 1843, in B. Warner (ed.), *The Cape Diary and Letters of William Mann. Astronomer and Mountaineer, 1839-43*, Cape Town: Friends of the South African Library, 1989, p. 58: 'As La Caille's arc . . . is too small (about 75 miles) to give a very satisfactory idea of the shape and dimensions of our globe'.
36. Ibid.; CA, A 515, Maclear Mann Papers, 14, Wallich to Thomas Maclear, 4 November 1842.
37. CNH, Wallich letters, Versfeld to Wallich, 18 December 1842.

38. Ibid.
39. William Mann to Sarah Mann, 21 June 1843, in Warner (ed.), *Cape Diary*, p. 58.
40. Warner, *Cape Diary*, passim.
41. William Mann to Sarah Mann, 21 June 1843, in: Warner (ed.), *Cape Diary*, p. 62.
42. Ibid., pp. 58f. 'the old Dr was a most delightful companion: about 35 years of his life had been spent in India and in travelling in the East, so as you may conceive, he was a person from whom one could not fail obtaining abundance of information.'
43. Ibid., p. 63. 'here we were upon entirely new ground from last year, and to judge from appearances were fast leaving the civilized and inhabited part of the Colony'.
44. Ibid., pp. 70f.
45. Ibid., p. 76.
46. Ibid. pp. 76f.
47. CA, A 515, Maclear Mann Papers, 14, Wallich to Thomas Maclear, 23 March 1843.
48. Ibid., 26 March 1843.
49. Ibid., 22 March 1843; ibid. 27 March 1843.
50. CA, 515 A, Maclear Mann Papers, Wallich to Arabella Roupell, (c. February 1844).
51. Desmond, *Joseph Dalton Hooker*, p. 84.
52. CNH, Wallich letters, Baron Ludwig to Wallich, 14 April 1843.
53. CNH, Wallich letters, J.D. Hooker to Wallich, 14 April 1843.
54. CA, A 515, Maclear Mann Papers, 74, Wallich to Mary Maclear, 5 August 1844; ibid, 78, Mrs Maclear's Diaries, 12 October 1843.
55. Ibid., 78, Mrs Maclear's Diaries, 29 June 1843.
56. Ibid. 28 August 1843.
57. Ibid., 74, Wallich to Mary Maclear, 13 August 1843.
58. CA, A 515, Maclear Mann Papers, 14, Wallich to Thomas Maclear, 3 November 1843: 'My health never better in my life. I am actually and literally getting stout. Think only!'
59. Gunn & Codd, *Botanical Exploration*, p. 369; CA, A 515, Maclear Mann Papers, 74, Wallich to Mary Maclear, 23 June 1847.
60. Ibid., Arabella Roupell to Wallich, 20 February 1844.

CHAPTER 15

Farewell to India

WILLIAM GRIFFITH

The previous years had clearly shown that Wallich's days in India were numbered. He no longer enjoyed the full confidence of the Government, and he had failed to keep up with the general progress of his profession as a botanist.[1] As early as by November 1842, he wrote from Cape Town to his friend Hooker: 'and not a month, certainly not more than a month shall elapse from the day of my return to Bengal, before I am off for a good on my final return home to Europe'.[2] All this was to contribute significantly to the fact that immediately after his return from Africa, a fierce dispute flared up with William Griffith, his former protege and now acting Garden Superintendent. The tensions that had first erupted on the Assam expedition had healed superficially at best, and both had since drifted even further apart in both practice and theory. While Griffith not only asserted himself in India as the leading representative of the natural system and the new plant physiology, he had also made large and highly important herbarium collections on his extensive travels in Southeast Asia, Assam, Bhutan and Afghanistan, while Wallich stuck to Linnaean systematics and a more conventional research ethos.[3] The number of strict Linnaean adherents was by now extremely small and in the end communication between them and the modernists broke down. The medium of botanical exchange had also altered and while Wallich still relied on correspondence and patronage networks, the march of botanical journals from the 1820s onwards had continued apace, accompanied by a significant institutionalization of botanical research.[4] In

Britain were periodicals such as Hooker's *Journal of Botany*, but scientific journals were now also being published in India, including the *Gleanings in Science*, the *Journal of the Asiatic Society of Bengal* and, above all, the *Calcutta Journal of Natural History* started by John McClelland in 1841.

For Wallich, it had been nothing short of treason that the Governor-General, Lord Auckland, had entrusted Griffith with the temporary management of the Garden after Voigt's departure.[5] The appointment was undoubtedly an expression of Auckland's disapproval of Wallich, and Griffith supported him in a highly critical report on the state of the Botanic Garden, which he submitted soon after taking office.[6] In this, Griffith expressed his displeasure of its outward appearance, such as the lack of a proper fencing that left the garden unprotected and vulnerable to destruction, but far worse, its whole design was unsystematic. One part had, in his opinion, rather the

Plate 15.1: William Griffith, lithography.
(State and University Library Göttingen)

character of a landscape garden, another part was structured according to the long-outmoded Linnaean order and, in general, the large number of trees overwhelmed the overall concept.[7] Griffith completely misjudged, or at least overlooked, one of the traditional functions of the garden as a place of recreation for the people of Calcutta.

Griffith immediately launched into a significant re-design, which totally overrode Wallich's research into economic plants and also his aesthetic principles. Not only teak, but mahogany, cinnamon and cloves fell victim to the transformation, as Wallich lamented that: 'The noblest, most superb trees, which even in this prolific climate, require a man's whole life to rear, have been rooted up by the score . . . roads, paths, broken up'.[8] In June 1844, shortly before his return, Griffith submitted another report in which he defended the changes he had made to the garden, library and herbarium and made further proposals. To Wallich's understandable annoyance, the Government ordered all Griffith's further recommendations to be implemented.[9]

Wallich was bitter, and he and Griffith parted on bad terms. Even worse, the conflict was never to be resolved for Griffith left Calcutta for Malacca in December 1844 and died there soon afterwards of liver disease at the age of only thirty-four.[10] Despite Griffith's death, Nathaniel carried the conflict on into his London retirement, but did not realize that by now personal conflicts had become a deep-seated aspect of his character. He continued to nurse his grudge against the deceased and tried to force some of his companions to take sides, which merely embarrassed them. The physician and botanist Francis Boott told Hooker at the end of 1846 that the battle with the dead must, once and for all, end,[11] but even three years later he noted his frustration with Wallich's behaviour and that, in the meantime, a dispute had arisen between Wallich's son David and one of his own sons at St. Bartholomew's Hospital and the College of Surgeons. Wallich avoided Boott for months.[12] Martius, Wallich's Munich friend, tried to calm him down only to receive complaints about 'deadly and murderous calamities and persecutions of me'.[13] The disagreement with Robert Wight reared its head again and contact was accordingly cut for some time, but Hooker managed to prevent this from becoming public.

Wallich did his utmost, in as far as possible, to erase the name of Griffith from history and posterity. Even though their contact had been close and confidential for many years, not even one of his letters can be found in the Wallich correspondence today. Following his return from South Africa, the bitterness made Wallich think more and more about retirement and on 8 February 1845 he wrote to his old companion Sir William Hooker that he had finally had enough of India.[14]

THE GALATHEA IN CALCUTTA

Mentally, he was already on his way to retirement when, on the morning of 6 November 1845, a reminder of Denmark appeared literally in front of his study as the Danish frigate *Galathea* glided on the incoming tide towards Calcutta. The ship had left Copenhagen four and a half months earlier on a scientific circumnavigation of the world, which was also intended to strengthen the Danish claims to the Nicobar Islands. The initiator of the expedition was the Kiel anatomist and zoologist Wilhelm Friedrich Georg Behn who originally wanted to persuade the Danish monarch Christian VIII to allow him to undertake a research voyage on a merchant ship. In the end, for political reasons, Christian VIII approved the sending of a well-equipped national scientific expedition. Natural research had long since become a matter of prestige and Denmark intended to do the same as Britain, even if on a smaller scale. The fact that such a project involving Copenhagen and the German-speaking university of Kiel was possible is proof of the viability and innovative strength of the as yet multinational Danish state, which was to break down later in national unrest and civil war.

One task of the expedition was to hand over the Danish colony Tranquebar to the British. Shortly earlier, a sale contract had been signed in Calcutta, by which the remaining Danish possessions in India, Tranquebar and Serampore, were to be transferred to the British, marking the end of more than two centuries of Danish colonial history on the Indian mainland. By this Wallich's first place of work was to change hands but after so many years in Calcutta, he kept quiet about the matter.

On the very day of his arrival in Calcutta, the botanist of the *Galathea*, Bernhard Caspar Kamphøvener, who was in poor health, appeared at Shibpur. During the ship's stay in Calcutta, he was supposed to spend most of his time at the Garden. Wallich found in Kamphøvener an excellent botanist and an interesting conversationist and was delighted to be able to chat in Danish again after such a long time.[15] Even Admiral Bille, commander of the Danish expedition, did not miss the opportunity to visit Wallich's floral kingdom: 'The botanical garden was my Sunday stay'.[16]

Before the *Galathea* continued its voyage towards the Nicobar Islands, East Asia and across the Pacific Ocean to South America, the composition of the scientific party underwent changes in Calcutta. Besides some sailors, the sick Kamphøvener left the expedition to return home, where he died soon afterwards. Nevertheless, he had participated in the compilation of the first dispatch of natural history objects to Copenhagen and Kiel, including from India a large amount of herbarium material which still survives.[17]

Agreement to the departure of Kamphøvener would undoubtedly not have been reached so quickly had Rudolf Amandus Philippi not been available on the spot as a replacement. Philippi, who was born in Berlin, had studied medicine in his hometown, then spent time in Italy for health reasons, where he undertook botanical research. From 1835, he taught natural sciences at the Polytechnic University in the German town of Kassel for almost ten years, before leaving to botanize in India and later to join the 'Galathea expedition'. However, today he is known only for his later research relating to Chile.[18] Philippi had travelled to the coasts of the Malay Peninsula before reaching Calcutta by steamer on 29 November, where

the *Galathea* had been lying for more than three weeks. His
first call was the Botanic Garden where he was welcomed by
Wallich, especially since he brought with him a letter from a
new correspondent: Alexander von Humboldt. Wallich enjoyed
his company and learned to appreciate Philippi and wrote in
one of his few letters to Humboldt: 'He is an extremely intel-
ligent and amiable gentleman'.[19] Wallich gave Philippi plant seeds
for the famous scholar in Berlin—'according to the expression
of Dr Wallich, silver gold and platinum, i.e. very valuable things.
The seeds arrived here fresh from the Himalayas'.[20]

On 24 December 1845, the *Galathea* set off from Calcutta
towards the Nicobar Islands. The visit had lasted six weeks in
all, and the farewell was to be a magnificent one. The day
before departure the ship's officers invited the elite of Calcutta
to a ball on board the ship. On the upper deck there was a tent
around which was a simulation of tropical jungle. Steen Bille
reported in his journal: 'The good Dr Wallich had looted the
botanical garden, and sent several boatloads full of greenery
and flowers, which our painter, Mr Plum, tastefully placed
between the tent openings'.[21] The dancing went on until two
o'clock in the morning.

RETIREMENT

Perhaps, this recent contact with his homeland and countrymen
strengthened Wallich's intention at last to turn his back
on India. On 19 November 1845, he officially informed the
Government of his intention to retire and return to Europe at
the beginning of the following year.[22] Less than a month later,
he informed Humboldt that he intended to leave either in
February or at the latest in March, if he were still alive by then.[23]

The only reason that kept him for a while was his beloved
daughter Hannah, who was pregnant again. Hannah, with
her son, followed her seriously ill husband William Biddulph
with the troops through northern India.[24] Practically unable to travel, she was constantly plagued by severe pain. On
27 January a little girl was born, named Sophia after her

grandmother; the mother's health hardly improved, as Nathaniel came to know by her letters.[25] His hope was for Biddulph to be granted a home leave so that they all could travel to Europe together.[26] But the departure of his daughter and her family was delayed. Biddulph was reluctant to be declared invalid, or to resign from the service, but was forced to take ever higher doses of opium for his pain. To Nathaniel's great joy, Hannah and the two children, nevertheless, arrived at the beginning of February to visit him in Calcutta. Full of pride, he relished his role as grandfather and wrote to Thomas Maclear of the grand-children: 'as fine and sweet children as it is possible to see, also in excellent health'.[27]

The *Galathea* had also brought private mail, including letters from his brother Arnold and his wife, but by the time they reached Calcutta Arnold was no longer alive.[28] When news of his death reached him, full of sadness, Nathaniel had to say goodbye to his beloved brother from a distance.[29] Arnold, although the older brother, had always been perceived as the younger in terms of strength and health and had never been seriously ill. With him, went one of the last representatives from Wallich's early Copenhagen period and one of the last bridges that connected him with his native land.[30]

In the choice of his successor, Wallich was to have no influence. He was to be replaced by John McClelland who had taken Griffith's side both on their trip to Assam. However, McClelland's tenure proved to be brief and in 1847, he was replaced by Hugh Falconer, previously Superintendent of the botanic garden at Saharanpur, under whose care a large part of the Garden was gradually restored to its former state.[31] The tree felling that Griffith had perpetrated, however, was still apparent and when Joseph Hooker visited the garden in 1848, he was horrified by a shadowless collection of plants.[32]

In early April 1846, Wallich's resignation was approved and after almost three decades, he was no longer Superintendent.[33] On 8 April the *Hindustan* left for the Red Sea with him on board.[34] After crossing the land bridge between Suez and Alexandria, the journey continued by boat to Marseilles, which was reached on 17 May. The journey to Europe now took less than six weeks ('I believe that no letter had ever before travelled quicker from Bengal to Europe')—no comparison with the seven and a half months that the young Dane had spent on the *Prince of Augustenburg* 39 years earlier.[35]

The return journey served to allow the making of personal contact with some of the members of his European botanical network. In Paris, he was given an almost triumphant reception, received by some of his famous colleagues and patrons including Baron Benjamin Delessert and Professors Jussieu, Richard, Gaudichaud and Mirbel. His two younger sons, Leonard and David, were also awaiting him there.[36] Nathaniel felt anxious about social interactions in Europe after so many years in India, especially since he had never visited France before. To Delessert he wrote: 'I am such a regular old Indian that I feel awkward in travelling out of the country'.[37] He then continued on to Caen, where his wife Sophia and their daughters awaited him.[38]

FAMILY REUNITED

After many years, most of the family was reunited with only their son George Charles, and daughter Hannah with her family, remaining in India. For years, the burden of the education of the younger children had rested solely on Sophia, while Nathaniel himself could only participate by correspondence. In the last years of his life, he would be even more committed to looking after their future careers and finding adequate spouses for them. Wallich wanted to reach London as quickly as possible; under no circumstances did he want to retire to the provinces, as Buchanan had done. Lehmann's assumption that Wallich would now be well-off and settle with a respectable pension in his native city Copenhagen was mistaken.[39] Nonetheless, in London, it was important for Wallich to reassure himself as to whether his name still counted for anything and to revive old personal contacts.

In London, he once again took up residence in the Bloomsbury district at 5 Gower Street near Bedford Square, where he was to spend the last years of his life. The household was manageable, with the three unmarried daughters Mary, Anne, and Fanny, who lived there with their parents.

In addition to the Gower Street household, the home of Sophia's wealthy sister Mary and her husband, the Hull merchant John Smith, who lived at Welton Garth near Hull, offered a haven of peace. Nathaniel always had words of respect for both, who were not only emotionally close to him, but had also committed considerable sums of money to the welfare of his children.[40] After many years of loneliness, Nathaniel also enjoyed a convivial Christmas with his family at Welton in 1846 and appreciated the warm hospitality of his sister-in-law. The last such relaxed family celebration he had experienced was in 1843 at the Cape Town Observatory, as he wrote to his hostess on that earlier occasion, Mary Maclear.[41]

The fact that Hannah was still in India remained a constant source of regret. The last news of her came at Christmas 1846, which said that she and her family would soon be leaving the mountains for Calcutta to make the journey to Europe. William's severe neuralgia had not improved, and he was still suffering from severe pain. Between Christmas and New Year, Wallich sat down at Welton to pen a few lines to Hannah: 'Next year, if I live so long (I trust you will all be among us long before the season arrives again) nothing will be wanting in my happiness'.[42] He believed she would return via Cape Town and so sent the letter to the Maclears; however, it was never picked up there and it is now in the Maclear papers in the West Cape State Archives. It was not until the spring of 1847 that the Biddulphs arrived back in Britain, only to settle not in Gower Street as Wallich had hoped, but at William's mother and sister's house at Frankton near Rugby.[43]

The three younger daughters Mary Sophia, Ann, and Fanny were still not of marriageable age, but careers had to be found for the younger sons Leonard Calder (born in India in 1823), and Nathaniel David (born at sea in 1825 and accordingly nicknamed by his father 'Hottentot'). Wallich made no secret of the fact that he saw their future in the service of the East India Company and to this end intended to make use of his ongoing contacts with the Court of Directors. While Leonard was intended to pursue a career as a clergyman, David was to follow in his father's medical footsteps (as had his brother George, who by now was established in India).

Against this backdrop, Nathaniel was able to build on the educational achievements nurtured by his wife. Long before his return, Leonard had begun to study theology at Cambridge and in January 1846 he had passed his examinations with distinction.[44] Afterwards, he took up a post as deacon in Poringland near Norwich. Wallich said that he was fortunate to have such a good position at the start of his career, but his father's efforts were directed towards finding him a clerical position in India. Finally, however, Leonard stayed in England.[45]

On Wallich's return, his younger son David had just completed his training as a surgeon at the teaching hospital of St Bartholomew's in London and in 1847 he passed his examination at the Royal College of Surgeons. While Leonard was meanwhile in good hands at Poringland, his father now tried to secure a position for David in India and turned to Henry Alexander, one of the Company Directors. Alexander immediately promised to try to secure one of the scarce medical positions for David for the following year—an indication that Wallich retained the trust of the Company.[46] But soon his plans were challenged from another direction, for David was engaged and his future father-in-law, Mr Bateman, did not want his only daughter to move to Asia.[47] In the end, Wallich's wishes prevailed and David found himself Assistant Surgeon to Sir Charles Napier's Camel Corps in Sind in the extreme west of India.[48]

Without doubt, Wallich's greatest hopes were placed in his eldest son, George Charles. It had always been expected that he would follow his father not only as a surgeon but also as a scientist. When Wallich had last heard from him, just before leaving Calcutta, George was with the troops on the Sutlej near the city of Lahore. He was interested not only in curing the sick, but also in the country and its people. With anticipation and a certain amount of pride, the father awaited in London the manuscript of a *History of Lahore*, which had been announced but appears never to have been published. Wallich made it clear to the Maclears that he considered his elder son to be exceptionally gifted: a scientific career had been pre-programmed, he said, and in the end, he was to be proved correct.[49]

Long forgotten were George's escapades with the wife of a comrade, which almost cost him his career in India. George finally settled down and married Caroline Elisabeth Norton during a holiday in Lowestoft, Suffolk in September 1851. His parents may have had a hand in the arrangement as the previous year the whole family had spent several weeks in the seaside town of Lowestoft.[50]

Plate 15.2: Thomas Herbert Maguire, Nathaniel Wallich in his sixties, lithography, 1849. (the author)

The last alliance forged during Wallich's lifetime was the marriage of his daughter Ann to the Danish-English merchant Charles (or Carl Severin) Møller. This union reflected an old connection, as Charles's Jutland-born father had been a fellow student with Wallich at the Surgical Academy.[51] Connection was re-established when Wallich had met Charles, who was involved in the trade and ship brokerage business between England and Denmark. His company headquarters were in Muscovy Square in London's Tower Hill district and had been used by Wallich for the shipping of herbarium specimens. The match for Ann was apparently a good one and on 1 March 1853 the wedding took place in the Old Church of St Pancras.[52]

Nathaniel did not live to see the marriage of his son Leonard Calder to Fanny Wilkinson. Fanny came from near Hull, close to Sophia Wallich's sister's family, the Smiths. They had known each other since childhood and were to be extremely well set up financially. Shortly before his death, Wallich settled an inheritance of a considerable £5000 in Fanny's name, while her father did the same in favour of Leonard—an arrangement which was heavily subsidized by Sophia's sister Mary Smith. Nathaniel summed up the financial security of his son: 'am I not warranted in saluting Leonard as a most lucky dog indeed?'[53]

Bracing North Sea air, whether at Lowestoft or Hull, was good in other respects, as Wallich suffered from health problems from the first day of his life in retirement. The humid, cool climate of Britain, and the bad air of London in particular, were far from beneficial. The much-travelled botanist, who had survived the jungles of the Tarai, and many a malaria attack, was increasingly struck down by the mildest of colds. Already in the first autumn, he began to suffer from severe respiratory problems, and he was ill for almost the whole of the first half of 1847.[54] A persistent inflammatory cold—the croup, as his physician Francis Boott suspected—was associated with cramps and the expulsion of bloody mucus.[55] Temporary improvement was achieved by treatment with leeches and emetics. He also had to change his diet and be sure to wear warm clothes. The sickbed had almost become a deathbed, as he wrote to Mary Maclear at that time. On one visit Boott found Wallich coughing and emaciated.[56] A visit to the seaside led to an improvement and a health trip could easily be extended to a relaxing family holiday, as he wrote to Martius in the summer of 1847.[57] Indeed, the North Sea air and the large family circle proved of great benefit and for some time he felt better and was satisfied with his state of health.[58]

HURRAH FOR OLD DENMARK!

When Wallich finally reached Europe, the continent was on the verge of revolution. In addition to the demand for liberal constitutions in some countries, Denmark struggled with increasing national tension between Danes and German subjects of the Danish King. In 1845, the visit of the *Galathea* had been both a reminder and a testimony to the importance to Wallich of his Danish homeland. Three years later, Denmark was in danger of sinking into chaos. Traditional sentiments of respect towards the international and formerly peaceful Danish monarchy were heavily shaken and it was difficult for the elderly Wallich to come to terms with the new political situation. His old companions in Denmark were all dead; his old teacher Jens Wilken Hornemann having died in 1841.

Wallich, who was gradually marginalized in botany, was looking for a new field to express himself and found one in the current political debate. For some time, he had probably considered himself a Briton-by-choice, writing and speaking largely in English, but, facing the revolution, he rediscovered his Danish heart. He was never one to forget personal affronts, and even in old age probably felt a deep bitterness when he thought of the name Schmidt-Phiseldeck, who, decades ago, had almost wrecked his career in India before it had even begun.

Wallich was always well-informed about developments on the continent through his regular reading of newspapers, especially the Copenhagen *Berlingske Tidende*. He formed his own opinion, but it was strongly influenced by the Danish bias of that paper. When the first news of the civil war in the

Danish Duchies of Schleswig and Holstein reached him, his feelings ran high. This was compounded by his personal disappointment as, after his health had eventually improved, he had planned to travel to Copenhagen in 1848, and this was now prevented by the outbreak of unrest.[59]

While Wallich's national Danish feelings remained subdued with his German correspondents, he expressed himself freely to his Danish compatriots and to the Maclears in Cape Town. Even though the tide turned dramatically in favour of the Germans for some time, Wallich declared a minor military encounter to be a brilliant Danish victory: 'Hurrah, for old Denmark! The Volunteer Rebels of Slesvick have had glorious trashing—and under God's justice they will have more',[60] as he wrote to Cape Town. The behaviour of the Germans of Schleswig and Holstein, which historically had almost always belonged to Denmark, was nothing but treason. Never had the world seen a greater betrayal than that committed by the duchies.[61]

At the end of April 1848, the balance of power was reversed and troops from the German state of Prussia occupied almost the entire Duchy of Schleswig.[62] Even to Martius, who was otherwise spared by Wallich's political views, he now openly expressed his feelings: 'My Danish blood is up in this weather beaten half-withered frame of mine'.[63] Wallich's initial cheers, however, faded away in the Prussian cannon thunder and only a short time later, he was much more realistic about the situation to the Maclears: in the end, Denmark would at least get its fair share of the Danish-speaking parts of Schleswig, but retribution there must be: 'But I could wish that some of the Traitor Dukes, Counts, and Commoners of both provinces might be hanged on the highest trees there'.[64]

The subject was particularly sensitive to Lehmann in Hamburg. A deep rift ran through his family, as he wrote to London at the end of 1848. His eldest brother, who lived in Copenhagen, was 'all German', while one son was the now notorious leader of the Danish nationalists, and his eldest son went 'as a volunteer to the war against the Danes'. Lehmann could express only sadness: 'So the closest relatives faced each other as enemies.' He himself, unlike the politicized Wallich, chose the path of inner contemplation: 'I still live for science'.[65] To Wallich, whose Danish attitude cannot have remained hidden from him, he trusted that: 'Whether my attitude is Danish or German—as they say—that is indifferent to our relationship, thank God.[66]

Even though Wallich identified himself ideologically as a Dane from 1848 to 1850, he saw himself almost completely socialised as British. Such attitudes were not necessarily mutually exclusive, for Denmark and Britain were considered natural allies. A lifetime had passed since British troops had attacked Copenhagen and taken over Serampore, thereby robbing him of his position as Royal Danish Surgeon. For many years he had identified himself with the British Empire, for which he was prepared—at least on paper—to offer great personal sacrifices: 'and my last drop of blood will I shed for it if required'.[67] Above all, he saw his adopted home as a rock in the global surf in a time of revolution.[68]

In 1846-7, the so-called Seventh Frontier War was fought between the British and Xhosa; and Wallich had as little sympathy with the Xhosa Kingdom in South Africa as he had for the German Schleswig-Holsteiners. Here, too, he saw what he viewed as 'vile conspirators at work who threatened the existing, and supposedly God-given, order'. The Xhosa tribes living in the peripheral regions of the Cape Colony, had increasingly suffered from a lack of land due to the expansion of European settlements. Violent incidents with the settlers occurred again and again, which finally led to an open and extremely bloody war when 12,000 Xhosa fighters penetrated deep into the Cape Colony. The mood in South Africa was heated, but even more so in England.[69]

After a period of calming down the war broke out again in the early 1850s. In Britain, however, reports of brutalities by British soldiers against the locals were now in circulation. The liberal public opposed Governor Sir Henry Smith, who was blamed for the atrocities, but not so Nathaniel Wallich, who had his own thoughts on 'this most awful Coffre war'. Shortly before his death, and in contrast to the majority opinion, he spoke out in favour of a hard line: 'a peace treaty should never be concluded with hyenas and wolves and Solemn treaties with Kafirs! Fear or extermination—no other terms upon which such tribes can be kept under the thumb'.[70] In his London retirement Wallich, who had once worked closely with Indians, Nepalis, Burmese and South Africans, developed into a hardliner, with unmistakable nationalist and racist undertones.

LINNAEAN HEIR

While botany as a science could easily seem 'pure' and supposedly 'free' of political discourse, Wallich understood his research had supported the imperial power of the British in India. Since his return to Europe, he no longer supervised a herbarium,[71] however, part of the large collection he had brought from India in 1828 was still with Bentham in its original state.[72] In the one and a half decades that had passed since his first stay in London, Wallich had no contact with Bentham. Bentham was surprised—and perhaps disappointed—that Wallich seemed to have forgotten him almost completely after their parting in Hamburg in 1832: 'I . . . often recur to the absolute silence which had taken place since we parted at Hamburgh now nearly fifteen years ago . . . never having had a single line from yourself or even a message in letters to our mutual friends'.[73] None of the relevant sources report a rift, and Wallich's long silence can probably be attributed to an increasing workload and ultimate dissatisfaction with his situation in India. The first news in many years reached Bentham in early 1847 in Florence, where he spent the winter months with his wife after a journey through Europe. In his reply, despite a palpable breath of bitterness, Bentham generously offered to assist Wallich in completing the distribution from his house.[74] Personal contact was resumed and in the following autumn work began at Pontrilas on the remaining specimens. Once again precious packages were sent on their way, such as palm leaves for Martius in Munich.[75] In November 1849, two decades after it had been commenced, the distribution of the East India Company herbarium was finally completed and the last entry in the *Wallich Catalogue* bears the number 8,517.[76]

As a 'grand-pupil' of Linnaeus, Wallich was a Fellow of the Linnean Society of London, the guardian of the heritage of the great Swedish botanist. Its fortnightly meetings were held in Soho Square in the former home of Sir Joseph Banks, now owned by Robert Brown (it was not until several years after Wallich's death that the Society moved to Burlington House, where it is still based today).[77] Wallich attended meetings regularly, but initially made no contributions of his own.[78] The occasion was a suggestion of the Council of the Society to commemorate Linnaeus with a translation of his personal notes of the *Almanach På Åhret efter Iesu Christi nåderika Födelse 1735*. In the introduction to the text, which was translated from Swedish and read at a meeting of the Society on 5 December 1848, Wallich pointed out the continuing importance of Linnaeus for botanical research. For him Linnaeus was the true 'princeps botanicorum', rather than Robert Brown, as Humboldt would have it. Even the smallest text by Linnaeus was important and Wallich later also published a translation from Swedish of a report that Charles Hartman had made on the manuscript of Linnaeus's *Iter Dalecarlium* owned by the Society.[79] In this way, even in old age, he again clearly declared himself a follower of the Linnaean tradition. The translations led to a more active involvement with the Linnean Society, and he undertook other translation work for the Society, such as a paper by Martius on 'Remarks on the scientific purpose and performance of our greenhouses', which appeared in Hooker's *Journal of Botany and Kew Gardens Miscellany* in 1853.[80]

On 4 December 1849, Robert Brown was elected President of the Linnean Society and two weeks later appointed his vice-presidents for the year: Thomas Horsfield, Sir William Hooker and his old friend Nathaniel Wallich.[81] However, after this appointment Wallich did not join every session, due largely to his deteriorating health, which increasingly tied him to the house. In addition to his membership of the Linnean Society, Wallich remained a Fellow of the Royal Society, to which he had been elected while on his furlough in 1829. He also received social recognition with election as a member of the prestigious Athenaeum Club.[82]

NOTES

1. Arnold, *Plant Capitalism and Company Science*, p. 926.
2. CNH, Wallich letters, Wallich to W.J. Hooker, 6 November 1842.
3. Thomas, *Calcutta Botanic Garden*, p. 126; Arnold, *The Tropics and the Traveling Gaze*, p. 16.
4. Harrison, 'Calcutta Botanic Garden', p. 243.
5. RBG Kew, Director's Correspondence, 55/393, Wallich to W.J. Hooker, 8 February 1853.
6. W. Griffith, *Report on the Honorable Company's Botanic Garden*, Calcutta, 1843.
7. Thomas, *Calcutta Botanic Garden*, p. 127.
8. See Bradlow, *Nathaniel Wallich*, p. 102
9. Thomas, *Calcutta Botanic Garden*, pp. 127-31.
10. Candolle & Radcliffe-Smith, 'Nathaniel Wallich', p. 343.
11. RBG Kew, Director's Correspondence, 63/85, Boott to W.J. Hooker, 22 December 1846.
12. Ibid., 63/116, Boott to W.J. Hooker, 27 January 1849; ibid., 31 December 1849.
13. BSB, Martiusiana, II A 2, Wallich to Martius, 14 February 1848.
14. Candolle & Radcliffe-Smith, 'Nathaniel Wallich', p. 343.
15. Royal Library Copenhagen, Manuscript Collection, Wallich to Schouw, 6 November 1845: 'Han er en ypperlig Botaniker og i enhver Henseende en interesting Mand'.
16. Bille, *Steen Billes' Bericht*, p. 129.
17. E. Rostrup, article 'Kamphøvener, Bernhard Casper', *Dansk Biografisk Leksikon*, vol. 9, ed. C.F. Bricka, Copenhagen: Gyldendal, 1895, pp. 95f.
18. G. Zirnstein, article 'Philippi, Rudolf Amandus', *Neue Deutsche Biographie*, vol. 20, Berlin: Duncker & Humblot, 2001, pp. 391f.

19. CNH, Wallich letters, Wallich to Humboldt, 10 December 1845.
20. Biblioteka Jagiellońska, Cracow, Collection of Autographs, Alexander von Humboldt, Philippi to Rother, 6 December 1845.
21. Bille, *Steen Billes Bericht*, p. 164.
22. BL IOR, F/4/2186, Board's Collections, Wallich to Halliday, 19 November 1845.
23. CNH, Wallich letters, Wallich to Humboldt, 10 December 1845 'As I hope life being spared'.
24. CA, A 515, Maclear Mann Papers, 14, Wallich to Thomas and Mary Maclear, 26 February 1845.
25. Ibid., 74, Wallich to Mary Maclear, 19 November 1846.
26. CNH, Wallich-letters, Wallich to Irvine, 12 December 1845.
27. Ibid.
28. CA, A 515, Maclear Mann Papers, 14, Wallich to Thomas Maclear, 4 February 1846.
29. Ibid., 'I have had a deep sorrow – and have still by the death of the dearest oldest and best friend I ever possessed – my beloved brother at Copenhagen'.
30. Ibid.
31. Candolle & Radcliffe-Smith, 'Nathaniel Wallich', p. 344.
32. Ibid.
33. CNH, Wallich letters, General Order by the Hon'ble President of the Council of India in Council, 3 April 1846.
34. Ibid., Secretary of the Agricultural and Horticultural Society of Madras to Wallich, 7 April 1846.
35. CA, A 515, Maclear Mann Papers, 74, Wallich to Mary Maclear, 19 November 1846; BSB, Martiusiana II A 2, Wallich to Martius, 28 November 1847.
36. CA, A 515, Maclear Mann Papers, 74, Wallich to Mary Maclear, 19 November 1846.
37. CNH, Wallich letters, Wallich to Delessert, 7 January 1846.
38. Ibid.
39. Hamburg State and University Library, Lehmann's papers, vol. 14, A II, 43.4, Lehmann to N.N., 1 July 1846.
40. Ibid.
41. CA, A 515, Maclear Mann Papers, 74, Wallich to Hannah Biddulph, 28 December 1846; ibid., Wallich to Mary Maclear, 18 January 1847.
42. Ibid. Wallich to Mary Maclear, 18 January 1847.
43. Ibid. 74, Wallich to Mary Maclear, 23 July 1847.

44. Ibid., 19 November 1846.
45. Ibid., 14, Wallich to Thomas and Mary Maclear, 8 March 1854.
46. Ibid., 19 November 1846.
47. Ibid., Wallich to Hannah Biddulph, 28 December 1846.
48. Ibid., 14, Wallich to Thomas and Mary Maclear, 8 March 1854.
49. Ibid., 74, Wallich to Mary Maclear, 18 January 1847, 'We have good reason to believe that he has become a study man in all respects'.
50. BSB, Martiusiana II A 2, Wallich to Martius, 29 November 1851; CA, A 515, Maclear Mann Papers, 14, Wallich to Thomas and Mary Maclear, 8 March 1854.
51. RAK, Kirurgisk Akademi, 3405-01, Matricul-Protocoll, Matricul 1785-1839, p. 68.
52. CA, A 515, Maclear Mann Papers, 14, Wallich to Thomas and Maclear, February 1853, 'One of my daughters, Anne 20 years, is going to be married early next month, to Mr Charles Möller, a Danish gentleman, the son of one of my oldest friends at Copenhagen, the only survivor of my Examination contemporaries at the Royal Academy of Surgeons in 1806 . . . Mr C. Möller is 36 years old and a Merchant in London, with whom there is my hope that my dear child will be happy'.
53. Ibid., Wallich to Thomas and Mary Maclear, 8 March 1854.
54. Ibid., 17, Wallich to Mary Maclear, 19 November 1846.
55. Kind notice by Mark Watson, Edinburgh, 14th November 2020: 'Franics Boott was another Linnean Society connection. Edinburgh trained Boott had previously been Secretary at the LS and later would be Treasurer. By the time of the late 1840s he had inherited enough money to retire from medicine, but presumably treated Wallich as a close friend.'
56. RBG Kew, Director's Correspondence, Boott to W.J. Hooker, 13 May 1847; ibid., 14 May 1847; ibid., (c.1847).
57. BSB, Martiusiana II A 2, Wallich to Martius, 28 November 1847.
58. Ibid. 3 May 1848; RBG Kew, Director's Correspondence, Gardner to W.J. Hooker, 7 May 1848
59. CNH, Wallich letters, Lehmann to Wallich, 30 December 1848.
60. CA, A 515, Maclear Mann Papers, 14, Wallich to Thomas Maclear, 20 April 1848.
61. Ibid.
62. Schultz Hansen, 'Demokratie oder Nationalismus', p. 443.
63. BSB, Martiusiana II A 2, Wallich to Martius, 3 May 1848.
64. CA, A 515, Maclear Mann Papers, 14, Wallich to Thomas Maclear, 10 July 1848.

65. CNH, Wallich letters, Lehmann to Wallich, 30 December 1848.
66. CNH, Wallich letters, Lehmann to Wallich, 29 January 1849.
67. CA, A 515, Maclear Mann Papers, 14, Wallich to Thomas Maclear, 20 April 1848.
68. BSB, Martiusiana II A 2, Wallich to Martius, 9 June 1848.
69. Welsh, *South Africa*, p. 187-190; CA, A 515, Maclear Mann Papers, 74, Wallich to Mary Maclear, 18 January 1847.
70. CA, A 515, Maclear Mann Papers, 14, Wallich to Thomas and Mary Maclear, 8 March 1854.
71. CNH, Wallich letters, Lehmann to Wallich, 30 December 1848.
72. CA, A 515, Maclear Mann Papers, 74, Wallich to Mary Maclear, 30 October 1847.
73. CNH, Wallich letters, Bentham to Wallich, 16 February 1847.
74. Ibid.
75. BSB, Martiusiana II A 2, Wallich to Martius, 28 November 1847.
76. Numerical List of Dried Specimens, http://wallich.rbge.info/, (retrieved 1 August 2017).
77. Gage & Stearn, *Bicentenary History*, pp. 29, 50-3.
78. *Proceedings of the Linnean Society of London*, vol. 1, November 1838–June 1848, London 1849, pp. iii–ix.
79. Ibid. vol. 2, November 1848–June 1854, London 1855, pp. 5-12; 114-17.
80. *Hooker's Journal of Botany and Kew Gardens Miscellany*, vol. 5, 1853, pp. 301-4.
81. *Proceedings of the Linnean Society of London*, vol. 2, p. 64.
82. CNH, Wallich letters, Brown to Wallich, 26 January 1847.

CHAPTER 16

Final Days

London continued to grow and consolidated its reputation as a world metropolis. In 1851 the first world exhibition took place in Hyde Park, for which the architect Joseph Paxton built the legendary Crystal Palace. Always full of admiration for the latest technology, Wallich visited the palace while it was under construction in 1850 and enthused to the Maclears: 'The Crystal Palace! Do imagine to Yourself anything that is gorgeous, interesting, grand, inexhaustible'.[1] Here the highest level of British manufactures were to be presented in a global context. His enthusiasm for technology knew limits only where practicality failed, as, for example, in a cooling unit driven by oxen designed by Charles Piazzi Smyth, Wallich's acquaintance from South African days, by now working as an astronomer in Edinburgh.[2] Wallich wrote somewhat disparagingly to their mutual friends Mary and Thomas Maclear: 'His, the professor's refrigerating apparatus for India . . . is very clever, very scientific—and most exceedingly good for nothing as far as regards its practical applicability'.[3] It was the enormous dimensions of the apparatus that he saw as its biggest obstacle and decades were to pass before the idea became a functional air conditioning system.

In 1851, Wallich celebrated his sixty-fifth birthday. Weeks of strength and health were increasingly replaced by phases of indisposition. More and more the wet, foggy winter days caused him problems. He complained to his correspondents about inflammation in the bronchi and throat: the botanist was gradually becoming a victim of the London smog.[4] In autumn 1852, and during the following winter, he was in permanently poor health. For two months he was confined to the house with bronchitis, from which he recovered only very slowly.[5] Only lively correspondence and the occasional visit from friends and companions now connected him with the outside world.

Medical care was given to him by George Leith Roupell of St. Bartholomew's Hospital, brother of his friend Thomas Roupell from happier South African days. But even this talented doctor was soon at his wits' end and sought additional advice from other celebrated London doctors. Comfort was not only provided by medical attention, but also by the tireless care of his beloved daughter Hannah, who, during her long visits to London, always arranged for a warm fire in his bedroom.[6] Wallich was apparently of the opinion that only a stay in warmer climes could help, and again and again his thoughts took him to his beloved, but unreachable South Africa.[7] Only rarely did he feel in good enough health to undertake even the short excursion to Kew.[8]

In the spring of 1853, Nathaniel felt strong enough to spend two weeks on Jersey with Hannah.[9] At the end of November 1853, he attended a dinner at the Philosophical Club of the Royal Society, where he also met his long-time friend from Indian days, John Forbes Royle.[10] In the following December, he could hardly leave the house again, suffering from severe pain, coughing fits and insomnia. Taking laudanum, an analgesic and soothing opiate tincture not without considerable side effects, did at least enable Wallich to sleep through the night again, as he wrote to Sir William Hooker in January 1854.[11] The birth of Anne's child prompted him to leave the house on only a single occasion.[12] His last winter had come.

At the end of February, after a long time, Wallich felt better for a while and was able to devote himself to writing letters again.[13] On 8 March, he wrote his last letter to the Maclears in Cape Town. He no longer felt able to use a pen and had long since switched to the easier-to-use carbon pencil.[14] In April, his health deteriorated to such an extent that he was now unable to write letters on his own and his wife Sophia took over all correspondence. But in the end, she too had no choice but to report to her friends about the now obvious physical deterioration of her husband.[15] As a doctor, Wallich himself foresaw his end: the symptoms of approaching death had been all too familiar to him throughout his life as a surgeon. A last, but nevertheless handwritten note, was sent with good wishes to the Fellows of the Linnean Society, which was still very important to Wallich. But it was to be the final one.[16]

Nathaniel Wallich died on 28 April 1854 in his house in Gower Street. The funeral took place a week later at Kensal Green Cemetery, attended by Robert Brown and other companions. With sadness the Linnean Society took note of the death of its long-standing and prominent member and at its meeting on 2 May, in view of his position as one of the Vice-Presidents and his life's work in the field of botany, the meeting was dissolved, out of respect, without further agenda following the election of some corresponding members.[17] His obituary was read out at the meeting of 24 May. In addition to presenting a long curriculum vitae, the manifold tasks he had accomplished were highlighted: the management of the Calcutta Botanic Garden, his numerous research trips, his botanical collections. It also emphasized his special ability to involve local collaborators to the advantage of scientific ends. There was also gratitude that ownership of the great herbarium of the East India Company had been given to the Society through Wallich's intercession in 1832.[18] However, what was not said is perhaps the more significant. The conflict with William Griffith was probably still vivid in the minds of many Fellows. The German-language magazine *Bonplandia* also noted this trait: 'Dr Wallich was at times somewhat violent and eccentric in character', though ultimately the positive qualities outweighed the negative: 'but he had a good heart and, therefore, had a large following among men of science. He was serious and energetic, and his manners were seasoned with a rich sense of humour, as well as something very peculiar that gave him just enough originality'.[19]

Just what was this 'something very peculiar'? Surely, some

special aspect of Wallich's character that on the one hand was characterized by great human warmth and on the other, especially in old age, also by violent antipathies. There is a sense in which Wallich had outlived his day and belonged to a time long past, the time of Linnaeus, of the multinational Danish state and the heyday of the East India Company. But these worlds had long been in a state of decay: the natural system had long since established itself in botany, and mere collecting and describing was no longer sufficient; four years after his death, the great uprising in India in 1857 swept away the rule of the East India Company, and another six years later the Danish monarchy lost its rebellious Duchies of Schleswig and Holstein.

NOTES

1. CA, A 515, Maclear Mann Papers, 14, Wallich to Thomas Maclear, 14 May 1850.
2. Carroll Gantz, *Refrigeration: A History*, Jefferson, North Carolina, 2015, p. 43.
3. CA, A 515, Maclear Mann Papers, 14, Wallich to Mary and Thomas Maclear, 8 March 1854.
4. For example, RBG Kew, Director's Correspondence, Wallich to W.J. Hooker, 12 December 1852.
5. Ibid., 55/385, 29 December 1852.
6. Ibid., 55/386, 7 January 1853.
7. CA, A 515, Maclear Mann Papers, 14, Wallich to Thomas Maclear, 11 February 1853.
8. RBG Kew, Director's Correspondence, 55/381, Wallich to W.J. Hooker, 12 December 1852.
9. Ibid. Director's Correspondence, 55/432, Wallich to Liebmann, 23 June 1853.
10. Ibid., Wallich to W.J. Hooker, 55/462, 6 December 1853; ibid. 55/467, 28 January 1854.
11. Ibid., 55/465, 16 January 1854.
12. Ibid., 55/467, 28 January 1854.
13. Ibid., 55/470, 27 February 1854.

14. CA, A 515, Maclear Mann Papers, 14, Wallich to Thomas and Mary Maclear, 8 March 1854.
15. RBG Kew, Director's Correspondence, R.J. Fayrer to W.J. Hooker, 23 April 1854.
16. See *Proceedings of the Linnean Society*, vol. 2, p. 317.
17. Ibid., p. 295.
18. Ibid., pp. 314-18.
19. Bonplandia, vol 2, no. 12, 15 June 1854, p. 139.

Sources and Secondary Literature

MANUSCRIPT SOURCES

'Asiatisk Kompagni København, Skibsprotoller', 752-3, Printzen af Augustenborg, Danish National Archives, Copenhagen.

'Asiatisk Kompagni, Factorierne i Frederiksnagore og Patna', 1807-8, 2031, Resolutionsprotokoller, Danish National Archives, Copenhagen.

'Asiatisk Kompagni, Faktorierne i Frederiksnagore og Patna', 1807-8, 2144, Regnskabsjournal, Danish National Archives, Copenhagen.

'Assistant Surgeons' Papers', 1838-9, L/MIL/9/386, India Office Records, British Library, London

'Bengal Proceedings', 15 March 1825, P/124/14, India Office Records, British Library, London.

'Bengal Public Letter', 1817-19, F/4/621/15534, India Office Records, British Library, London.

'Board's Collections', 1827, F/4/1068, India Office Records, British Library, London.

'Board's Collections', 1828-30, F/4/1139, India Office Records, British Library, London.

'Board's Collections', 1834, F/4/1586, India Office Records, British Library, London.

'Board's Collections', 1845, F/4/2186, India Office Records, British Library, London.

'Board's Collections', 1820, F/4/655/15, India Office Records, British Library, London.

'Collection Römer', NL 134 M 62, Leipzig University Library, Leipzig.

'Committee of Correspondence', 1839, F/4/1139, India Office Records, British Library, London.

'Det. Kgl. Ostind. Guvernement i Tranquebar', 1816, 1378h, Rapport fra Overdragelses Kommission, Danish National Archives, Copenhagen.

'Director's Correspondence', 52-5, Library and Archives at Royal Botanic Gardens, Kew.

'Extract Bengal Public Consultations', 1822, F/4/712/19459, India Office Records, British Library, London.

'First Report of the Plantation Committee', 25 March 1823, P/11/2, India Office Records, British Library, London.

'Fourth Report of the Plantation Committee', 18 September 1823, P/11/10, India Office Records, British Library, London.

'Håndskriftsamlingen, various letters to Nathaniel Wallich', 1823-54, Royal Library, Copenhagen.

'Herschel Letters', 1828-50, HS 18, 28-34, Royal Society, London.

'Kirurgisk Akademi', 1785-1839, 3405-1, Matricul-Protocoll, Danish National Archives, Copenhagen.

'Last Will of Nathaniel Wallich', 11 April 1854, PROB 11/2192/77, National Archives, Kew.

'Letters from Wallich', 1810-53, Natural History Museum, Copenhagen.

'Letters of Johann Georg Christian Lehmann', vol. 14, A II, Hamburg State and University Library, Hamburg.

'Lorentz Bie, Periodiske Annotationer paa Serampore i Bengal', 1809-22, Maritime Museum, Helsingør.

'Maclear Mann Papers', 14, 74, 78, A 515, West Cape State Archives, Cape Town.

'Martiusiana II A2', Bavarian State Library, Munich.

'Ostindisk Kompagni', 1674-1778, 2034b, Bengalske dokumenter, Danish National Archives, Copenhagen.

'Proceedings of the Agricultural and Horticultural Society', vol. 1, Agricultural and Horticultural Society, Kolkata.

'Revenues at Serampore', F/265/5862, India Office Records, British Library, London.

'Second Report of the Plantation Committee', 26 June 1823, P/11/6, India Office Records, British Library, London.

'Seventh Report of the Plantation Committee', 5 January 1824, P/11/17, India Office Records, British Library, London.

'Tenth Report of the Plantation Committee', 5 December 1825, P/11/46, India Office Records, British Library, London.

'Wallich letters', 1794–1846, Central National Herbarium, Botanical Survey of India, Kolkata.

'Wallich, Nathaniel', 1814, L/Mil/9/366/148, India Office Records, British Library, London.

QA-035, Engelholm Gods, 1811-52, Familie Wolf privatarkiv, correspondence, 29-8, Landsarkivet for Sjælland, Copenhagen.

PRINTED SOURCES

Anker, Peder, *En samling af mythologiske Antiquer, Bragt fra Hindustan af generalmajor Anker*, London, 1806.

Asiatic Journal and Monthly Register for British and Foreign India, China, and Australasia, New Series, vol. 10-36, London, 1833-41.

Banks, Joseph, *The Indian and Pacific Correspondence of Sir Joseph Banks, 1768-1820*, ed. Neil Chambers, vol. 8, London: Pickering & Chatto, 2014.

Bartels, Johann-Heinrich and J.C.G. Fricke, 'Amtlicher Bericht über die Versammlung Deutscher Naturforscher und Aerzte in Hamburg im September 1830', Hamburg: Perthes & Besser, 1831.

Bastin, John, 'The Letters of Sir Stamford Raffles to Nathaniel Wallich 1819-24', *Journal of the Malaysian Branch of the Royal Asiatic Society*, vol. 54, no. 2, 1981, pp. 1-73.

Bentham, George, *Autobiography 1800-34*, ed. Marion Filipauk, Toronto, Buffalo, and London: University of Toronto Press, 1997.

Bie, Lorentz, 'Periodiske Annotationer paa Serampore i Bengalen', *Personalhistorisk Tiddskrift*, vol. 52, no. 9, 1931, pp. 102-14.

Bille, Steen, *Steen Bille's Bericht über die Reise der Corvette Galathea um die Welt in den Jahren 1845, 46 und 47*, translated into Danish and ed. W. von Rosen, Copenhagen: Reitzel, Leipzig: Lorck, 1852.

Bonplandia, *Zeitschrift für die gesammte Botanik*, vol. 2, no. 12 and no. 15, 1854.

Bowrey, Thomas, A *Geographical Account of Countries Round the Bay of Bengal, 1669 to 1679*, New Delhi: Munshiram Manoharlal, 1997.

Bricka, Carl Frederik, ed., *Fonden ad Usus Publicus. Aktmæssige bidrag til belysning af dens virksomhed*, published by the Danish National Archives, vol. 2, Copenhagen, 1902.

British Parliamentary Papers, 1839, Report on the Tea Plant of Upper Assam, India Revenue Consultations, 20 June 1836. vol. XXXIX, Paper 63.

British Parliamentary Papers, 1839; India Revenue Consultations, 20 June 1836; Report on the Tea Plant of Upper Assam, by Mr Assistant-Surgeon William Griffith, Madras Establishment, late Member of Assam Deputation.

Buchanan-Hamilton, Francis, *An Account of the Kingdom of Nepal and of the Territories Annexed to this Dominion by the House of Gorkha*, New Delhi, 2007.

Burkill, Isaac Henry, 'William Jack's Letters to Nathaniel Wallich',

Journal of the Malayan Branch of the Royal Asiatic Society, vol. 7, 1916, pp. 147-268.

Callisen, Adolph Carl Peter, *Medicinisches Schriftsteller-Lexicon der jetzt lebenden Ärzte, Wundärzte, Geburtshelfer, Apotheker, und Naturforscher aller gebildeten Völker,* vol. 16, Copenhagen, 1833.

Charlton, Andrew, *Correspondence Regarding the Discovery of the Tea Plant of Assam*, Calcutta, 1841.

Crawfurd, John, *Journal of an Embassy from the Governor-General of India to the Court of Ava in the Year 1827*, London: Colburn, 1829.

Crawfurd, John, *Journal of an Embassy from the Governor-General of India to the Courts of Siam and Cochin China; Exhibiting a View of the Actual State of those Kingdoms*, 2nd edn, vol. 1, London: Colburn, Bentley, 1830.

Dansk Litteratur-Tidende for Aaret 1819, Copenhagen, 1819.

Flora oder Botanische Zeitung, vol. 6, no.1, 7 January 1823.

Gordon, Robert (ed.), *Copy of Papers from India relating to the Measures adopted for Introducing the Cultivation of the Tea Plant within the British Possessions in India*, London, 1839.

Griffith, William, *Journals of Travels in Assam, Burma, Bootan, Afghanistan, and the Neighbouring Countries*, ed. John McClelland, Calcutta, 1847.

Griffith, William, *Report on the Honorable Company's Botanic Garden*, Calcutta 1843.

Griffith, William, *Report on the Tea Plant of Upper Assam*, Calcutta, [ca. 1838].

Hanitsch, Richard, 'Letters of Nathaniel Wallich Relating to the Botanical Garden in Singapore', *Journal of the Malayan Branch of the Royal Asiatic Society*, vol. 65, 1913, pp. 39-48 (reprint: *Journal of the Malayan Branch of the Royal Asiatic Society*, vol. 42, no. 1, 1969, pp. 145-54).

Herder, Johann Gottfried, *Persepolis. Eine Muthmassung*, vol. 15. of *Herders Sämmtliche Werke*, ed. Bernhard Suphan, Berlin, 1888, pp. 571-621.

Holmes and Co., ed., *The Bengal Obituary; or a Record to Perpetuate the Memory of Departed Worth*, London and Calcutta: W. Thacker & Co., 1851.

Hooker, William Jackson, *Hooker's Journal of Botany and Kew Gardens Miscellany*, vol. 5, London: Reeve,1853.

Humboldt, Alexander von, *Ideen zu einer Geographie der Pflanzen nebst einem Naturgemälde*, Tübingen: F. G. Cotta, 1807.

———, *Kosmos. Versuch einer physischen Weltbeschreibung*, vol. 1, Stuttgart and Augsburg, 1845.

Jacquemont, Victor, *Letters from India. Describing a Journey in the British Dominions of India, Tibet, Lahore and Cashmeer*, 2nd edn, vol. 1, London: Edward Churton, 1835.

Johnson, George William, *The Stranger in India; or Three Years in Calcutta*, vol. 1, London: Henry Colburn, 1843.

Kjøbenhavns Veiviser, *eller Anviisning til de Fleestes Boepæle i Kjøbenhavn og Forstæderne*, Copenhagen, 1798-1815.

Kvist, Palle, ed., *Mellem København og Tranquebar: på rejse med asiatisk kompagnis skib Kronprindsessen af Danmark 1748-1750*, Copenhagen: Selskab for Udgivelse af Kilder til Dansk Historie, 2011.

McClelland, John, *Some Inquiries in the Province of Kemaon, Relative to Geology, and Other Branches of Natural Science*, Calcutta: Thacker & Co., 1835.

Montefiore, Joshua, *Commercial Dictionary of the Present State of Mercantile Law, Practice, and Custom*, London, 1803.

N.N., *Min Stemme i Anledning af Dagens Stridsskrifter om den jødiske Ungdoms Opdragelse*, 1796.

Nair, P. Thankappan, ed., *Proceedings of the Asiatic Society*, vols. 2-4, Calcutta, 1995-2000.

Nyerup, Rasmus, *Beschreibung der Stadt Kopenhagen*, ed. & trs. into German M. Müller, Copenhagen: Schultz, 1807.

———, *Catalogus Librorum Sanskritanorum, quos Bibliothecae Universitatis Havniensis vel dedit vel paravit Nathaniel Wallich, Doctor Medicinae et Philosophias, Ordinis Danebrogii Eques, Horti botanici Calcuttensis in India Praefectus*, Copenhagen: Gyldendal, 1821.

———, *Oversigt over Fædrelandets Mindesmærker fra Oldtiden, saaledes som samme kan tænkes opstillede i et tilkommende National-Museum. Et forsøg*, Copenhagen, 1806.

Politisk og oekonomisk Lommebog, eller Kjøbenhavns Stats- og Handels Veiviser, Copenhagen, 1787-90.

Proceedings of the Linnean Society of London, vol. 1: Nov. 1838–June 1848, London: R. and E.J. Taylor, 1849.

Proceedings of the Linnean Society of London, vol. 2: Nov. 1848–June 1854, London: Taylor and Francis, 1855.

Rask, Rasmus Kristian, *Den Ældste Hebraiske Tidsregning indtil Moses, efter kilderne på ny bearbejdet og forsynet met et Kårt over Paradis*, Copenhagen: Schultz, 1828.

Roxburgh, William, 'Directions for Taking Care of Growing Plants at

294   *Sources and Secondary Literature*

Sea', *The Annual Register or a View of the History, Politics and Literature for the Year 1810*, 2nd edn, London, 1825, pp. 619–20.

Simmond's Colonial Magazine and Foreign Miscellany, ed. P.L. Simmonds, London, vol. 6, September-December 1845.

The Magazine of Natural History, vol. 2, 1829.

Wallich, Nathaniel, 'Af et brev fra Dr N. Wallich, Directeur ved den botaniske Have af Calcutta, til Professor J.W. Hornemann', *Tidsskrift for Naturvidenskaberne*, vol. 1, no. 2, 1822, pp. 257-64.

——, 'Brief Excursion to the Hills to the East of Ava in November 1826', *SOAS Bulletin of Burma Research*, vol. 3, no. 2, 2005, pp. 476-82.

——, 'Descriptions of two new species of *Sarcolobus*, and of some other Indian Plants', *Asiatick Researches*, vol. 12, 1816, pp. 566-71.

——, *A Numerical List of Dried Specimens of Plants in the East India Company's Museum, Collected under the Superintendence of Dr. Wallich of the Company's Botanic Garden at Calcutta*, London, 1828-49.

——, *Observations on the Cultivation of the Tea Plant, for Commercial Purposes, in the mountainous Parts of Hindustan; drawn up at the Desire of the Right Honourable C. Grant, President of the Board of Control for Indian Affair*, in Parliamentary Papers,/39,1839, Document 63.

——, *Plantae Asiaticae Rariores: or, Descriptions and Figures of a Select Number of Unpublished East Indian Plants*, vols. 1-3, London: Treuttel and Würtz, 1829-32.

——, *Tentamen Florae Napalensis Illustratae, Consisting of Botanical Descriptions and Lithographic Figures of Select Nipal Plants*, vols. 1 & 2, Calcutta-Serampore: Asiatic Lithographic Press, 1824-6.

——, 'An account of a new species of a Camellia growing wild at Napal', *Asiatick Researches*, vol. 13, 1820, pp. 428-32.

Wallich, Wulf Lazarus, *Forslag til Forbedring i den Jødiske menigheds Forfatning i Kiøbenhavn*, Copenhagen, 1795.

Ward, William, *Sermon Preached on the 1st of August, 1813, in the Settlement Church at Serampore on Occasion of the Erection of a Monument to the Memory of the Lady of N. Wallich*, Serampore: Mission Press, 1813.

Warner, Brian, ed., *The Cape Diary and Letters of William Mann, Astronomer and Mountaineer. 1839-43*, Cape Town, 1989.

SECONDARY LITERATURE

Aagaard, Otto C. & Spärck, R., Art. 'Jacobson, Ludvig Levin', Poul Engelstoft, ed., vol. 11 of Dansk Biografisk Leksikon, Copenhagen: J. H. Schultz, 1937, pp. 342-5.

Aalund, Fleming and Simon Rastén, *Indo-Danish Heritage Buildings of Serampore. Survey Report by the Serampore Initiative of the National Museum of Denmark*, Copenhagen, 2010.

Alberti, Eduard, *Lexikon der Schleswig-Holstein-Lauenburgischen und Eutinischen Schriftsteller von 1829 bis heute*, vol. 2, Kiel: Biernatzki, 1868.

Allen, Charles, *The Prisoner of Kathmandu. Brian Hodgson in Nepal, 1820-43*, New Delhi: Speaking Tiger Publishing, 2016.

Arasaratnam, Sinnappah, *Maritime India in the Seventeenth Century*, Oxford and New Delhi: Oxford University Press, 1994.

Arnold, David, 'Plant Capitalism and Company Science. The Indian Career of Nathaniel Wallich', *Modern Asian Studies*, vol. 42, no. 5, September 2008, pp. 899-928.

——, *Colonizing the Body. State Medicine and Epidemic Disease in Nineteenth-Century India*, Berkeley: University of California Press, 1993.

——, *The Tropics and the Traveling Gaze: India, Landscape, and Science, 1800-56*, Seattle and London: University of Washington Press, 2006.

Aung-Thwin, Michael, *A History of Burma*, New York, 1967.

Aung-Thwin, Michael and Aung-Thwin, Maitrii, *A History of Myanmar since Ancient Times. Traditions and Transformations*, London: Reaktion Books, 2012.

Banerjea, Dhrubajyoti, *European Calcutta, Images and Recollections of a Bygone Era*, 3rd edn, New Delhi: USB Publishers' Distributors, 2008.

Bastin, John, 'Sir Stamford Raffles and the Study of Natural History in Penang, Singapore and Indonesia', *Journal of the Malaysian Branch of the Royal Asiatic Society*, vol. 63, no. 2, 1990, pp. 1-25.

Bhattacharya, Jayanta, 'From Hospitals to Hospital Medicine. Epistemological Transformation of Medical Knowledge in India', in *Außereuropäische und europäische Hospital- und Krankenhausgeschichte*, ed. Gunnar Stollberg, Christina Vanj, Ernst Kraas, Berlin: LIT Verlag, 2013, pp. 45-75.

Bie, Lorentz, 'Juliane Marie Wallich. Et tidsbillede fra Dansk Ostindien', *Personalhistorisk Tidsskrift*, vol. 62, no. 11, 1941, pp. 236-43.

Bird, Allan, *Arabella Roupell. Pioneer Artist of Cape Flowers*, Johannesburg: South African Natural History Publication Company, 1975.

Blunt, Wilfred, *The Art of Botanical Illustration*, London: Collins, 1967.

Bobé, Louis, 'Conrad Georg Friederich Elias v. Schmidt-Phiseldeck', in *Dansk Biografisk Leksikon*, ed. Carl Frederik Bricka, vol. 15, Copenhagen: Gyldendalske Boghandels Forlag, 1901, pp. 233ff.

Borgen, Liv, *Botanisk Hage 1814-2014. Historien om en Hage*, Oslo: Press Forlag, 2014.

Bradlow, Edna, 'Nathaniel Wallich: A Man for all Seasons', *Quarterly Bulletin of the South African Library*, vol. 52, no. 3, 1998, pp. 96-108.

Bregnsbo, Michael, 'Der Friedensvertrag und seine Unterzeichnung in Kiel am 14. Januar 1814', in *Der Kieler Frieden 1814. Ein Schicksalsjahr für den Norden*, ed. Sonja Kinzler, Neumünster: Wachholtz, 2013, pp. 47-57.

Buescher, Hartmut, *Catalogue of Sanskrit Manuscripts*, Copenhagen: NIAS Press—Det Kongelige Bibliotek, 2011.

Burkill, Isaac Henry, *Chapters on the History of Botany in India*, Delhi: Botanical Survey of India, 1965.

Candolle, Roger de and Alan Radcliffe Smith, 'Nathaniel Wallich, MD, PhD, FRS, FLS, FRGS, (1786–1854) and the Herbarium of the Honorable East India Company, and their Relation to the de Candolles of Geneva and the Great Prodromus', *Botanical Journal of the Linnean Society*, vol. 83, 1981, pp. 325-48.

Carøe, Kristian, *Den Danske lægestand*, Copenhagen and Christiania (Oslo): Nordisk Forlag and Gyldendalske Boghandels Forlag, 1905.

Carter, Harold B., *Sir Joseph Banks 1743-1820*, London: British Museum, 1988.

Christensen, Carl, 'Hornemann, Jens Wilken', in *Dansk Biografisk Leksikon*, vol. 10, ed. Poul Engelstoft, Copenhagen: J. H. Schultz, 1936, pp. 599-603.

——, 'Vahl, Martin', in *Dansk Biografisk Leksikon*, vol. 25, ed. Poul Engelstoft, Copenhagen: J. H. Schultz, 1943, pp. 12-18.

——, *Den Danske botaniks historie med tilhørende bibliographie*, vol. 1, Copenhagen: H. Hagerups Forlag, 1924-6.

Christensen, Dan Ch., *Naturens tankelæser. En biografi om Hans Christian Ørsted*, 2 vols., Copenhagen: Museum Tusculanum, 2009.

Clerke, Agnes Mary, 'Herschel, Johann Frederick William', in *Dictionary of National Biography*, vol. 26, New York: Macmillan and Co., 1891, pp. 263-8.

Collin, Jonas, 'Cantor, Theodor Edvard', in *Dansk Biografisk Lexikon*, vol. 3, ed. Carl Frederik Bricka, Copenhagen: Gyldendalske Boghandels Forlag, 1889, p. 352.

Crawford, Dirom Grey, *A History of the Indian Medical Service 1600-1913*, 2 vols., London: W. Thacker, 1914

Dasgupta, Subrata, *Awakening. The Story of the Bengal Renaissance*, London: Random House, 2011.

Deb Lal, Nilina, *Calcutta. Built Heritage Today. An INTACH Guide*, Kolkata: INTACH Calcutta Regional Chapter, 2006.

Degn, Christian, *Die Schimmelmanns im Atlantischen Dreieckshandel. Gewinn und Gewissen*, 3rd edn, Neumünster: Wachholtz, 2000.

Delfs, Tobias, ' "What shall become of the mission when we have such incompetent missionaries there?" Drunkenness and Mission in 18th century Danish East India', in *A History of Alcohol and Drugs in Modern South Asia. Intoxicating Affairs*, ed. Harald Fischer-Tiné and Jana Tschurenev, London: Routledge, 2014, pp. 65-89.

Desmond, Ray, *Sir Joseph Dalton Hooker. Traveller and Plant Collector*, 2nd edn, Woodbridge, Suffolk: Antique Collectors' Club, 2006.

——, *The European Discovery of the Indian Flora*, Oxford: Clarendon Press, 1992.

——, *The History of the Royal Botanic Gardens*, London: Harvill Press, 1998.

Deuntzer, Johan Henrik, 'Af det Asiatiske Kompagnis Historie', *Nationaløkonomisk Tidsskrift*, vol. 46, 1908, pp. 368-417.

Dukesz, Eduard, 'Daniel Jechiel Wallich, gestorben 1789, Großherzoglich mecklenburgischer Hofagent, sowie anderer wesentlich bedeutenderer Hamburg-Altonaer Großkaufleute', in *Jahrbuch für die jüdischen Gemeinden Schleswig-Holsteins und der Hansestädte*, vol. 4, 1932-3, pp. 49-57.

Dutta, Krishna, *Calcutta. A Cultural and Literary History*, New Delhi: Interlink Books, 2003.

Encyclopedia Judaica, 'Wallich', vol. 16, Jerusalem: Keter, 1971, pp. 256f.

Etzemüller, Thomas, *Biographien. Lesen, erforschen, erzählen*, Frankfurt am Main: Campus, 2012.

Farrington, Anthony, *Catalogue of East India Company Ship's Journals and Logs 1600-1834*, London: British Library, 1999.

Feldbæk, Ole, 'No Ship for Tranquebar for Twenty-Nine Years, or: The Art of Survival of a Mid-Seventeenth-Century European Settlement in India', in *Emporia, Commodities and Entrepreneurs in Asian Maritime Trade, c. 1400-1750*, ed. Roderich Ptak and Dietmar Rothermund, Stuttgart: F. Steiner, 1991, pp. 29-36.

——, 'Revolutionskriege und Gesamtstaat. Das Ende der Neutralitätspolitik', *Zeitschrift des Vereins für Schleswig-Holsteinische Geschichte*, vol. 116, 1991, pp. 107-23.

——, *India-Trade under the Danish Flag 1772-1808. European Enterprise and Anglo-Indian Remittance and Trade*, Odense: Studentlitteratur, 1969.

Findeisen, Jörg-Peter and Hosum, Poul, *Kleine Geschichte Kopenhagens*, Regensburg: Pustet, 2008.

Fischer-Tiné, Harald, *Pidgin-Knowledge. Wissen und Kolonialismus*, Zurich and Berlin: Diaphanes, 2013.

Förster, Stig, *Die mächtigen Diener der East India Company. Ursachen und Hintergründe der britischen Expansionspolitik*, Stuttgart: F. Steiner, 1992.

Foster, William, *The East India House. Its History and Associations*, London: John Lane, 1924.

Frahm, Jan-Peter and Jens Eggers, *Lexikon deutschsprachiger Bryologen*, Norderstedt: BOD, 2001.

Francis, W., *The Nilgiris*, Madras: Government Press, 1908.

Frasch, Tilman, 'Autonomie im Griff des Kolonialismus. Südostasien', in *Die Welt im 19. Jahrhundert*, ed. Michael Mann, Vienna: Mandelbaum, 2009, pp. 155-88.

Fraser-Jenkins, Christopher R., *The First Botanical Collectors in Nepal. The Fern Collections of Hamilton, Gardner and Wallich. Lost Herbaria, a Lost Botanist, Lost Letters and Lost Books Somewhat Rediscovered*, Dehradun, 2006.

Friis, Ib, 'Martin Vahl's videnskabelige løbebane i København og betydning for botaniken', in *Martin Vahl. 250 års minnet*, ed. Per M. Jørgensen, Bergen, 2000, pp. 12-46.

Gage, Andrew Thomas and William Thomas Stearn, *A Bicentenary History of the Linnean Society of London*, London, 1988.

Gait, Edward, *A History of Assam*, Dibrugarh-Guwahati-Tezpur-Jorhat, 2010.

Gantz, Carroll, *Refrigeration. A History*, Jefferson, North Carolina, 2015.

Gerlach, Dieter, *Geschichte der Mikroskopie*, Frankfurt am Main, 2009.

Glamann, Kristof, 'The Danish Asiatic Company, 1732-72', *The Scandinavian Economic History Review*, vol. 8, no. 2, 1960, pp. 109-49.

Glass, Ian Steward, *The Royal Observatory at the Cape of Good Hope*, Cape Town, 2015.

Gøbel, Erik, 'Danish Companies' Shipping to Asia, 1616-1807', in *Ships, Sailors and Spices. East India Companies and their Shipping in the 16th, 17th and 18th Centuries*, ed. Jaap R. Bruijn and Femme S. Gaastra, Amsterdam, 1993, pp. 99-120.

——, 'Det Seramporske Collegium. Skoler og College i Serampore 1800–1845', in *Skole, Kirke, Arkiv*, ed. Børge Riis Larsen, Odense, 2004, pp. 27-39.

——, *De styrede rigerne. Embedsmændene i det Dansk-Norske civile central-administration 1660-1814*, Odense, 2000.

Goldberg, Bettina, *Abseits der Metropolen. Die jüdische Minderheit in Schleswig-Holstein*, Neumünster, 2011.

Grau, Jürke, 'Palmen und 8000 brasilianische Pflanzen. Der Botaniker Carl Friedrich Philipp von Martius', in *Christian Gottfried Nees von Esenbeck. Die Bedeutung der Botanik als Naturwissenschaft in der ersten Hälfte des 19. Jahrhunderts. Methoden und Entwicklungswege*, ed. Daniela Feistauer, Uta Monecke, Irmgard Müller, and Bastian Röther, Stuttgart, 2006, pp. 189-98.

Gribbin, Mary and Gribbin, John, *Flower Hunters*, Oxford-New York, 2009.

Gröschl, Jürgen, 'Missionaries of the Danish-Halle and English-Halle Mission in India 1706-1844', in *Halle and the Beginnings of Protestant Christianity in India*, ed. Andreas Gross, Y. Vincent Kumaradoss, and Heike Liebau, vol. 3, Halle, 2006, pp. 1497-1527.

Grove, Richard, *Green Imperialism. Colonial Expansion, Tropical Island Edens and the Origins of Environmentalism*, Cambridge, 1997.

Guha, Amalendu, *Medieval and Early Colonial Assam*, Calcutta & New Delhi, 1991.

Gunn, Mary and Codd, Leslie Edward, *Botanical Exploration of Southern Africa. An Illustrated History of Early Botanical Literature on the Cape Flora. Biographical Accounts of the Leading Plant Collectors and their Activities in Southern Africa from the Days of the East India Company until Modern Times*, Cape Town, 1981.

Harrison, Mark, 'The Calcutta Botanic Garden and the Wider World, 1817-46', in *Science and Modern India*, ed. Uma Das Gupta, Delhi, 2011, pp. 235-53.

Helbig, Jörg, ed., *Brasilianische Reise 1817-20. Carl Friedrich Philipp von Martius zum 200. Geburtstag*, Munich, 1994.

Henningsen, Bernd, 'Henrik Steffens' Kopenhagener Philosophie-Vorlesungen 1802/03. Zur Einführung', in Steffens, Henrik *Einleitung in die Philosophischen Vorlesungen*, Freiburg and Munich, 2016, pp. 7-21.

Herbert, Eugenia W., *Flora's Empire. British Gardens in India*, Philadelphia, 2011.

Hohenegger, Beatrice, *Liquid Jade. The Story of Tea from East to West*, New York, 2006.

Hoppe, Brigitte, 'Das naturwissenschaftliche Werk von C.G.D. Nees von Esenbeck als Beitrag zur Entwicklung der Botanik, insbesondere der Systematik', in *Christian Gottfried Nees von Esenbeck: Die Bedeutung der Botanik als Naturwissenschaft in der ersten Hälfte des 19.*

Jahrhunderts. Methoden und Entwicklungswege, ed. Daniela Feistauer, Uta Monecke, Irmgard Müller & Sebastian Röther, Stuttgart, 2006, pp. 21-54.

——, 'Von der Naturgeschichte zu den Naturwissenschaften. Die Dänisch-Halleschen Missionare als Naturforscher in Indien vom 18. zum 19. Jahrhundert', in *Mission und Forschung. Translokale Wissensproduktion zwischen Indien und Europa im 18 und 19. Jahrhundert*, ed. Heike Liebau, Andreas Nehring & Brigitte Klosterberg, Halle, 2010, pp. 141-66.

Hüttemeister, Nathanja, "Königlich schwedischer Professor der Weltweisheit und Arzneygelahrtheit'. Dr Schnaber-Levison und seine Kollegen. Grabinschriften für Ärzte und Hebammen', in *Verborgene Pracht. Der jüdische Friedhof Hamburg-Altona*, ed. Michael Brocke, Altona and Dresden, 2009, pp. 295-300.

Indian Museum, ed., *The Indian Museum 1814–1914*, Calcutta, 1914, rep. Kolkata, 2004.

Jensen, Jørgen, *Thomsen's museum. Historien om Nationalmuseet*, Copenhagen, 1992.

Jørnæs, Bjarne, *The Sculptor Bertel Thorvaldsen*, Copenhagen, 2011.

Kampen, Christan, *Min Wolffske familie*, manuscript.

Karsten, Mia C., *The Old Company's Garden at the Cape and its Superintendents*, Cape Town, 1951.

Klein, Christian, ed., *Handbuch Biographie. Methoden, Traditionen, Theorie*, Stuttgart-Weimar, 2009.

Krieger, Martin, 'Dänische Kaufleute in Balasore. Die Entwicklung einer europäischen Handelsniederlassung im indischen Orissa', *Scripta Mercaturae*, vol. 2, 1995, pp. 65-95.

——, 'Der dänische Gesamtstaat im Zeitalter der Napoleonischen Kriege', in *Der Kieler Frieden 1814. Ein Schicksalsjahr für den Norden*, ed. Sonja Kinzler, Neumünster, 2013, pp. 32-45.

——, 'Serampore Around 1800', in *Urbanization in the Oldenburg Monarchy, 1500-1800*, ed. Thomas Riis, Kiel, 2012, pp. 63-80.

——, *European Cemeteries in South India (Seventeenth to Nineteenth Centuries)*, New Delhi, 2013.

——, *Kaufleute, Seeräuber und Diplomaten. Der dänische Handel auf dem Indischen Ozean (1620-1868)*, Cologne, Weimar & Vienna, 1998.

——, *Tee. Eine Kulturgeschichte*, Cologne, Weimar & Vienna, 2009.

Kulke, Hermann and Dietmar Rothermund, *Geschichte Indiens. Von der Induskultur bis heute*, Munich, 1998.

Lange, Axel, 'Frederik Ludvig Holbøll', in *Dansk Biografisk Leksikon*, vol. 10, ed. Poul Engelstoft, Copenhagen: J.H. Schultz, 1936, pp. 370ff.

Larsen, Kay, *De Danske Ostindiske koloniers historie*, vol. 2, Copenhagen, 1908.

Lenger, Friedrich, *Industrielle Revolution und Nationalstaatsgründung*, Stuttgart, 2003.

Lock, H. Walter, 'Nees von Esenbeck und die Biodiversität von Gefäßpflanzen', in *Christian Gottfried Nees von Esenbeck. Die Bedeutung der Botanik als Naturwissenschaft in der ersten Hälfte des 19. Jahrhunderts. Methoden und Entwicklungswege*, ed. Daniela Feistauer, Uta Monecke, Irmgard Müller & Bastian Röther, Stuttgart, 2006, pp. 157-71.

Lowther, David, Ann Sylph & Mark Watson, 'Hodgson's Tibetan Mastiffs. Survival at Sea, Twice Presented to the London Zoo, and Tragic Demise', *Britain / Nepal ZSL*, 12 May 2014.

Lübker, Detlev Lorenz and Hans Schröder, *Lexikon der Schleswig-Holstein Lauenburgischen und Eutinischen Schriftsteller von 1796 bis 1828*, vol. 1, Altona: K. Busch Nachfolger, 1829.

Macfarlane, Alan and Iris Macfarlane, *Green Gold. The Empire of Tea. The Remarkable History of One of the Most Important Plants Known to Mankind*, London, 2004.

Mägdefrau, Karl, *Geschichte der Botanik. Leben und Leistung großer Forscher*, Stuttgart, Jena & New York, 1992.

Mann, Michael, 'Vom Werden eines Imperiums', in *Die Welt im 19. Jahrhundert*, Vienna, 2009, pp. 125-54.

Mann, Michael, *Flottenbau und Forstbetrieb in Indien 1794-1823*, Stuttgart, 1996.

Mariss, Anne, *'A World of New Things'. Praktiken der Naturgeschichte bei Johann Reinhold Forster*, Frankfurt am Main, 2015.

Marshman, John Clark, *The Life and Times of Carey, Marshman, and Ward. Embracing the History of the Serampore Mission*, vol. 1, London, 1859 (rep. Serampore, 2005).

McDonald, Donald, 'The Indian Medical Service. A Short Account of its Achievements 1600-1947', *Proceedings of the Royal Society of Medicine*, vol. 49, no. 1, 1956, pp. 13-17.

Medicinsk-historisk Museum af Københavns Universitet, ed., *Academia Chirurgorum Regia. Det kongelige kirurgiske Akademi 1787-1987*, Copenhagen, 1988.

Mentz, Søren, *The English Gentleman Merchant at Work. Madras and the City of London 1668–1740*, Copenhagen, 2005.

Mitra, Rajendralal, *History of the Society. Centenary Review of the Asiatic Society of Bengal 1784-1884*, vol. 1, Calcutta, 1885, rep. 1986.

Möbius, Martin, *Geschichte der Botanik. Von den ersten Anfängen bis zur Gegenwart*, Jena, 1937.

Mount, Ferdinand, *The Tears of the Rajas. Mutiny, Money and Marriage in India 1805-1905*, London, 2015.

Müller, Sigurd, 'Wallick, Ahron Wulff'; in *Dansk Biografisk Leksikon*, vol. 18, ed. Carl Frederik Bricka, Copenhagen: Gyldendalske Boghandels Forlag, 1905, p. 227.

Nielsen, Aage Krarup, *En Østerlandsfærd*, Copenhagen, 1923.

Nielsen, Yngvar, 'General-Major Peter Anker, Guvernør i Trankebar', *Norsk Historisk Tidsskrift*, vol. 1, 1871, pp. 273-384.

Nilsson, Sten, *European Architecture in India 1750-1850*, London, 1968.

Noltie, Henry J., *Journeys in Search of Robert Wight*, Edinburgh: Royal Botanic Garden Edinburgh, 2007.

——, *Raffles' Ark Redrawn. Natural History Drawings from the Collection of Sir Thomas Stamford Raffles*, London and Edinburgh, 2009.

——, *The Botany of Robert Wight*, Ruggell, 2005.

——, *The Life and Work of Robert Wight*, Edinburgh: Royal Botanic Garden Edinburgh, 2007.

Norrie, Gordon, 'Jødernes kamp for adgangen til universitet og den medicinske doctorgrad i Danmark', *Bibliotek for Læger*, vol. 87, no. 7, 1892, pp. 117-38.

Pedersen, Karl Peder, 'Tranquebars Historie', *Architectura. Arkitekturhistorisk Årsskrift*, vol. 9, 1987, special issue Tranquebar, pp. 11-49.

Pilon, Maxine and Danièle Weiler, *The French in Singapore. An Illustrated History (1819-today)*, Singapore, 2001.

Plug, C., Artikel 'Maclear, Sir Thomas', in *Biographical Database of Southern African Science*, http://www.s2a3.org.za/bio/Biograph_final.php?serial=1791, retrieved 7. February 2017.

Raman, Anantanarayanan, 'Georges Guerrard-Samuel Perrottet. A Forgotten Swiss French Plant Collector, Experimental Botanist and Biologist in India', *Current Science*, vol. 107, no.9, 2014, S. 1607-12.

Rasch, Aage, *Vore Gamle Tropekolonier: Dansk Ostindien 1777-1845*, ed. Johannes Brøndsted, vol. 7, 2nd edn, Copenhagen, 1967.

Ray, Pradyot Kumar, *Dewan Ram Comul Sen and his Times*, Calcutta, 1990.

Rivière, Marc Serge, 'From Belfast to Mauritius. Charles Telfair (1778-1833), Naturalist and a Product of the Irish Enlightenment', *Eighteenth Century Ireland. Iris an dá chultúr*, vol. 21, 2006, pp. 125-44.

Robinson, Tim, *William Roxburgh. The Founding Father of Indian Botany*, Chichester, 2008.

Rocher, Rosane and Ludo Rocher, *The Making of Western Indology. Henry Thomas Colebrooke and the East India Company*, London and New York, 2012.

Rostrup, E., 'Hofman (Bang) Niels', in *Dansk Biografisk Leksikon*, ed. Carl Frederik Bricka, vol. 1, Copenhagen: Gyldendalske Boghandels Forlag, 1887, pp. 504ff.

——, 'Kamphøvener, Bernhard Casper', in *Dansk Biografisk Leksikon*, vol. 9, ed. Carl Frederik Bricka, Copenhagen: Gyldendalske Boghandels Forlag, 1895, pp. 95f.

Sanwal, Bhariava Dat, *Nepal and the East India Company*, 1965.

Schultz Hansen, Hans, 'Demokratie oder Nationalismus. Politische Geschichte Schleswig-Holsteins 1830-1918', in *Geschichte Schleswig-Holsteins. Von den Anfängen bis zur Gegenwart*, ed. Ulrich Lange, Neumünster, 1996, pp. 427–85.

Schultze, H., 'Geschichte der Familie Wallich', *Monatsschrift für Geschichte und Wissenschaft des Judentums*, 1905, issue 1: pp. 57-77, issue 2: pp. 183-92; issue 3: pp. 272-85; issue 4: pp. 450-58; issue 5: pp. 571-80.

Schwarz Lausten, Martin, *Jøder og Kristne i Danmark. Fra middelalderen til nyere tid*, Frederiksberg, 2012.

——, *Oplysning i kirke og synagoge. Forholdet mellem kristne og jøder i den danske Oplysningstid*, Copenhagen, 2002.

Secord, Anne, 'Botany on a Plate. Pleasure and the Power of Pictures in Promoting Early Nineteenth-Century Scientific Knowledge', *Isis. An International Review Devoted to the History of Science and its Cultural Influences*, vol. 93, 2002, pp. 28-57.

Sheppard, Francis, *London 1808-70. The Infernal Wen*, London, 1971.

Sivaramakrishnan, K., *Modern Forests. Statemaking and Environmental Change in Colonial Eastern India*, Stamford, 1999.

Sommer, Marianne, Müller-Wille, Staffan and Reinhardt, Carsten, eds., *Handbuch Wissenschaftsgeschichte*, Stuttgart, 2017.

Sprecher von Bernegg, Andreas, *Der Teestrauch und der Tee. Die Mate- oder Paraguayteepflanze*, Stuttgart, 1936.

Stahncke, Holmer, *Altona. Geschichte einer Stadt*, Hamburg, 2014.

Studemund-Halevy, Michael, *Im jüdischen Hamburg, Ein Stadtführer von A-Z*, Munich and Hamburg, 2011.

Szöllösi-Janze, Margit, 'Lebens-Geschichte—Wissenschafts-Geschichte. Vom Nutzen der Biographie für Geschichtswissenschaft und Wissenschaftsgeschichte', *Berichte zur Wissenschaftsgeschichte*, vol. 23, 2000, pp. 17-35.

Thomas, Adrian Peter, *Calcutta Botanic Garden. Knowledge Formation and the Expectations of Botany in a Colonial Context, 1833-1914*, Diss. Phil., London, 2016.

Vicziany, Marika, 'Imperialism, Botany and Statistics in Early Nineteenth-Century India. The Surveys of Francis Buchanan (1762-1829)', *Modern Asian Studies*, vol. 20, 1986, pp. 625-60.

Warming, Eugen, 'Ecklon, Christian Friedrich', in *Dansk Biografisk Leksikon*, vol. 4, ed. Carl Frederik Bricka, Copenhagen: Gyldendalske Boghandels Forlag, 1890, pp. 417f.

Watson, Mark F. and Henry J. Noltie, 'Career, Collection, Reports and Publications of Dr Francis Buchanan (later Hamilton), 1762-1829. Natural History Studies in Nepal, Burma (Myanmar), Bangladesh and India', *Annals of Science*, vol. 71, no. 4, 2016,

Welsh, Frank, *A History of South Africa*, London, 2000.

Wunschmann, Ernst, 'Lehmann, Johann Georg Christian', in *Allgemeine Deutsche Biographie*, vol. 18, Munich, 1883, pp. 143-5.

Wurtzburg, C.E., *Raffles of the Eastern Isles*, London, 1954.

Yong, Tan Tai, 'Early Entrepôt Portal. Trade & Founding of Singapore', in *Maritime Heritage of Singapore*, ed. Aileen Lau & Laure Lau, Singapore, 2005, pp. 80-97.

Zirnstein, Gottfried, 'Philippi, Rudolf Amandus', in *Neue Deutsche Biographie*, vol. 20, Berlin, 2001, pp. 391f.

DATABASES/ONLINE RESOURCES

Archer, Jeremy, C.B. General William Munro, 39th Regiment –Soldier and Plantsman, Homepage The Keep Military Museum. Home of the Regiments of Devon and Dorset, http://www. keepmilitary museum.org/info/general+william+munro+c+b++39th+regiment+-+soldier+and+plantsman, retrieved 5 September 2016.

Database Jüdische Grabsteinepigraphik, Steinheim Institut, http://www.steinheim-institut.de/cgi-bin/epidat

Folketællinger, Dansk Demografisk Database, RAK, http://www. ddd.dda.dk/

Larsen, Kay, Dansk-Ostindiske Personalier og Data, Dansk Demografisk Database http://www.ddd.dda.dk/dop/sogeside.asp.

Naturhistorisk Riksmuseet Stockholm, title: Christian Friedrich Ecklon and Karl Ludwig Philipp Zeyher, http://www.nrm.se/en/

forskningochsamlingar/botanik/botaniskhistoria/error.13420.html, retrieved 7 February 2017.

A Numerical List of Dried Specimens of Plants in the East India Company's Museum, collected under the Superintendence of Dr Wallich of the Company's Botanic Garden at Calcutta, Online Version of Royal Botanic Garden Edinburgh, http://wallich. rbge. info/

Index